Oct. 1, 1981
To My Brother — ALBERT M. GOODRICH

WORDS OF WISDOM TO LIVE BY————————

As a man thinketh in his heart so is he.

The
MAJESTY
of
BOOKS

The MAJESTY of BOOKS

STERLING W. SILL

Published by Deseret Book Company, Salt Lake City, Utah, 1974

Library of Congress Catalog Card No. 74-81407
ISBN 0-87747-532-6

Lithographed by

DESERET PRESS

in the United States of America

Contents

SECTION V: Books of Inspiration

Section

I

The Majesty of Books

1

The Majesty of Books

T HAS been said that it is very difficult to think effectively until we have a language to think with. Language comes from a combination of ideas. And ideas are made up of words which have a different intensity of emotion, a different degree of meaning, and a different brightness of color. Words are the smallest units of language which have meaning within themselves. Like people, words come in both high and low rank and have different degrees of integrity and intensity. Then some great soul may put the best of these lofty words together into stimulating ideas to make a great book which may be the marvel of creation.

In Alan J. Lerner's play *My Fair Lady,* Professor Higgins says, "Think what you're dealing with. The majesty and grandeur of the English language. It's the greatest possession we have. The noblest sentiments that ever flowered in the hearts of men are contained in its extraordinary, imaginative, and musical mixtures of sounds."

One of the very lofty words in our language is the word *majesty.* We use this word in referring to the grandeur of the mountains, the greatness of kingship, the nobility of great expression. It is a quality or state that inspires reverence. It carries with it an attitude of imposing stateliness. It is also an elevation of manner or style as it appears in great human beings. The dictionary says that majesty stands for the dignity, authority, or power of a sovereign. "Your Majesty" is a term of address or acknowledgment of the highest of dignity, rank, and power in human life. And it is sometimes used to represent the supreme authority and glory of God.

In his book *Heroes and Hero Worship,* Thomas Carlyle points out that actually all people are natural hero worshipers. There are very few things that ever give us the thrill of satisfaction that we get from the contemplation of a great human being at his best. We like to identify with someone who knows where he is going and how he is going to get there. We are inspired by those who have developed within themselves those great powers that enable them to reach any possible goal, and we ourselves live according to how we think.

The greatest good fortune of our lives is that God created man in his own image and has endowed him with his attributes and potentialities. The Creator has given us these potentially magnificent brains, these physical bodies, the wonder and function of which we do not even comprehend. He has given us these miraculous personalities, which makes God our only fellow in the universe.

One of the greatest of our endowments is that we have been given an upward reach, a God instinct, an ambition to be better than we are. Man has a consuming passion for grandeur. Actually, one of the greatest needs of the human heart, wrote E. H. Lawrence, is for splendor, fulfillment, a godly price, glory, and lordship. The scriptures project our future by saying, "Ye are Gods; and all of you are children of the most High." (Psalm 82:6.) What we know about God's laws of heredity and the information given in the scriptures all tell us that the offspring of God may eventually become like their eternal parents. It is said that three of the most important requirements of life are: (1) to love, (2) to be loved, and (3) to feel that our own lives are worthwhile. However, Mr. Lawrence points out that in his opinion we need to feel these qualities of success and worthwhileness even more than we need love or bread.

And it is one of the great privileges of man not only to worship God, but also to personally identify with him and strive to become like him. Victor Hugo once said that nothing is as powerful as an idea whose time has come, and an idea's time always comes when we get a harness on it and set it to work in our interest in its most constructive purpose. And if we were going to try to identify this great word, *majesty,* we might think first of the majesty of God; second, of the majesty of great human beings living at their best, and third, of something more inspiring than the majesty and glory contained in a great book, which, if properly used, may create us in its own image.

One of the marvels of our world is that the words and attitudes and enthusiasms of God himself may be transformed, preserved, and presented on the pages of a great book through which we may be born again as many times as we like. When we hear great ideas spoken, they are only retained in some fragment, and that which we do get withers away in time. But the great commandments of God as they were given out of the fires of Sinai have been retained in a book so that they remain as fresh to us today as they were when first recorded, and by our reading and memorizing they may become a part of us. That is, a great book may transfer its majestic traits to us as it creates us in its own image. We put our money in banks, we put our food in the storeroom, we put our clothing in our clothes closets, but God has put his own wisdom, his directions, his commandments in books. That is also where we may find preserved the best of great men and women.

Books serve as our storehouses of wisdom. They contain the inspiration of the great literature, the inspiring music, the beautiful poems of the finest minds. By the proper use of books, we may learn great leadership, great occupational know-how, great wisdom, great religion, great happiness, and the way to eternal life. Through the majesty of books, we may transfer the glory of God into the eternal lives of his children.

2

"What We Need to Know Is in Books"

IT IS very significant that we live in the greatest age of wonders and enlightenment that has ever been known in the world. Our forefathers lived on a flat, stationary earth, and many of them lived in caves or tents. They plowed their ground with a wooden stick and sowed their grain a handful at a time.

But we live on an earth of power steering and jet propulsion. We fly through the stratosphere faster than sound. With television on our eyes, we can see every part of the earth. With radio on our ears, we can hear people when they speak to us from the surface of the moon. With our modern machinery, we can do the farm work previously done by 10,000 men. We have available the most advanced education on every subject; we live in the most magnificent homes and enjoy the finest food. Our knowledge of medicine gives us strong bodies and clear minds. Our life expectancy has been increased from nineteen years for those who lived in Jerusalem 2,000 years ago to seventy-one years in our own day. And many people today would count it an incredible hardship to live as Solomon lived in all of his glory.

With a modern submarine, we can sail under the polar ice cap or live in perfect comfort in the depths of the sea. The great knowledge explosion taking place in our day has been on the drawing boards of the universe since time began. And we who live with its benefits need to develop character and personality qualities to make the most of the God-given opportunities of our time.

Some time ago I talked with a man who had charge of the work of 300 scientists employed by one of America's greatest corporations. These men do constant research on how to improve the goods and services of their company, and all of their discoveries are written down for the benefit of everyone. And this man pointed out that there were enough new inventions and new developments taking place in the world every day to fill an entire set of the *Encyclopedia Britannica*. This indicates quite a change in pace from the occasion just a few years ago when there was great clamor to close up the United States Patent Office because it was thought that all of our inventions had already been discovered.

One of this scientist's honorary societies had asked him to write a paper on the greatest inventions of the last ten years. I asked him what, in his opinion, was the greatest invention of all time. And I was very interested that he did not mention the wheel, or the lever, or radium, or television, or the electronic computer, or the airplane, or nuclear fission. Without any hesitation or question, he said the greatest invention of all time is the book.

Someone has said that books are among life's most precious possessions. They are the most remarkable creation of man. Nothing else that man builds ever lasts. Monuments fall, civilizations perish, but books continue. The perusal of a great book is, as it were, an interview with the noblest men of past ages who have written it.

Charles Kingsley said, "There is nothing more wonderful than a book. It may be a message to us from the dead, from human souls we never saw who lived perhaps thousands of miles away. And yet these little sheets of paper speak to us, arouse us, teach us, open our hearts, and in turn open their hearts to us like brothers. Without books, God is silent, justice dormant, philosophy lame."

John Milton said, "Books are not dead things but contain a certain potency of life in them as active as the soul whose progeny they are. They preserve as in a vial the purest efficacy of the living intellect that bred them."

A recent news dispatch seemed almost to have some connection to the vision of Daniel the prophet in ancient Babylon over 2,500 years ago when the Lord said to him: "But thou, O Daniel, shut up the words, and seal the book, even to the time of the end: many shall run to and fro, and knowledge shall be increased." (Daniel 12:4.) This newspaper dispatch indicated that of all the scientists who have ever lived in the world, 80 percent live in our day. And these great men were reserved to come forth in our time for our benefit to help prepare our earth for the greater things which are to come. These scientists who are masters in their various fields spend their lifetimes making our modern conveniences available to us. They have written down their discoveries in books that we may get for a few cents. We have the great books of science. We have the great books of literature. We have the great leadership books. We have books giving us the finest occupational know-how, and we have books that tell us how to live successfully both here and hereafter. Much of our education and religion comes from books. Books contain much for us by way of culture, morality, and faith. If we read the right kind of books, we may improve the quality of our patriotism, our loyalty, and our ambition.

Abraham Lincoln once said, "What I want to know is in books, and my best friend is the one who will get me a book I haven't read." He said, "I will prepare myself now and take my chances when the opportunity comes." Lincoln went to great lengths to get the few books that were available to him in his day, and then he spent all of his spare time in study. There were two books that influenced Lincoln's life most. One was the Holy Bible and the other was the *Life of Washington* by Mason Locke Weems. And while Lincoln had little formal education or cultural background for his reading, yet he studied and mastered these books in the evenings on the dirt floor of a backwoods cabin before an open fire.

Today we don't have access merely to the books of the present day. We also have many great books containing the ideas and ideals which the greatest men in every field have written since time began. With our books, aided by a little imagination, we can go backward or forward across time, much as an aviator goes through space. We can go back to the very beginning of time and watch the creation of our earth take place. We feel the brooding, unbroken darkness that covered the deep and feel what it must have been like when, in the march of progress, God first said, "Let there be light."

And then through our great books we may reenact this miracle of creation, which brings light and progress and understanding and pleasure into our minds and hearts. Through books we become the heirs of all the ages and can turn the calendar forward or backward according to our will and good pleasure. We can sightsee in Babylon. We can stand at the foot of Mount Sinai while we reabsorb the spirit of the Ten Commandments, or we can be inspired by going to the high mountain where Jesus appeared in shining garments with Moses and Elias as he was transfigured before Peter, James, and John.

Out of books we get the great literature, the great biography, the great religion. One of the wonders of our world is American business. The great businessmen have written down their important success secrets having to do with selection, recruiting, induction, training, supervision, and motivation. The most powerful ideas, the finest logic, the best good judgment are made immediately available to us. We can learn how to think, how to plan, how to organize, how to worship, and how to work. We have the holy books of scripture through which we may learn about God himself and become familiar with his great doctrines, his standards of value, and his will concerning us.

The great attitudes and skills that have been developed by one set of people can be made negotiable in the bloodstream of others. We learn to organize, discipline, and project our own strengths by the use of books. It has been said that planning is the place where man shows himself most like God. Just try to think of someone more God-like than the planner. He is the organizer, the thinker, the one who draws the blueprint and builds the roadway on which his every success must travel. And we may have access to the most expert books teaching us how to plan.

Once every year, the Harvard Graduate School of Business sponsors a national business conference attended by prominent businessmen from all over America and abroad. Participating on the programs are some of the world's top executives and administrators as well as Harvard's own business experts, who devote their life to the study and development of successful business principles and procedures. And then these successful ideas are written down so that the experience, plans, and programs of these top executives and administrators are made available without charge to everyone who may be interested.

At one of these conferences some years ago, General Lucius D. Clay, who was chairman of the board of directors of Continental Can Company, delivered an address entitled "The Art of Delegation." This is one of the most important subjects in all of the fields of administration and executive responsibility. General Clay made many excellent suggestions about how this could be done either on the battlefield or in carrying on the business of the world.

As the central theme of his talk, he used an example from the Old Testament that had taken place in the early part of the history of the children of Israel. It seems that Moses was working from dawn until dark trying to do all of the work personally involved in listening to the troubles and complaints of his people. But many others were standing around in groups wanting to be heard. This caused dissension and murmuring among them. Jethro, the father-in-law of Moses, observing the confusion, said to Moses, "The thing that thou doest is not good." Then he advised Moses to select able men and make them judges of thousands, judges of hundreds, judges of fifties, and judges of tens, and let them judge and teach the people. That is, under the direction of Moses they were to bear the burdens of leadership on every level except the highest. Moses accepted the counsel of Jethro and placed parcels of his authority upon others. When a problem arose it was solved, if possible, on the lowest level. More important problems rose to a higher level. But only those issues which could not be handled by anyone else came up to Moses. (Exodus 18: 13-27.)

This idea of delegation is as fresh today as it was then. We see the interesting picture of one of our effective modern leaders reaching back over the centuries for an idea with which to inspire Harvard professors and students. And out of that same ancient book, we get some of our greatest literary ideas, our most powerful motivating activities, and also authoritative suggestions for saving our souls.

As Lehi and his colony were preparing to leave the Old World, the Lord made it clear to him that he should not go without taking the scriptural records that had been written up to that time, because the Lord knew of the great disasters that could come into the lives of people when they tried to live without books.

Books are important in self-improvement. They form the basis of our public relations. We have medical books, law books, and books of great literature. We have books of inspiration and books by which we save our souls. But we must get them out of the bookstore and into our hearts. We must take them down from the shelves and make them negotiable in our own lives. And we might say with Abraham Lincoln: "What we need to know is in books. And if we prepare now, we will be ready when the opportunity arises."

3

Our Great Literature

FAIRLY EARLY in my life I heard a lecture on the value of great literature. The lecturer had a wonderful appreciation of the value of great human thought, which he was trying to share with the members of his class. This one lecture has had a profound effect in my life since that time. Certainly the right kinds of ideas and ideals are among the most valuable of all possible possessions. But they also represent one of the opportunities that we most frequently fail to take advantage of.

The word *literature* generally means light. Light of any kind is important. But the kind of mental, spiritual, and moral light that can come from our great literature can nourish our faith and give a tone to our lives that almost nothing else can. Light may have been a luxury in the Dark Ages, but it is a necessity in our age of wonders and miracles.

We frequently miss the benefits of reading by the destructive excuse that we do not have time, but every life is given an equal allotment of time. Each week brings us 168 brand new, unused hours. If we use 40 of these hours in making a living, we still have 128 left, and certainly we need to allocate some of them for the enlightenment of our souls and the improvement of ourselves.

Jesus is the authority for the direction that men cannot live successfully by bread alone. Real success in life demands a substantial portion of inspiration in the daily diet; and to bring our lives to their constructive best, we need to raise our mental blinds and let in more light. There are some things that are optional in success, but we proceed at great risk when we allow our mental pores to close and try to get along without a substantial intake of new and stimulating ideas. One of our greatest needs is that particular kind of nourishment for the spirit that we know as inspiration. It was a wise counselor who said:

If of thy mortal goods thou art bereft
And from thy slender store two loaves alone to thee
   are left,
Sell one, and with the dole
Buy hyacinths to feed thy soul.

—Saadi, "Garden of Roses"

The human mind itself is a possession of uncalculated value, but it needs to be lighted, charged, and vitalized. The mind can get balance, reason, foresight, and understanding from the thoughts of others. The right kinds of ideas, properly introduced into the mind, breed initiative, moral courage, the will to grow, and a love of fairness. When the mind is not properly pollenized and vitalized by the inspiration of stimulating thoughts and uplifting ideals, much of its power is wasted. A chemist, a lawyer, or an inventor does not depend upon his own discoveries for his occupational success; he appropriates for his own use all of the tested methods and good ideas of all of the best men in his field. If utilizing the most helpful past experiences of others is a necessity for business or professional success, why shouldn't the ideas of others be used just as profitably in the larger and more important field of life itself? What a tremendous opportunity we have to set aside a regular part of each day to enlighten the mind, teach the heart, enrich the soul, and charge the ambition with power.

Suppose, then, that each of us selects the ten authors that we would most like to resemble. We have no obligation to choose those that appeal to someone else. Our ten should be those with the greatest power to move us personally. Then suppose that we proceeded to exhaust each of them one at a time. That is, we first select our man and then read everything that he has ever written. We consider his every idea, we rethink his every thought, we live his life over again. We try to understand his moods and the reasons behind them. We probe and search and pry into every corner of his life. We leave no mental pockets unsearched, no spiritual files unexplored. As we proceed, we can isolate and adopt his most stimulating procedures for our own use. We may be thrilled by his example and capture the spirit of his success. Our hero may have spent eighty years in successful living, but the essential parts of his experience have been distilled for us in a book that we may absorb in a few hours.

Alexander Hamilton has often been referred to as a genius.

He has given us his formula. He said, "Men give me some credit for genius. All the genius I have lies just in this: When I have a subject in mind, I study it profoundly. Day and night it is before me. I explore it in all its bearings. My mind becomes pervaded with it. Then the effort which I make the people are pleased to call the fruit of genius. It is the fruit of study and labor."

A regular period set aside each day over a few years could make each of us a "genius" in living. It could make us the beneficiaries of all of the great and good who have ever lived. Reading is the process by which we take possession of this fabulous inheritance. It enables us to live a thousand lives in one. We can get the profit from any great man's life without its risk; we may have the experience without the danger. By reliving his success, new visions, new experiences, new ambitions, and new accomplishments can be introduced into the most ordinary life.

The power in others can be used to motivate us. Their goodness can be used for our profit. As we increase our intake from great lives, we develop a new ability to think for ourselves. We can borrow ready-made virtues at our convenience and pleasure without the obligation of taking a single vice.

During his lifetime William Shakespeare wrote thirty-seven plays. He staffed them with a thousand characters. Each of his characters is the personification of some personality trait. Shakespeare's Julius Caesar is the personification of courage. Cassius said of Caesar:

> Why, man, he doth bestride this narrow world
> Like a Colossus; and we petty men
> Walk under his huge legs, and peep about
> To find ourselves dishonorable graves.
>
> Now in the names of all the gods at once,
> Upon what meat doth this our Caesar feed,
> That he is grown so great?
> —Act 1, scene 2

That is a very good question, for greatness does not feed on a certain diet. Caesar fed on courage. He said:

> Cowards die many times before their deaths;
> The valiant never taste of death but once.
> Of all the wonders that I yet have heard,
> It seems to me most strange that men should fear;

> Seeing that death, a necessary end,
> Will come when it will come.
> Danger knows full well
> That Caesar is more dangerous than he:
> We are two lions litter'd in one day,
> And I the elder and more terrible:
> And Caesar shall go forth.

—Act 2, scene 2

From Caesar we may take courage to our heart's content.

From Portia in the *Merchant of Venice* we borrow mercy. In the same play we may learn from the generosity of Antonio and the avariciousness of Shylock. Most of our education comes through the experiences of others, and the greatest education is the awakening of the heart and the arousing of the spirit. It is by these processes that we add to our own stature and increase the dimensions of our own lives. And as Oliver Wendell Homes has pointed out, "A mind once stretched to a new idea never returns to its original dimensions."

Through literature we may have access to the greatest ideas that have ever been thought in the world, and all of them that we can master belong to us. Seneca once said, "Whatsoever has been well said by anyone is my property." It is equally true that whatever has been well done is our property also. Emerson said, "Next only to him who first voices a great truth is him who quotes it." And next to him who first discovers a good idea is he who puts it to work. Thomas A. Edison once said that even he had never had very many original thoughts. He had only taken the ideas already known and fitted them together into new combinations to make new applications. Our success in life is determined not so much by our own mental invention and manufacture as by how well we apply those thoughts already available and use them to fill our own life's needs.

Emerson pointed out one of the most important of these needs when he said, "I have never seen a whole man." What he meant was that he had never seen any man as complete as the man he could imagine. There are dozens of perfect birds, there are hundreds of perfect flowers, there are thousands of things that fulfill their life's mission in such a way that no improvement could be asked for. But there are no perfect men. Mostly we are only parts of men with many needs that are yet to be filled. From the great literature of the world we may select the particular ideas that can best make up our individual deficits, and great literature is about the only place where we may find every virtue in any quality. Through the white light of great literature we may see into every corner of experience from the most advantageous points of view. We may see the most tragic failures side by side with the greatest successes. In the pages of literature we may live with the lowly or think the thoughts of the mighty. We may travel with Napoleon or live with Hitler at his worst. We may feel the possibilities of both the evil and the good in their true perspective. Then we may perfect our own lives quite as much from the one as from the other.

Through the printed page we may live with criminals and try to understand the forces that brought them to where they are, without suffering the consequences that would attach to that kind of personal experience.

What a disadvantage it would be to live in a world in which there was no great literature! I have always felt very sorry for those who have lived in the earlier ages of the world because they had little account of the good and bad in other lives to help them to see the consequences of their actions of right and wrong. Through literature even the pain and grief of others may be made to work for our benefit. By the law of antithesis, sinners may provide the stimulation to serve us as a passport to paradise. On the other hand, they may drag us down to hell, depending upon our attitude toward them. We have within us every potentiality, and our literature may help us to make the right decisions and get our attitudes headed in the right direction. The logic of the law of opposites is that we see dark objects best on a light background, and when we have before us both evil and good possibilities, we are able to choose more wisely.

Goethe said, "I have in me the germ of every crime." We are all potential criminals as well as potential heroes, depending on which motivation we apply. Through the great literature we may make our choices of life's values under the most favorable circumstances. Of course, the very heart of great literature is the holy scriptures. As our great literature represents the finest expressions of great men, so the holy scriptures bring us an expression from the divine. What an opportunity it should be to hold regular communion with the great spirits who have been ordained of God to speak to us in his name.

Suppose, then, that we select some of their experiences as recorded in the scriptures and then relive them, one at a time. What a privilege it would be even in imagination to go with Moses to the sacred top of Mount Sinai and be his companion for those memorable forty days while God gave him the law for ancient Israel. Or suppose that we get on intimate terms with the other great prophets and rethink their thoughts and relive their lives. Suppose that we prepare our own attitudes by memorizing the greatest passages of the prophets. Suppose that with determined minds and faithful hearts we follow Jesus during those three years of his earthly ministry while he trod the dusty roads of this earth. Suppose that we try to follow him in his faith and in his righteousness. What change would it make in us if we saturated our minds with the Sermon on the Mount? Suppose that we follow Jesus in living the Golden Rule and the Lord's Prayer. Suppose that we follow his direction in loving our enemies and seeking first the kingdom of God. Suppose that we live by his parables and fill our minds with his doctrine. Suppose that we adopt the spirit of his life and then rearrange our personal program accordingly.

It seems perfectly clear that the quality and volume of our reading is one of the greatest of our life's opportunities. Certainly it is one of our foremost responsibilities.

4

Bibliotherapy

THE OTHER day I learned a brand-new word that serves as the title of this chapter. However, there is no need to try to look it up in the dictionary, as it may be some time before the dictionary catches up to the progressive psychologist who put it together. This nice big helpful word, *bibliotherapy,* was compounded from some Greek words meaning "books" and "treatment." Briefly it has to do with a particular kind of self-improvement. It is a literary remedy for our problems and denotes a cure brought about by the effective use of good ideas. An idea in action is the most powerful thing in the world, and the most abundant source of supply of ideas is found in the organized habitual reading of good books.

Over the door of the library in the ancient city of Thebes an Egyptian king had inscribed these words: "Medicine for the Soul." Bibliotherapy can be the most important part of keeping ourselves well physically; it is also the most important part of our business success. It is very helpful in farming. It is a vital part of our religion. A good bibliotherapy probably represents our greatest field of personal opportunity. For no matter what our objectives may be, we can greatly help our accomplishment if we have a good brand of bibliotherapy in successful operation in our individual program.

Most of us are vaguely aware that there are tremendous values in great books, but very few of us ever actually take enough of the treatment to bring about a realization of our potentiality. It is thought that the best place to begin any program of accomplishment is to believe in it. And a great step forward is taken when we really make up our minds about the uses of good books.

Personally, I have always felt very sorry for those who have lived in the periods when there was no great world literature. It may have been that if Cain had read the right kind of good books in his spare time as did Abraham Lincoln, he might not have killed his brother Abel and started the first crime wave. Of course, the Bible and the other religious books form the very center of our literature, and yet even the word of the Lord doesn't help us much unless we know what it says and are willing to take the treatments that it prescribes, for we learn to do by doing. Our bookshelves are loaded with the most helpful volumes, and yet ignorance and the violation of tested and proven principles remains one of the greatest curses of mankind.

Some time ago a man told me that during the last ten years he had not read one single book. He had spent a great deal of money for liquor and tobacco, but not a cent for enlightenment or mental or spiritual improvement. His kind of life would have been a tragedy even in the Dark Ages. But how unfortunate that such a condition can exist in this great age of wonders and enlightenment that we call the dispensation of the fulness of times! The thick blackness of the Dark Ages has not yet been generally dispersed, for a recent Gallup Poll indicated that 56 percent of all American adults never completely read a single book after their formal education has been completed. Upon the cross Jesus said, "Father, forgive them, for they know not what they do." (Luke 23:34.) That is still our biggest problem, as almost all of the sins of the world are the sins of ignorance, and these sins could all be cured by the right treatment from good books.

For example, the one who in direct violation of the word of the Lord allows the vicious alcohol habit to get its chains wrapped around him clearly does not know what he is doing. The person who makes immoral practices a part of his life's program doesn't realize that this will downgrade his life for all eternity. The one who never takes the time to really prepare for his life's work doesn't know what he is doing.

I know a man who just seems to make every mistake. He has all kinds of unnecessary problems because he doesn't understand. There are some wonderful books that contain exactly what he needs, and on more than one occasion he has been provided with these books and urged to study them, but he refuses the ideas, the motives, and the lessons; and the therapy that could reform his life has been continually avoided so that his problems and troubles still humiliate him by keeping him negative, sinful, and unsuccessful.

On the other hand we have heard of men and women who have risen to great heights by the faithful use of only a few minutes a day devoted to significant study. One man recently told how Dr. Norman Vincent Peale's book *The Power of Positive Thinking* had changed the outcome of his life at its most critical period. A similar program would do the same for us if we would only take the treatment. Dale Carnegie once wrote a book entitled *How to Win Friends and Influence People,* which is chock-full of the finest soul medicine.

Someone once asked Wendell Phillips when he was born. He said, "It was one Sunday afternoon when I was twenty-five years old, just after I had finished reading a great book." That new birth has happened on innumerable occasions in the past and it will happen to many people in the future.

Jesus said that everyone should be born again. In a little different way there are many people who need to be reborn a dozen times. Our minds need to be renewed, our hearts need to be reawakened, and our ambitions need to be recharged. Most of the things we need for a successful and happy life are within our easy reach, if we could only learn to take our medicine. Frequently we find ourselves in the position of Ferdinand Magellan, who in 1519 started the first trip around the world. En route a large number of his men died of scurvy because of a deficiency in their diet. However, at the very time they were dying, Magellan had on board a cargo of limes that he had picked up along the way that contained the very vitamins necessary to have saved his sailors' lives if he had only known it. It is equally possible for us to die mentally, financially, and spiritually while all of the time the means for curing our diseases are in the good books that are right under our noses.

One of our biggest problems is how to get information, ideals, and ambitions in force in our lives. Too frequently we follow a procedure similar to the one used by Pilate when he said to Jesus, "What is truth?" And then without waiting for the answer he turned and walked out of the room. (John 18:38.) Mostly we don't have the answers because we have not been willing to invest the time and study necessary to find the truth, and we fail in our goals because we do not generate sufficient industry to get the ideas in force. Only he who fails to seek fails to find, and only he who fails to practice fails to become.

Woodrow Wilson pointed out one of the greatest problems involved in bibliotherapy when he said, "The greatest ability of

the American people is their ability to resist instruction." Most
of us have more of that unfortunate talent than is good for us,
especially when it applies to religion. When the mind is left un-
stimulated, it loses its power. But we develop a twin vice when we
fail to practice that which we already know. Even the wisest instruction has little value unless it is put to work.

Thomas A. Edison touched upon this side of the problem
when he said, "There is no limit to which a man will not go to
avoid thinking." Thinking is one of the hardest, most unpleasant
things that some of us ever have to do, and yet Solomon said,
"As [a man] thinketh in his heart, so is he." (Proverbs 23:7.) I
don't know just where that leaves us, but if we are what we think
and if we don't think, we have a problem. Someone compared
our situation with the experience that Goliath had with David.
You remember that David used his slingshot to throw a rock,
which embedded itself in Goliath's forehead; and after the whole
thing was over, someone said that such a thing had never entered Goliath's head before. We need to get more things into our
heads; we need to get more things into our hearts, and more things
into our bloodstreams. And the entry is easier through our
eyes and our ears than through our foreheads.

One man said that there were only two books in the world
from which he had ever received any benefit. One was his mother's
cookbook and the other was his father's checkbook. As early as
possible we need to learn that there are some other values in
books besides these two. Our problem usually comes in getting
the ideas out of the books and into us. This is not as easy as it
may at first appear; at least most of us don't do it very well. For
example, most Christians are what someone has called Bible Christians. That is where most of the Christianity remains in the Bible
and not very much gets into the person.

Emerson had some of these people in mind when he said,
"On the brink of an ocean of life and truth we are miserably
dying. Sometimes we are furthest away when we are closest by.
We stand on the brink of an ocean of power but each must take
the steps that would bring him there." So frequently it is true
that we are furthest away when we are closest by. Think how
near they were who lived contemporaneously with Jesus. They
lived in the same time and space as the Savior of the world. They
had the scriptures foretelling his life. They saw him as he passed
among them. They knew his miracles. They heard him in the tem-

ple. His saving power was within their easy reach, and yet they were so far away. They didn't believe. They didn't understand. They didn't get his message in force in their lives. They didn't take the steps that would bring them to where they should have been. As a consequence they pronounced their own doom upon themselves by saying, "His blood be on us, and on our children." (Matthew 27:28.)

And so it has been, and so it may be with us. We are so near; we live in the greatest age ever known in the world. Our educational standards are the highest. We have the holy scriptures, and yet what good do they do if we don't know what they say? Whereas a little study can give us a complete mastery of the greatest scriptures and a little bibliotherapy can put celestial glory within our easy reach, yet with all of this we may be so far away. Isn't it strange that in spite of our wonderful opportunities, in spite of the wonders and the marvels of our time, yet there is among us a tremendous increase in crime, delinquency, moral failure, nervous breakdowns, and disobedience to God—all because we have not learned to take our medicine.

If we have the right soul medicine, we can cure our every ill, but it is of no use unless we take it. If we utilize the treatments available in great ideas, we can reform our lives in any way we desire. Just think what would happen if we would actually live the Golden Rule or put the Ten Commandments in operation in our lives, or practice the ideals spotlighted in the parables, or adopt the spirit of the Beatitudes, or get the Sermon on the Mount into our bloodstream.

There is a physician in Birmingham, Alabama, who goes around writing prescriptions for sick people to be filled not at drugstores but at bookstores, because he knows what all of us know: that most of the people who occupy sick beds are there because of some mental or emotional disturbance which they themselves have set into motion. Someone has said that no one ever gets stomach ulcers because of what he eats; we get stomach ulcers because of what is eating us. Sins, guilt complexes, wrong thinking, and harmful activities produce poisons that make both the body and the spirit sick. These can all be cured by some treatments from the great scriptures. The spirit languishes and fails because it lacks mental stimulation and spiritual nourishment.

Jesus called himself the great physician. His mission was to make men whole and holy. He put into the book the greatest of all prescriptions when he said, "Come, follow me." The final success of every human life will finally be determined by how much of that prescription we take. We need to follow him in his faith. We need to follow him in his understanding, and we need to follow him in actually doing the will of our Father in heaven. We need to read more and think more and live more and do more and be more. Jesus said that we should live by every word that proceedeth out of the mouth of God. What a healthy, holy, happy, successful people we would be if we adopted that kind of bibliotherapy in our everyday lives. Our only salvation lies in the possibility we may learn to take our medicine.

Section

II

Books to Read From

5

Books to Read From

AMONG THE great experiences in anyone's life, one of the greatest has to do with reading. This is a rather mysterious kind of process whereby we get ideas, philosophies, enthusiasms, and faith out of the greatest minds into our own. This important experience should always begin before the reader himself can read. It was a very fortunate man who said:

> You may have tangible wealth untold;
> Caskets of jewels and coffers of gold,
> Richer than I you can never be—
> I had a mother who read to me.
> —Strickland Gillilan

Charles Laughton once conducted a class where he read the Bible for half an hour and those who attended were charged $3.50 each. One of those who attended was asked why he paid $3.50 to hear Charles Laughton read the Bible when he could read it himself for nothing. The student said that when he heard Charles Laughton read the Bible, he not only got the Bible but he also got Charles Laughton. To hear one man read the dictionary or the telephone book might be more profitable than to hear someone else read the book of wisdom itself. And for one's mother to read to him is one of the very best ways of getting a clear title both to the subject matter and to his mother.

Reading is also a good way to get the most important benefits from the greatest men, and anything that is read can all be clear profit, as there is no obligation to take anything but the best. The first eight years of my formal reading experience took place while I was attending grammar school. Once each day during this period the teacher conducted a reading class. Each year, during most of these eight grades, we were issued a book at the beginning of the year entitled *Studies in Reading*. These books were written by W. Searson, professor of English at the University of Nebraska, and George E. Martin, president of the State Teachers College at Kearney, Nebraska.

These books were made up of some great poetry, some especially selected prose, and other bits of wisdom. These books had some great stories of patriotism; other ideas pointed toward good citizenship; still others glorified the family and honored God. We studied Victor Hugo's *Les Miserables,* Patrick Henry's *Call to Arms,* the speech of John Adams favoring the adoption of the Declaration of Independence, the Bible, Abraham Lincoln's story of the "Soldier's Reprieve" by R. D. S. Robbins, William Cullen Bryant's "Thanatopsis," James Russell Lowell's "Vision of Sir Launfal," and Joseph Addison's "Mountain of Miseries." Some of the other authors were Oliver Wendell Holmes, Edgar Allan Poe, Francis Scott Key, Robert Louis Stevenson, Alfred Tennyson, Lord Byron, J. G. Holland, William Wordsworth, Ralph Waldo Emerson, William Shakespeare, and hundreds of others.

Back in those days we memorized a great deal. I can still recite many of those great literary treasures that I learned by heart over fifty years ago. Later, while serving as a teacher, it was my pleasant privilege to direct some of these reading classes, and as one of my most treasured possessions I still have copies of these old readers from the fifth through the eighth grades. Apparently these particular books were first published in 1910. And it is a very pleasant experience for me now to think of the "old days" and the inspiring material that was taught during this period. Naturally those things that we learn while we are young and impressionable have a very important effect upon us for the rest of our lives. And from the preface of one of these books I have copied the following introduction.

"Reading with appreciation is a fine art. It is the purpose of this volume to provide the means whereby the reader may obtain a more intelligent appreciation of some of the inspiring short poems and the selected prose that are to be found in the English language. The poems are selected to cover a wide range of appeal in every good grade and uplifting variety of emotion. Each subject presented for study has a helpful introduction. Next comes the selection itself. In third place are some suggested questions which may be studied for additional understanding and appreciation. And finally there is a list of references calling attention to other helpful related selections."

The introduction brings the reader's mind into a constructive attitude and provides the atmosphere in which the selection may be most appreciated. The questions at the end afford the student the means of deepening and intensifying that appreciation. Notes are given to make sure that he understands those references that may not at first be clear to him. The titles of other helpful and related material that follow permit him to widen his appreciation into other fields. With such directed effort he can learn to read the selection with genuine appreciation. He is taught how to study and how to do his homework, and through the class recitation period he is taught expression and complete familiarity with the best thought and highest feelings known in our age. This reading activity should bring the student face to face with the fundamental truths and beauty of such selections as "America the Beautiful," Paul's speech on Mars Hill, "The Chambered Nautilus," and "Columbus."

There are hundreds of other important selections of ideas which have been dressed up in the elegant language of verse and prose, where ideas have been cast in words that have been measured, metered, rhymed, and in many cases set to music. It is probable that all of the authors and those who had anything to do with these great selections of literature have already passed away, and yet these magnificent volumes are as fresh and dynamic as they were when first published in 1910. I have had a powerful experience with books since that time. But I think nothing since then has been as valuable to me as this hour a day engaged in these studies in reading during the grammar grades.

Instead of books, I imagine this shelf in my library to contain a great collection of human beings where I may have the best of each one as his service is needed. These great men may have set down in writing only the best one percent of themselves, and it is in my book where they reach their greatest height of power and usefulness. None of them could have been more helpful if they had engraven their message in the rock forever saying, "This is the best of me." For the rest of these men's lives they may have eaten, and drunk, and slept, loved, and hated, like other people. But in writing in my book each one says to me, "This is my best. This is the greatest of what I saw, knew, and believed during my lifetime. If anything of mine is worth your memorizing and remembering, this is it."

The compilers and publishers have put the best of many men together into a composite. The contribution of each may be brief in itself, but whatever he may have possessed of inspiration, dedication, and righteousness now belongs to me without the necessity of my taking anything from him that is ordinary. There are other ways to amplify and carry the voice, but my book eternally preserves the intellect itself, and each author has something to say that he perceives to be true and useful and helpfully beautiful. So far as he knows, no one else has ever said it this way. Perhaps no one else can say it; that is his call, and he is bound to say it clearly, melodiously, and helpfully.

In this very important hour a day that we formerly spent in reading great literature, so many people now read of the crime waves, the sex orgies, the errors in government, and the bitterness in human relations, or, if we will, we may gossip with a neighbor or discuss the weather with a friend. Of course, the opportunity is still available where, through the great books, we may talk with the kings and queens of intellect so that we can more fully satisfy ourselves with our claims for high companionship and self-respect. It is not necessary to jostle with the common crowd for an entry here or an audience there, because all the while this eternal high court is open to us with its society as wide as the world and as multitudinous as all of its days. We may have fellowship and rank with the chosen and the mighty of every place and time according to our own wish. And if we want to be the companions of nobles, all we need to do is to make ourselves noble. We do not need to lack for conversation with the wise; if we understand wisdom, we shall hear it on every hand. We have only one limitation; and that is, if we do not rise to them, they cannot stoop to us.

The influence of great books upon us is miraculous. They can make us into their own image, and you may judge a man more truly by the books and the papers that he reads than the company that he keeps. Emily Dickinson said:

> There is no frigate like a book
> To take us lands away,
> Nor any coursers like a page
> Of prancing poetry.
> This traverse may the poorest take
> Without oppress of toll;
> How frugal is the chariot
> That bears a human soul!

One's associates are often imposed upon him, but his reading may be the result of his own choice. And the man who chooses the right class of books and papers unconsciously becomes more accurate in his thinking, more rooted in his convictions, and his mind becomes greater in its strength.

The life and feelings of a young girl who is fascinated by some glowing love romance has her attitude colored and shaped by the page that she reads. If the writing be false and weak and foolish, she may become false and weak and foolish too; but if it be true and tender and inspiring, then some of this truth, tenderness, and inspiration will grow into her soul and will become a part of her very self. The boy who reads about deeds of manliness or bravery or of noble daring feels a spirit of emulation grow within him and the seed is planted which will bring forth fruit of heroic endeavor and an exalted life.

About books, Ralph Waldo Emerson once said, "Consider what you have in the smallest chosen library. A company of the wisest and wittiest men that could be picked out of all civil countries, in a thousand years, have set in best order the results of their learning and wisdom. The men themselves were hid and inaccessible, solitary, impatient of interruption, fenced by etiquette; but the thought they did not uncover to their bosom friend is here written out in transparent words to us, the strangers of another age."

If we need encouragement or to be motivated in our faith, we may read from some treasured volume the philsophy of our choice. In his poem "The Day Is Done," Henry Wadsworth Longfellow said:

> The day is done, and the darkness
> Falls from the wings of Night,
> As a feather is wafted downward
> From an eagle in his flight.
>
> I see the lights of the village
> Gleam through the rain and the mist,
> And a feeling of sadness comes o'er me
> That my soul cannot resist:
>
> A feeling of sadness and longing,
> That is not akin to pain,
> And resembles sorrow only
> As the mist resembles the rain.

Come, read to me some poem,
Some simple and heartfelt lay,
That shall soothe this restless feeling,
And banish the thoughts of day.

We not only lend to the rhyme of the poet the beauty of our own voice, but we also lend the imagination of our own interest to fill the night with music and the day with success. In addition to the great poems, we have the great stories. There are stories of patriotism, of heroism, and of success.

Horatio Alger wrote some 235 books, filled with the rags to riches variety of success stories which may actually draw us upward. We have stories of industry where the labor thrust may be transferred to our own personalities. We have human interest stories in every field, and stories of great motivation.

Robert Louis Stevenson once gave us a very interesting idea for our general success when he said that everyone should always have available for his use two sets of books: one to read from and one to write in.

One of the wonders of our world is the many kinds of books that we have to read from. This also constitutes one of the greatest good fortunes of our lives. There are more treasures in books than in all of the gold mines in the world put together. There are some great books of science. There are books filled with occupational know-how. We have some books that tell us how to live. There are others that tell us how to die. There are some books of poems that serve a very constructive place in our lives. There is an important literary area called useful fiction. There are books of inspiration by which we run great emotional charges of ambition, faith, and righteousness through our lives.

As someone has said, 'You can live without reading, but not very well." How else but in a book can one go back into the past for a visit in ancient Rome or Gethsemane or Gettysburg? How can we share the wealth of the great thinkers who bring about the progress of the world? Books may contain the distilled essence of the greatest lives. They abound in inspiration and provide a motivation for the most magnificent accomplishment.

Through the great books of scripture, we may even know the mind and will of God himself. Above almost every other thing, may God help us to read well.

6

The Standard Works of the Church

IT HAS already been pointed out that the most important invention of all time is a book. Most of our knowledge, many of our ambitions, our enthusiasms, and our attitudes come from that source. This is where we get our occupational know-how and learn about effective public relations. There are books of science, books of poetry, books of wisdom, books of knowledge. We study medicine to learn how to keep ourselves well physically. We study psychology and psychiatry and the other studies of the mind to learn how to keep ourselves well mentally. Agriculture is how we feed ourselves. Sociology is how we live agreeably together. Law is how we keep our lives orderly. Business is how we deal profitably with each other. And then we have this great science of religion to teach us how to keep ourselves well spiritually. One of our most important sets of books is those important volumes that God himself has caused to be written for our benefit.

He has been very particular to see to it that insofar as has been possible, the people of the world in all ages should have his word in writing. This has been his instruction to many of the greatest prophets, and because of this, we now have four collections of sacred and official gospel writings.

There is a sacred upper room in the Salt Lake Temple where some of the most important councils are held by the General Authorities of the Church. On a table in front of the First Presidency can always be found these four books, which are officially called the standard works of the Church. These are all accepted by The Church of Jesus Christ of Latter-day Saints and its members as scripture. They contain the word of the Lord. They comprise the authoritative rules for faith and practice for the Church. And while every Church member should have a set of these books for his own, yet this particular set on the table in front of the First Presidency seems to me to be a kind of symbol for the other sets that are possessed by the general Church membership. This particular set exists in a kind of holy of holies situation.

The standard works of the Church contain a great credenda of the life-saving doctrines of Deity. They also record our greatest human concepts and give us those instructions that would save our souls.

The scriptures tell of our antemortal existence, the purpose of our mortality, and the glory of our eternal lives after this life has been finished. Through them we know many of the details of that grand antemortal council held in heaven. They also tell the purpose of life, the atonement of the Son of God, the great doctrines of free agency, the immortality of the human personality, the eternal progression of our lives, and the possible everlasting glory of the human soul. The holy scriptures also tell us what we ought to do about them.

We live in the greatest and final dispensation. Consequently, we now have much of the scriptures given to various peoples in different locations and in different ages of the world's history. The Holy Bible is a record of God's dealings with his people upon the eastern continent. The Old Testament consists of 39 books of 703 pages written by the ancient prophets. The New Testament consists of 27 books with a total of 214 pages. Ninety-seven of these pages, or 45 percent of the New Testament, are taken up in the four Gospels. Twenty-eight pages are devoted to the Acts of the Apostles and make up 14 percent of the New Testament. Sixty-two pages, or 29 percent of the New Testament, are made up of the letters Paul wrote to various branches of the church and to individuals. Peter, James, and John, who served as the chief apostles, wrote a total of 12 pages, and one page was written by Jude, for a total of 6 percent. And 13 pages were written by John the Revelator, for another 6 percent. Jesus was very active for a ministry of some three and a half years, and yet all of his direct recorded remarks could be read in approximately thirty minutes.

Some 600 years before Christ was born, a group of people was led away from Jerusalem to re-people the western continent. Under direct command from God, they brought with them as many of the Old Testament writings as were available. The Lord appointed prophets among them and required of them, as he had done in the East, that they write their messages down so that the people could keep them in mind. Then in the year A.D. 320 the Lord called a young man by the name of Mormon to do something similar in the West to what King James had done in the East: to assemble these records, do whatever translating and abridging were necessary, and prepare these records that we might have them when the western civilization had been destroyed, which destruction the Lord foresaw and foretold.

As a consequence we have the Book of Mormon, made up of 15 books in 522 pages. One of these books is Third Nephi, which is a kind of fifth gospel, as it contains the record of the postmortal visit of Christ to the western continent. Here, after his resurrection, he organized his church as he had done in the East during the three years of his mortal ministry. Everyone is fully familiar with the fact that Jesus himself was crucified after a short ministry, and every one of his twelve apostles met a violent death except John the Revelator, who was banished to the rocky little island of Patmos in the Aegean Sea. Without inspired men the church soon degenerated to a purely human institution where a lot of unauthorized ministers fulfilled the prophecy of Isaiah foretelling that the people would transgress the laws, change the ordinances, and break the everlasting covenant.

Upon the western continent the church flourished and made great progress for a time. But eventually its members also fell away by the same processes of apostasy. Therefore, on both continents apostasy reigned and brought the dark ages upon both hemispheres.

Because this alienation from God was more severe in the West, one section of the people degenerated into a warlike, half-savage state. And in their last battle in the year A.D. 384 they wiped out what had been the more righteous part of the people. Long before that event, however, one of their prophets was permitted to look down to the time when Columbus would be inspired by God to rediscover America. And the prophet saw the growth of a great nation upon the western continent in the latter days. He beheld that our Pilgrim fathers brought with them as the basis of their culture the Holy Bible from the eastern continent, to be united with the record of the people who had existed in America and to fulfill the prophecy made in chapter 37 of Ezekiel so that the stick of Judah and the stick of Joseph should become one in the hands of the Lord.

Now in our day, we have a kind of one-world situation where, because of wireless, radio, airplanes, and other technology, the two hemispheres are only minutes or hours apart. This is the greatest and final of all dispensations. It is foretold in the scriptures that many things that should happen in our day. Some of these are that for the last time the Lord should organize his church upon the earth, that the great doctrines of salvation should again be taught, and that all the scriptures should be gathered together—the Holy Bible from the East and the Book of Mormon from the West. And in our own day we also have what are probably the two most important volumes of scriptures for us and our time. One of these is entitled the Doctrine and Covenants and the other is the Pearl of Great Price, magnificent and tremendously important books for every person who ever lives upon the earth.

7

The Holy Bible

THE GREATEST single possession of our world is undoubtedly the Holy Bible. It contains the word of the Lord given for our benefit. It outlines the covenants God has made and would like to make with every person who ever has lived or who ever will live upon the earth. Some 34 centuries ago, God gave the fundamental basic law, including the Ten Commandments, by which the world should be governed. The Bible is the world's first book of religion. It is the world's first book of history. It is the world's first book of knowledge. It is the world's first book of wisdom. It is the world's first book of literature. It is the world's first book of success. It contains the fundamental philosophies of the Son of God himself.

Most books on science that were written ten or fifteen years ago are now almost completely out of date, and while the Bible was written at a time when the camel was our chief means of communication and transportation, yet it is more up to date than if it had been written yesterday. It not only has in it God's dealings with his children upon the earth in the past; it also points to the great events that will take place in the future. It foretells in detail such tremendous events as the glorious second coming of Jesus Christ to cleanse our earth of its sins and inaugurate his millennial reign upon it. It also foreshadows the literal bodily resurrection of every person, whether good or bad, who has ever lived upon the earth. It pictures the details of the eternal judgment. It describes those great life-saving principles of the atonement of Christ, the various kingdoms or degrees of eternal glory, and the things that are required for our eternal exaltation.

The Bible did not actually develop in Palestine, where so many of the events recorded in the Bible took place. Palestine was not a Christian land in the days of Jesus, nor has it been in any period from that time until the present. The Bible as we know it actually came from England. In the year 1604 King James the First of England appointed 50 scholars to select from available scripture the texts that should be included in the Bible.

They were assigned the job of translating them into English from the original tongues. Their assignment was completed in the year 1611, and the Bible was brought to America in the *Mayflower* with the Pilgrim fathers in 1620. It was as though God was waiting for the completion of this great book as a basis on which this new expedition should be launched and upon which the new nation should be established. He not only caused the Bible to be brought to America, but he also inspired those to come to the new world who believed in its principles. By the light of a smoking lamp on board the *Mayflower,* our Pilgrim ancestors wrote into the Mayflower Compact as follows:

"We, whose names are underwritten, . . . [have] undertaken for the Glory of God, and advance of the Christian Faith, . . . to plant the first colony in the northern Parts of Virginia. . . ."

The Huguenots settled in New England in God's name. William Penn claimed Pennsylvania in the name of the Nazarene, and the padres landed on the shores of California with the crucifix in their hands. And in a great latter-day revelation, the Lord said that he himself had raised up the wise men to establish the Constitution of the United States and had redeemed the land by the shedding of blood. Then under his direction the national U.S. government was founded upon the principles of the religion of Christ. How fortunate we are to have such men as the founding fathers to stand in the forefront of our civilization and give the new nation its start toward its divine destiny.

The Bible has been made available to every individual in the world. However, we miss most of its benefits because in so many cases it sits upopened on our shelves and we fail to understand or govern our lives according to its divine doctrines. Therefore, even though the Bible remains our greatest possession, we are still losing much of its values as we lack a full utilization of its religion. And when we follow this practice of partial enthusiasm and fractional obedience, we are wasting the greatest of our national resources. This might be more than ordinarily tragic because the benefits of the Bible are available to the most humble without the necessity of raising taxes, increasing the work week, lessening the gold reserves, or even trimming the family budget.

The Bible does not apply merely to the next world. It is the world's first book of success in this life. In the United States alone during the last ten years, more than 200 novels have been written based on Bible events. And in the next ten years other hundreds will be written. Every week thousands of ministers, statesmen, and philosophers use Bible texts and illustrations as the basis of their most scholarly preachments and dissertations. In a period of less than one year, the great *New York Times* ran 367 editorials based on Bible passages. But the wisdom of the Bible has scarcely been touched. There are thousands of inspiring stories, commandments, and philosophies capable of molding the lives and changing the attitudes and activities of everyone who will try to get on intimate terms with it.

Excluding those men who have spoken directly for God, most people usually think of Shakespeare as being the greatest writer who ever lived. Shakespeare looked with keen insight into human lives, and his *Hamlet* has been voted his greatest book. But while it has many great philosophies and great experiences, in no sense can it be compared to the holy scriptures. The great plays of Shakespeare and others have run for years at a time in the world's greatest theaters. Half of Shakespeare's plays were tragedies and the others were called comedies. In those days a comedy was not something that was funny. It was a play that had a happy ending for every human life who will accept it and live by its principles. Because the people in the days of Noah were disobedient to the Lord, they acted out the earth's greatest tragedy on a worldwide scale. But even this great calamity has an advantage, for it makes it unnecessary for us to repeat their mistakes; Jesus gave us one of our greatest warnings when he looked down to our day and made a comparison to us when he said, ". . . as the days of Noe were, so also shall the coming of the Son of man be." (Matthew 24:37.)

The Bible contains some other tragic performances built around the Tower of Babel, Sodom and Gomorrah, Greece and Rome, Babylon and Persia. We also have the individual tragedies of Cain, Nebuchadnezzar, King Saul, and Judas Iscariot to warn us against their repetition. These Bible plays furnish us the keys for developing in us those wonderful qualities of courage, excellence, and righteousness that will lead us to celestial glory in God's presence.

Some time ago in admiring a great portrait, I noticed that no matter where the viewer stood, the eyes of the person in the picture always seemed to be focused upon him. This is also an interesting characteristic of the Bible. It has a kind of personal focus that always puts the reader in an individual spotlight. There are many great books of science, philosophy, and fiction that have little meaning for us personally, but the Golden Rule, the Ten Commandments, and the Beatitudes seem to have been written for us individually. The doctrines of faith, repentance, baptism, spiritual excellence, eternal love, and everlasting happiness all have a personal and individual meaning for us.

A number of years ago an article was written about the Bible, entitled "The Book That Has Helped Most in Business." Again we see this strange paradox of a book being written before the printing press and before the establishment of any school of business, written among a people unnoted for their business procedures, but that has such a profound effect upon modern America in developing business techniques that are among the wonders of the world. The Bible has been a material factor in raising our standards of living far above anything ever known before. Many great American leaders use the Bible and its philosophies in their daily work.

The New Testament tells of that great event when the Son of God came here to the earth and established upon our world his church with the idea that everyone should belong to it. He gave those great life-saving principles that would ensure the eternal exaltation of every person. And then this young man from Nazareth went around giving some great philosophies. In the greatest statement of public relations that has ever been given, he instituted the Golden Rule, saying, "Whatsoever ye would that men should do to you, do ye even so to them." (Matthew 7:12.) He encouraged our accomplishment by saying: "All things are possible to him that believeth." "Be not afraid." "Be of good cheer." "Let not your heart be troubled." "Follow me." "Love your enemies; do good to them that hate you." "Blessed is he who is not offended." "Seek ye first the kingdom of God, and his righteousness; and all these things shall be added unto you." "He that loseth his life for my sake shall find it." And "He that shall endure unto the end, the same shall be saved."

These great scriptures point out that man does not live by bread alone. We need a good dose of inspiration occasionally. We need something to wind up our faith, increase our enthusiasm, and get us headed for success. The Bible is the world's first book of self-discipline. It is the world's first book of life. It contains the only program ever written on the greatest of all subjects, our own eternal progression. What a tremendous opportunity we have to be familiar with its principles, to be obedient to its spirit, to learn to love its great truths and memorize its great doctrines!

8

The Book of Mormon

THE SECOND of the standard works of the Church is the Book of Mormon, which contains the records of the great civilizations that flourished on the western continent during the period of 2200 B.C. to A.D. 421. We are aware that a great culture existed here in pre-Columbus days, and this book, written by inspired prophets, tells us about their great civilizations and the reason for their destruction. Foreseeing that these people would finally be destroyed, the Lord appointed an ancient prophet by the name of Mormon to gather up their scriptures, do some translating and abridging, and inscribe their records on golden plates so that we who should follow them would have their records and know the reasons for their destruction.

Mormon was born in the year A.D. 310 and was destroyed in the last great battle 74 years later. The records were hidden away under the direction of the Lord by Mormon's son Moroni. And then, as a resurrected being, under the instruction of the Lord he returned to the earth and in the year 1823 made known the records' hiding place in upper New York state to a young man by the name of Joseph Smith. The young prophet translated this record by the gift and power of God, and the first edition was published in 1830.

About this book, the Prophet Joseph Smith said, "I told the brethren that the Book of Mormon is the most correct of any book on earth, and the keystone of our religion, and that a man could get nearer to God by abiding by its precepts than by any other book." The book itself says that its purpose is that men may be persuaded that Jesus is the Christ, the eternal Son of God. What a tremendous purpose! It says that it should come in a time when men would be denying and doubting the Bible, and it would restore many of the great truths taught by Jesus that had been taken away.

Without this book and modern revelation, we are strangers in our own land. These great scriptures tell us that this land is a land choice above all other lands. It tells us about the great commitment that God had made to free agency. And when this land was re-peopled after the flood, God ordained that it should be a citadel of liberty, a sanctuary of freedom. This record says: "And he [God] has sworn in his wrath unto the brother of Jared, that whoso should possess this land of promise, from that time henceforth and forever, should serve him, the true and only God, or they should be swept off when the fulness of his wrath should come upon them. . . . And the fulness of his wrath cometh upon them when they are ripened in iniquity." (Ether 2:8-9.) And three great civilizations have already been destroyed for that reason upon our land before our own nation was established.

Some of their prophets knew in advance that their civilization was to be destroyed. The prophet Nephi was given a great vision of the future of this land, showing the rise of our own great nation, which should possess his land after the downfall of his own people. He saw Christopher Columbus as he was being inspired by God to rediscover this land, and he saw the specially selected Pilgrims, who had been directed to come here to lay our national foundation. He saw our great nation growing in wealth and power on this great land.

The prophet Nephi noticed that the people in his vision carried with them a book, and the angel said unto him, "Knowest thou the meaning of the book?" And Nephi said, "I know not." (1 Nephi 13:21-22.) Then the angel explained that this was the Holy Bible, which had been brought with our Pilgrim forefathers, furnishing the foundation principles upon which our great civilization should rest.

The Lord indicated to the prophet Ezekiel that a record should be kept of both of God's peoples—both in the East and in the West. He said: "Moreover, thou son of man, take thee one stick, and write upon it, For Judah, and for the children of Israel his companions: then take another stick, and write upon it, For Joseph, the stick of Ephraim, and for all the house of Israel his companions, And join them one to another into one stick; and they shall become one in my hand." (Ezekiel 37:16-17.)

America has not just been a favored land in our own day. America has always been a favored land, and certainly it is not hard to understand and believe that God would reveal his mind and will to the millions of people who lived and died upon the western continent, just as he did to the people in the various dispensations of time upon the eastern continent.

This record tells of a visit made here by the Savior of the world after his resurrection in Jerusalem. He taught the people the principles of the gospel and he organized his church among them. He taught them about his second coming. We know from the traditions, legends, and their own hieroglyphics that the people on the western continent knew a great many things about the principles of the gospel, as taught by Jesus in Jerusalem. Among the Indians there was a very prominent tradition that a white God had visited them here and that he had promised to return. When the Spanish conquerors came here and learned of these traditions, they took advantage of the situation, which made the Indians an easy prey to their pretensions.

The Book of Mormon and modern-day revelation describe the divine American mission as to keep freedom, righteousness, and human dignity alive in the world. Many generations ago, God made it known that he was sick and tired of dictators, and he wanted a strong, free nation to serve as a balance of world power. The Communists have boasted over and over again that they mean to take over the government of the world. Nikita Khrushchev expressed their ambition when he said that Russia would bury the United States. They have announced their intention of making slaves of the entire world, just as they have already done in Hungary, East Germany, and their other satellite nations, and which they would do with everyone else in the world, without a moment's hesitation, if they thought they could. One of the first things that Communist nations try to do is to banish God from their countries. God has made some firm commitments to freedom, beginning in the grand council of heaven. Because of the rebellion of Lucifer, we had the war in heaven, which was fought over the question of whether or not men should be free. If all of the people in the world could get the spirit of the Book of Mormon, they would get the spirit of freedom and the spirit of God.

The Lord, through Samuel the prophet, tried to discourage the ancient Israelites from doing away with their system of judges to install a king, but he was not successful. The Israelites wanted to be like other nations, and so the Lord permitted them to have a king. And America is the finest example of freedom and individual enterprise that has ever been known in the world.

America has had a great past. It is presently the greatest nation that has ever been known upon the earth, and it will have a brilliant future when Christ shall come in his glorious second coming to cleanse the earth of its sins. He will set up his own government over all of the earth, which will be a perfect theocracy, and he will reign upon the earth during its millennial period of a thousand years. He will have two capitals. One will be in America. Then out of Zion shall go forth the law and the word of the Lord from Jerusalem. Every person of every nation and color and creed anywhere in the world should continually pray for a strong, enduring United States of America. For if any combination of dictators should ever get control in the world, then none of our other problems would ever again seem of very great consequence, or, as Emerson, our early spokesman, said, "Of what avail is plow or sail or land or life, if freedom fail." For many reasons the Book of Mormon is a unique and tremendously important book, and we ought to be fully acquainted with what it says.

9

The Doctrine and Covenants

THE LORD has been very particular to make his written word available to as many people as possible. He provided the Bible for the ancient people of the eastern continent. The Book of Mormon served the same purpose for the ancients on the western continent. Both of these attempts to establish his church ended in apostasy on both continents. Because the world has mistaken apostasy for the death of God or his loss of interest in us, the word has been spread by uninformed and unauthorized people that the heavens are forever sealed and there will never be any more revelation from God.

However, in modern times, to meet our current needs and responsibilities, the Lord has given a great new book of scripture that applies specifically to our modern world and its future. The Lord has said of this one world, "And this gospel of the kingdom shall be preached in all the world as a witness unto all nations; and then shall the end come." (Matthew 24:14.) The Church has been restored to the earth after the long apostasy from God and the blackness of the dark ages, and a new volume of scripture has been written, entitled the Doctrine and Covenants, which contains many modern-day revelations from God.

In view of our great knowledge explosion, it would be a little ridiculous to think that the Lord would let his people go uninstructed in their religious affairs in this greatest and final dispensation of the fulness of times, when all things should be brought together in one. Our day is a day of restoration. Peter refers to our time as the time of the restitution of all things. The New Testament, which is the latest scripture known by most Christians, is composed of only 214 pages, and in acknowledging the brevity of the recorded words of Jesus, the apostle John said: "And there are also many other things which Jesus did, the which, if they should be written every one, I suppose that even the world could not contain the books that should be written." (John 21:25.)

If all of the words directly credited to Jesus during his entire ministry were put into a single discourse, it would require about thirty minutes to read. It would be wonderful if in our day of such extreme need we had a great many more of his unrecorded teachings, for a lot of new needs have arisen that make further instruction and enlightenment even more necessary. To enlighten us on the many wonderful things that we need to know about this greatest of all gospel dispensations, this great book of scripture called the Doctrine and Covenants has been written by direct command of the Lord. However, there are not very many people in the world who know very much about this great book of scripture.

The Doctrine and Covenants is made up of 136 sections or chapters containing a total of 257 pages, or about the size of or a little larger than the New Testament. Most of these are direct revelations from God, having to do with things that are important in our own day. For example, in April of 1830, the Lord gave a great revelation about the organization of the Church in these latter days. Among other things, he personally named the Church when he said: "For thus shall my church be called in the last days, even The Church of Jesus Christ of Latter-day Saints." (D&C 115:4.)

The Lord also indicated that April 6 rather than December 25 was the date of his birth, and the Church was organized in this dispensation exactly 1830 years after the time he had been born in Bethlehem. (D&C 20:1.) In section 119, given July 8, 1838, is found the Lord's command reinstituting the ancient law of tithing as the primary financial law of the Church. In section 101, the Lord tells us that the Constitution of the United States was written by wise men whom he had raised up for that very purpose and that he had redeemed the land by the shedding of blood.

The Lord has indicated that the cradle of civilization was in America. In section 116, he has designated Spring Hill, Daviess County, Missouri, as the place where our great progenitor, Adam, will come to visit his people. This is the place where the Ancient of Days (or the oldest man) shall sit, as spoken of by Daniel the prophet.

On February 27, 1833, at Kirtland, Ohio, the Lord gave to Joseph Smith a revelation called the Word of Wisdom, in which he said that tobacco and liquor and other strong drinks were not good for man and should not be used. And then, after giving a great many other details about our health and diet, the Lord said:

"And all saints who remember to keep and do these sayings, walking in obedience to the commandments, shall receive health in their navel and marrow to their bones;

"And shall find wisdom and great treasures of knowledge, even hidden treasures;

"And shall run and not be weary, and shall walk and not faint.

"And I, the Lord, give unto them a promise, that the destroying angel shall pass by them, as the children of Israel, and not slay them." (D&C 89:18-21.)

The Lord has reinstituted his ancient missionary program. That is, missionaries should go out two by two without pay carrying this life-saving message to the ends of the earth. (D&C 42:6.)

On December 25, 1832, the Lord gave a revelation on war (D&C 87). This was twenty-nine years before the beginning of the Civil War. He foretold many of the details of the Civil War, saying that it should begin with the rebellion of South Carolina and would eventually terminate in the death and misery of many souls, and then he told of the other wars and rumors of wars which should subsequently take place, and that war would eventually be poured out upon all nations.

The Lord mentioned the great wickedness in our day and said, "And thus, with the sword and by bloodshed the inhabitants of the earth shall mourn; and with famine, and plague, and earthquake, and the thunder of heaven, and the fierce and vivid lightning also, shall the inhabitants of the earth be made to feel the wrath, and indignation, and chastening hand of an Almighty God, until the consumption decreed hath made a full end of all nations." (D&C 87:6.)

On July 12, 1843, the Lord gave a great revelation on marriage. The family is an eternal organization, and marriage is solemnized not just until death do us part, but rather, for time and for all eternity. It is also indicated that this important ordinance should be performed only in the temples of God, which have been erected for this purpose. Everyone who concerns himself with the prospects of an eternal life is greatly interested in the conditions that may obtain with us after death.

About this the Apostle Paul wrote to the Corinthians and mentioned the three degrees of glory. One he likened to the glory of the sun, which he called the celestial. The second was a lesser glory, which he likened to the light of the moon and called the terrestrial. The lowest of the kingdoms of glory he likened to the twinkle of a tiny star. This kingdom is called the telestial.

And then there is a fourth kingdom which is not a kingdom of glory. This is the place prepared for the final confinement of Satan and his angels. To this group will be added those who fail most seriously in this life. They are called in the scripture the sons of perdition, or the sons of Satan. Then the Apostle Paul spoke of these three degrees of glory and said: ". . . for one star differeth from another star in glory. So also is the resurrection of the dead. . . ." (1 Corinthians 15:41-42.) This is important in-information to have, and yet it is given so briefly that the meaning is not very clear.

However, in a vision given to the Prophet Joseph Smith and Sidney Rigdon at Hyrum, Ohio, on February 16, 1832, the Lord gave a revelation covering over six pages, giving all of the details of exactly who qualifies for each one of these kingdoms. Elder Melvin J. Ballard of the Council of the Twelve said that this revelation in the 76th section of the Doctrine and Covenants is the greatest revelation that has ever been given in any age to men upon this earth.

In the Doctrine and Covenants there are a lot of other great truths that are scarcely mentioned in the New Testament, or they are discussed so briefly that the message is not always clear, which partially accounts for the fact that the various sects claiming to be successors of the original Christian church have been splintered into over 250 different segments, all teaching a variety of different kinds of doctrine. Wouldn't it be helpful for us if we had those other discussions and discourses of Jesus which John says if they were all written would fill the world? They would also fill our religious lives and help us to be a different kind of people.

Some of these more than 100 revelations give details on the glorious second coming of Jesus Christ, and tell about the great doctrines of the literal bodily resurrection, repentance, atonement, and other things that are vitally important to our understanding. In one of the greatest scriptures of all time having to do with the atonement and repentance, the Lord said,

"For behold, I, God, have suffered these things for all, that they might not suffer if they would repent;

"But if they would not repent they must suffer even as I;

"Which suffering caused myself, even God, the greatest of all, to tremble because of pain, and to bleed at every pore, and to suffer both body and spirit—and would that I might not drink the bitter cup, and shrink." (D&C 19:16-18.)

We are all aware of the great knowledge explosion that is presently taking place. A prominent scientist recently said that there are enough new discoveries every day to fill an entire set of *Encyclopedia Britannica*. A recent news dispatch said that of all of the scientists who had ever lived, 80 percent of them are alive today. We are aware that God has sent his greatest scientists and his greatest philosophers and his geatest businessmen to the earth in this greatest of all dispensations. And yet we foolishly imagine that the Lord would let this period go by without any new revelation from him. But this great book of Doctrine and Covenants indicates that exactly the opposite of this situation is true, and it tells some of the details of the many heavenly messengers that have been sent to the earth in our day to restore the principles and authorities that are necessary to operate the Church of Christ.

For example, John the Baptist, the forerunner of Christ, held the keys of the Aaronic Priesthood in the dispensation of Jesus. On May 15, 1829, John the Baptist appeared as a resurrected being to Joseph Smith and Oliver Cowdery. This angelic personage announced that he was acting under the direction of Peter, James, and John, the ancient apostles who held the keys of the Melchizedek Priesthood. He put his hands upon their heads and said:

"Upon you my fellow servants, in the name of Messiah I confer the Priesthood of Aaron, which holds the keys of the ministering of angels, and of the gospel of repentance, and of baptism by immersion for the remission of sins; and this shall never be taken again from the earth, until the sons of Levi do offer again an offering unto the Lord in righteousness." (D&C 13.)

As was promised, Peter, James, and John at a later date restored the keys of the Melchizedek Priesthood. Another angelic messenger visited the earth in the fulfillment of the prophecy of the Old Testament prophet Malachi. The Lord said through Malachi: "Behold, I will send you Elijah the prophet before the coming of the great and dreadful day of the Lord: And he shall turn the heart of the fathers to the children, and the heart of the children to their fathers, lest I come and smite the earth with a curse." (Malachi 4:5-6.)

In obedience to that ancient promise, Elijah the prophet, who was taken into heaven without tasting death and who appeared to Jesus on the Mount of Transfiguration, came again to the earth on April 3, 1836, and conferred upon Joseph Smith his authority in fulfillment of the promise of Malachi. On this occasion the resurrected Savior himself also appeared and gave his instructions concerning the newly dedicated temple in Kirtland, Ohio. Section 110 of the Doctrine and Covenants tells of the visits of several other heavenly messengers, each sent to restore the various gifts and authorities held by Him in his day. The Savior also reinstituted the sacrament of the Lord's Supper, and the verbatim prayers are given in section 20 as they were dictated by the voice of the Lord.

There are hundreds of tremendously important statements made for our benefit in this great book of modern scripture. For example, in section 130, the Lord says, "Whatever principle of intelligence we attain unto in this life, it will rise with us in the resurrection. And if a person gains more knowledge and intelligence in this life through his diligence and obedience than another, he will have so much the advantage in the world to come." (D&C 130:18-19.)

Or think of this great law of consequence. The Lord said, "There is a law, irrevocably decreed in heaven before the foundations of this world, upon which all blessings are predicated—And when we obtain any blessing from God, it is by obedience to that law upon which it is predicated." (D&C 130:20-21.)

The Lord said: "It is impossible for a man to be saved in ignorance." (D&C 131:6.) In section 109, the Lord has given a great statement saying: "And as all have not faith, seek ye diligently and teach one another words of wisdom; yea, seek ye out of the best books words of wisdom, seek learning even by study and also by faith." (D&C 109:7.)

The Lord has given us a great leadership principle in section 107, verses 99 and 100, when he said: "Wherefore, now let every man learn his duty, and to act in the office in which he is appointed, in all diligence. He that is slothful shall not be counted worthy to stand, and he that learns not his duty and shows himself not approved shall not be counted worthy to stand."

There are some people who may not be convinced that this book is of God, just as there are many millions who are not convinced that the Bible is of God. But it is a great book, just the same. And it just happens that both of these are of God, and every person in the world would be well advised to study them both carefully and to govern their lives according to the lifesaving principles and doctrines that are contained therein.

10

The Pearl of Great Price

IT IS generally acknowledged that Jesus Christ is the greatest teacher who has ever lived upon our planet. He gave us some great comparisons and parables that should motivate every part of our success. In one of these he said, ". . . the kingdom of heaven is like unto a merchant man, seeking goodly pearls: Who, when he had found one pearl of great price, went and sold all that he had, and bought it." (Matthew 13:45-46.)

To the ancients, pearls were among the most precious of all things. They were the most beautiful of the precious gems and were highly esteemed as ornaments. Their value was still further enhanced by the beauty of their symbolism. The pearl has long been considered the symbol of purity. It is the emblem of wisdom, and the word *pearl* is used to represent not only those things of great value, but it also stands for wisdom, purity, and beauty. It is only natural, therefore, that when some enterprising merchant would find a beautiful pearl of extraordinary magnificence, he would be willing to make great sacrifices in order to obtain it even if he was required to sell everything he had. And what could have been more appropriate for the Master of parables to use than a pearl of great price as a symbol for the kingdom of heaven, which any understanding person would be anxious to attain. Certainly the kingdom of heaven far surpasses in desirability any other value that we know anything about.

Jesus enlarged upon this idea when he asked, "For what shall it profit a man, if he shall gain the whole world, and lose his own soul?" Then he asks another related question for us to answer when he asked, "Or what shall a man give in exchange for his soul?" (Mark 8:36-37.) And we might echo the refrain and say, "What, indeed?" Certainly there is no effort too great if by it we can make ourselves eligible for those blessings represented by the kingdom of heaven.

In our own day we have been given a great additional resource in a little book of 58 pages which has been appropriately called the Pearl of Great Price. It has become one of the standard works of the church for our modern day, which Paul referred to as the dispensation of the fulness of times. This little book has four sections:

1. The Book of Moses
2. The Book of Abraham
3. The writings of the Prophet Joseph Smith, including an inspired translation of the 24th chapter of Matthew
4. The Articles of Faith, which are thirteen brief statements about some of the principal beliefs of the Church

The Book of Moses is made up of a very important revelation given to Moses only a part of which is found in the Holy Bible, and it makes more clear some very important points of doctrine that heretofore were not fully understood.

The Book of Abraham was taken from some ancient records that came from the catacombs of Egypt and were brought to Joseph Smith for translation. This concerns the writings of Abraham while he lived in Egypt, written by his own hand on papyrus. One of the very unusual things recorded in the Book of Abraham is an account he gives of a vision he received from God about the antemortal council held in heaven before the foundations of this earth, where Jesus was chosen by God and sustained by a two-thirds majority of the entire membership of heaven to be the Savior and Redeemer of the world. At this time, the creation of the earth itself was still on the planning boards. The Book of Abraham tells many things that happened in that eternal council, which helps us to understand the purpose of our mortal probation and the overwhelming significance of our eternal lives.

This great book of scripture also gives us an intimate, first-hand account of this great patriarch who was called the father of the faithful and the friend of God. He was not only the progenitor of the entire race of Israel, but several other peoples also look to him as their great ancestor. The section of the Pearl of Great Price to which I would particularly like to call your attention is the section written by Joseph Smith, who was one of the greatest prophets who ever lived—and how great a soul he must have been to have been chosen by God to be the leader of the greatest and final dispensation of time. He was given the specific responsibility for preparing the way for the glorious second coming of Christ and the end of our earth's existence as we now know it.

John the Baptist was the forerunner of Jesus in the meridian dispensation of time, and of him the Lord said, "For I say unto you, Among those that are born of women there is not a greater prophet than John the Baptist. . . ." (Luke 7:28.)

Joseph Smith was born December 23, 1805, in Sharon, Windsor County, Vermont. Later he moved with his family to Manchester in upper New York State. When Joseph Smith was in the fifteenth year of his life, a great religious revival was taking place in the community where he lived, which gave rise to much disorder, confusion, and feeling, with priests contending against priests and the members of the various sects striving with each other.

Young Joseph Smith was considerably aroused and confused by all this contest of opinions and disagreements in the doctrines believed in by the various Christian sects. In his confusion he made an appeal to the Bible, and he read in the book of James, first chapter, fifth and sixth verses, as follows:

"If any of you lack wisdom, let him ask of God, that giveth to all men liberally, and upbraideth not; and it shall be given him.

"But let him ask in faith, nothing wavering. For he that wavereth is like a wave of the sea driven with the wind and tossed."

Joseph said, "Never did any passage of scripture come with more power to the heart of man than this did at this time to mine. . . . I reflected on it again and again, knowing that if any person needed wisdom from God, I did; for how to act I did not know, and unless I could get more wisdom than I then had, I would never know; for the teachers of religion of the different sects understood the same passages of scripture so differently as to destroy all confidence in settling the question by an appeal to the Bible.

"At length I came to the conclusion that I must either remain in darkness and confusion or else I must do as James directs, that is, ask of God. . . ."

Finally Joseph selected a secluded spot where he kneeled down and offered up the problems of his heart to the Lord. In part he described what happened as follows. He said:

"... I saw a pillar of light exactly over my head, above the brightness of the sun, which descended gradually until it fell upon me. ... When the light rested upon me I saw two Personages, whose brightness and glory defy all description, standing above me in the air. One of them spake unto me, calling me by name and said, pointing to the other—*This is My Beloved Son. Hear Him!*

"My object in going to inquire of the Lord was to ask which of all the sects was right, that I might know which to join." Accordingly, Joseph asked the personages who stood above him in the light which of all the sects was right and which he should join. He said, "I was answered that I should join none of them, for they were all wrong; and the Personage who addressed me said that all their creeds were an abomination in his sight; that those professors were all corrupt; that: 'they draw near to me with their lips, but their hearts are far from me, they teach for doctrines the commandments of men, having a form of godliness, but they deny the power thereof.'

"He again forbade me to join any of them; and many other things did he say unto me, which I cannot write at this time. ... When the light had departed, I had no strength; but soon recovering in some degree, I returned to my home. ..." (Joseph Smith 2:12-19.)

His family accepted his message and gave him full support. But when he gave this information to a minister, the minister treated his communication with great contempt, saying that it was of the devil and that there were no such things as visions or revelations in these days, that all such things had forever ceased with the ancient apostles and that there would never be any more of them. This is what a large number of ministers are still saying, and we can well understand what might appear harshness on the part of the Lord in saying that the sectarian creeds were an abomination in his sight and that their ministers were all corrupt. For what greater sin could one be guilty of than to teach these false, unauthorized, and contending doctrines? The scriptures tell us of many revelations that are yet to take place in the world, including the glorious second coming of the Lord himself. Although at this time Joseph Smith was only an obscure boy between the ages of fourteen and fifteen, yet his experience excited a great deal of prejudice against him and was the cause of severe persecution.

In the midst of all this bitterness against this young boy, he said, "However, it was nevertheless a fact that I had beheld a vision. I have thought since, that I felt much like Paul, when he made his defense before King Agrippa, and related the account of the vision he had when he saw a light, and heard a voice; but still there were but few who believed him; some said he was dishonest, others said he was mad; and he was ridiculed and reviled. But all this did not destroy the reality of his vision. He had seen a vision, he knew he had, and all the persecution under heaven could not make it otherwise; and though they should persecute him unto death, yet he knew, and would know to his latest breath, that he had both seen a light and heard a voice speaking unto him, and all the world could not make him think or believe otherwise."

And Joseph Smith said, "So it was with me. I had actually seen a light, and in the midst of that light I saw two Personages, and they did in reality speak to me; and though I was hated and persecuted for saying that I had seen a vision, yet it was true; and while they were persecuting me, reviling me, and speaking all manner of evil against me falsely for so saying, I was led to say in my heart: Why persecute me for telling the truth? I have actually seen a vision; and who am I that I can withstand God, or why does the world think to make me deny what I have actually seen? For I had seen a vision; I knew it, and I knew that God knew it, and I could not deny it, neither dared I do it; at least I knew that by so doing I would offend God, and come under condemnation." (Joseph Smith 2:24-25.)

The Pearl of Great Price, which serves as one of the standard works of the Church, is small in size, and yet is one of the greatest books of the world. Jesus said, "And this is life eternal, that they might know thee the only true God, and Jesus Christ, whom thou hast sent." (John 17:3.) God revealed himself to Moses at Mount Sinai. The resurrected Jesus had his disciples handle him to make sure they understood the kind of being he was. The Lord appeared to John the Revelator and John again tried to describe what he looked like.

But for a long period since that time it had been the feeling of many people that for some mysterious reason God had gone out of business, that the heavens have been closed forever, and that there would never be any more revelation from God. And yet the very opposite is clearly taught in the scriptures. This great

Pearl of Great Price volume of scripture, supported by the testimonies of millions of people, indicates that again the heavens are open and that the work of the Lord is going forward; and while as of old, many are rejecting it, yet it is true.

It is easy for some people to dispose of some great doctrine or responsibility merely by saying that they disbelieve it. In case we are inclined to follow that course, we had better be pretty sure that we know what we are doing, because we cannot avoid the consequences that must follow disbelief in the word of the Lord or his authorized servants. It is one of the great truths of the world that every human being must be involved in the fact that God the Father and his Son, Jesus Christ, have again reappeared on the earth in our day to reestablish among men a belief in the God of Genesis, the God of Calvary, and the God of the latter days.

The Church of Jesus Christ *has* been restored to the earth in our day, with the God-given direction that every person in the world should belong to it and should obey all of his commandments concerning living its principles and practicing its ordinances. If believed and followed, the teachings of the Pearl of Great Price can help us to save our souls and bring about our eternal success and happiness.

11

Hamlet

L ITERATURE SERVES an especially
important need in our day of cul-
ture and education. Culture gives us polish and pleasure, and all
education is about ourselves. Great literature can be one of the
finest aids to our total success.

A number of years ago, an interesting literary survey was
made by Daniel Starck. He interviewed 100 of the most com-
petent literary judges in an attempt to identify the greatest
books that had ever been written. Excluding the scriptures, the
first ten books named in order of their popularity were:

1. Shakespeare's *Hamlet,* written in 1600.
2. *The Works of Aristotle,* written in 325 B.C.
3. Homer's *Iliad,* written in 800 B.C.
4. Darwin's *Origin of Species,* written in 1859.
5. Dante's *Divine Comedy,* written in 1300.
6. Plato's *Republic,* written in 400 B.C.
7. Goethe's *Faust,* finished in 1808.
8. *The Writings of Confucius,* written in 480 B.C.
9. Milton's *Paradise Lost,* written in 1667.
10. Cervantes' *Don Quixote,* written in 1605.

Excluding those men who have spoken directly for God,
most people usually think of Shakespeare as being the greatest
writer who ever lived. Shakespeare looked with keen insight into
human lives. He wrote thirty-seven plays and staffed them with a
thousand characters, each personifying some personality trait.
He said his purpose was to hold the mirror up to life to show virtue her own image and scorn her own likeness. In his plays we
can see our own lives in miniature as we watch his players act
and react upon each other. If *Hamlet* is the greatest of all
Shakespeare's works, it may be helpful for us to think about the
reasons why. The story of Hamlet is as follows:

Hamlet, the king of Denmark, was sleeping in his garden.
His brother, Claudius, poured a quick-acting poison into his ear

that went coursing through his blood and caused his death. The report was given out that the king had been bitten by a serpent. In less than two months, Claudius had married Hamlet's queen, ascended the throne, and taken over the rule of Denmark. Hamlet's son, Hamlet, was not a great admirer of his uncle, and he suspected that something was wrong.

While the young prince was trying to find out what it was, the report came to him that the late king's ghost had been seen in the dead of night, stalking the gloomy battlements of the castle. In a terrifying encounter Hamlet learns from the specter that his father was murdered by Claudius. The young prince is committed to avenge his father's death. The rest of the play has to do with his carrying out this oath, and in the process all of the principals in the play lose their lives.

In Shakespeare's day most plays were labeled as either comedies or tragedies. In those days, a comedy was not something that was funny; a comedy was something that had a happy ending. The fact that over one half of all Shakespeare's plays were tragedies may also indicate a ratio for our present lives.

Shakespeare was a great author for many reasons. He understood human nature. He said, "Conceit in weakest bodies strongest works." (*Hamlet*, Act 3, scene 3.) He knew how to appeal to human interest. Certainly he was not dull. He was great for the impetus he gave to self-improvement. He said, "Assume a virtue, if you have it not." (*Hamlet*, Act 3, scene 4.) He dealt with these important subjects of life and death and success. He knew the place of good and evil in human lives. He was an architect of speech and understood how to exalt and polish the most simple expression. He was an artist in making language beautiful and effective. Shakespeare was also a wise philosopher. He said:

> For, to the noble mind,
> Rich gifts wax poor when givers prove unkind.
> —Act 2, scene 3

> Neither a borrower, nor a lender be;
> For loan oft loses both itself and friend,
> And borrowing dulls the edge of husbandry.
> This above all: to thine own self be true,
> And it must follow, as the night the day,
> Thou canst not then be false to any man,
> —Act 1, scene 3

Hamlet greatly loved his father. He said, "He was a man, take him for all in all, I shall not look upon his like again." (Act 1, scene 2.) Again he said:

> ... What a piece of work is a man! How noble in reason! how infinite in faculty! in form, in moving, how express and admirable! in action how like an angel! in apprehension how like a god!
>
> —Act 2, scene 3

Shakespeare made some great utterances that were centered in human weakness. And those human frailties in young Hamlet's weak-willed mother helped to touch the young prince with a case of melancholia wherein he contemplated suicide. He was restrained by fear of the penalty that God has attached to taking one's own life. In his dilemma of despondency he said,

> O! that this too too solid flesh would melt,
> Thaw, and resolve itself into a dew;
> Or that the Everlasting had not fix'd
> His canon 'gainst self-slaughter! O God! O God!
> How weary, stale, flat, and unprofitable
> Seem to me all the uses of this world.
> Fie on't! 'tis an unweeded garden,
> That grows to seed; things rank and gross in nature
> Possess it merely. . . .
>
> —Act 1, scene 2

Hamlet's doubt that life was worthwhile prompted the famous soliloquy in which he said:

> To be, or not to be: That is the question:
> Whether 'tis nobler in the mind to suffer
> The slings and arrows of outrageous fortune,
> Or to take arms against a sea of troubles,
> And by opposing end them? To die: to sleep,
> No more; and, by a sleep to say we end
> The heart-ache and the thousand natural shocks
> That flesh is heir to, 'tis a consummation
> Devoutly to be wish'd. To die, to sleep;
> To sleep: perchance to dream: ay, there's the rub;
> For in that sleep of death what dreams may come
> When we have shuffled off this mortal coil,
> Must give us pause. There's the respect
> That makes calamity of so long life;
> For who would bear the whips and scorns of time,

The oppressor's wrong, the proud man's contumely,
The pangs of dispriz'd love, the law's delay,
The insolence of office, and the spurns
That patient merit of the unworthy takes,
When he himself might his quietus make
With a bare bodkin? Who would fardels bear,
To grunt and sweat under a weary life,
But that the dread of something after death,
The undiscover'd country from whose bourn
No traveller returns, puzzles the will,
And makes us rather bear those ills we have,
Than fly to others that we know not of?
Thus conscience does make cowards of us all.

—Act 2, scene 3

Hamlet's father had died in his sleep without any chance to repent. Therefore, according to a particular theology, his soul was sent to hell. In the midnight rendezvous with his son, the father touches our interest as he describes his situation. He said:

I am thy father's spirit;
Doom'd for a certain term to walk the night,
And for the day confin'd to fast on fires,
Till the foul crimes alone in my days of nature
Are burnt and purg'd away. But that I am forbid
To tell the secrets of my prison-house,
I could a tale unfold whose lightest word
Would harrow up thy soul, freeze thy young blood,
Make thy two eyes, like stars, start from their
    spheres,
Thy knotty and combined locks to part,
And each particular hair to stand on end,
Like quills upon the fretful porpentine.
But this eternal blazon must not be
To ears of flesh and blood. . . .

. . . Now, Hamlet, hear.
It's given out that, sleeping in mine orchard,
A serpent stung me; . . .
The serpent that did sting thy father's life
Now wears his crown.

List, Hamlet, O, list!
If thou didst ever thy dear father love—. . .
Revenge his foul and most unnatural murder.

—Act 1, scene 5

As the spirit scented the approach of morning air and knew he must depart, he bade a quick farewell to his son by saying, "Adieu, adieu! Hamlet, remember me."

Then under the stress of a most determined resolve the son replied,

> Remember thee!
> Ay, thou poor ghost, while memory holds a seat
> In this distracted globe. Remember thee!
> Yea, from the table of my memory
> I'll wipe away all trivial fond records,
> All saws of books, all forms, all pressures past,
> That youth and observation copied there,
> And thy commandment all alone shall live
> Within the book and volume of my brain,
> Unmix'd with baser matter.
>   —Act 1, scene 5

But first Hamlet decided to have more proof of his uncle's guilt. He reasoned that inasmuch as the devil had the power to assume a pleasing shape, the spirit he had seen may have been Satan trying to entice him to commit murder in order to damn him. He said, "Yea, and perhaps out of my weakness and my melancholy, as [Satan] is very potent with such spirits, abuses me to damn me." A group of traveling players were then in the castle, and Hamlet arranged for them to enact a similar murder play before his uncle, while he watched his uncle's face for the telltale indication of his guilt. He said:

> I have heard
> That guilty creatures sitting at a play
> Have by the very cunning of the scene
> Been struck so to the soul that presently
> They have proclaim'd their malefactions;
> For murder, though it have no tongue, will speak
> With most miraculous organ. I'll have these players
> Play something like the murder of my father
> Before mine uncle. I'll observe his looks;
> I'll tent him to the quick. If he but blench,
> I know my course.
>   —Act 2, scene 2

He said, "The play's the thing/Wherein I'll catch the conscience of the king." (Act 2, scene 2.) When the players reached the murder scene, the panic-stricken king arose from his seat, hast-

ily broke up the performance, and left the room. Hamlet's chance
soon came to kill his uncle when, unbeknown to Claudius, Hamlet
entered his room. But he found Claudius on his knees praying
aloud. Claudius prayed:

> O, my offence is rank, it smells to heaven;
> It hath the primal eldest curse upon't,
> A brother's murder. Pray can I not,
> Though inclination be as sharp as will.
> My strong guilt defeats my strong intent. . . .
> What if this cursed hand
> Were thicker than itself with brother's blood,
> Is there not rain enough in the sweet heavens
> To wash it white as snow? . . .
> Then I'll look up;
> My fault is past. But, O, what form of prayer
> Can serve my turn? "Forgive me my foul murder"?
> That cannot be; since I am still possess'd
> Of those effects for which I did the murder,
> My crown, mine own ambition, and my queen.
> May one be pardon'd and retain th' offence?
> —Act 3, scene 4

Hamlet felt that if he killed Claudius while Claudius was
praying, the latter's soul would then be clean and would go to
heaven, and his own revenge would be thwarted. He said:

> A villain kills my father, and for that
> I, his [sole] son, do this same villain send
> To heaven.
> Oh, this is hire and salary, not revenge.
> —Act 3, scene 4

Therefore he left the room to await a more appropriate time.
However, the king himself was not satisfied that his prayer was of
much help to him, as upon arising he said:

> My words fly up, my thoughts remain below.
> Words without thoughts never to heaven go.
> —Act 3, scene 4

Finally Hamlet killed the king with a poisoned sword point
that the king had prepared for the prince, and the tragedy of
Hamlet came to an end. In pointing out the comparison, Shakespeare says, "All the world's a stage, and all the men and women
merely players. . . . one man in his time plays many parts." (*As*

You Like It, Act 2, scene 7.) May each of us play his own part well, and may each of our lives have the most satisfactory happy ending.

12

The Picture of Dorian Gray

IN 1888, Oscar Wilde wrote his great masterpiece, *The Picture of Dorian Gray*. The dictionary says that fiction is fabrication. But fiction is sometimes more useful than fact. The characters may never have existed, but the principles involved may be pure truth.

Dorian Gray was the child of English aristocracy. His parents came to a tragic end when he was very young, but they left a large inheritance, ample to provide him with a life of luxury. Dorian Gray was a young man of almost-unheard-of physical attractiveness and personal charm.

One day he met a great portrait painter by the name of Basil Hallward. Because Hallward was a worshiper of beauty, he felt a most unusual attraction for Dorian Gray. He said, "I knew I had come face to face with someone whose mere personality was so fascinating that, if permitted, it would absorb my whole nature." Hallward desired above everything else to paint the picture of this unusual person. As he painted, his intoxication grew; his very soul seemed to be absorbed. The portrait was not only the masterpiece of his life, but it also revealed his worship of Dorian Gray.

Young Dorian Gray also loved beauty. To be the recipient of his unusual admiration helped to kindle in his soul a new flame. Life has its masterpieces just as does poetry or sculpture or painting. The stimulating adoration of the artist had touched a secret chord in his soul and had sent it vibrating and throbbing with quickened pulses. Dorian Gray felt that he was one of life's masterpieces, and he drank in feverishly the lilac perfume of his own importance.

When completed, the picture was beyond words. It was unthinkable that it should be owned by anyone except Dorian Gray himself. Dorian Gray received the gift with joy and was overwhelmed by its wonder. But as he worshiped before his own portrait, he was suddenly saddened by a new thought. He said, "How sad it is that I shall grow old and dreadful, but this picure will remain forever young and beautiful. It will never be older than at this particular minute. The experiences of life that will make my soul great will mar and wear out my body. Why should this portrait keep what I must lose? Every moment takes something from me, but nothing from it. O, if it were only the other way! If only I could remain young and have the picture grow old. I would give anything and everything if the picture could change and let me remain as I now am. For that I would give my soul."

Dorian Gray had fallen in love with Sibyl Vane, an actress who played Juliet. With her, he seemed as responsive as a violin. She seemed to spiritualize him, but one night Dorian Gray took two friends to the theater to see Sibyl play. She had become so enraptured with her newly found love that her interest in the theater had suddenly waned, and on this particular night, knowing that he was near, she had performed miserably. Dorian was embarrassed and humiliated. After the show he went to her dressing room and told her he never wanted to see her again. He was so brutal in his treatment that her heart was broken. After he had left the theater, she ended her life by drinking poison.

When Dorian Gray arrived home, he went to sit for a while, as was his custom, to worship before his portrait. But to his great amazement, the portrait did not seem the same. There was a different expression. He noticed a touch of cruelty in the mouth that he had never noticed before. It seemed as if he were looking at himself in a mirror at the very instant that he was doing some dreadful thing. The mind of his picture now seemed to be filled with brutality.

At first he thought it must be some horrible fancy, or maybe it was his conscience reproving him for his brutal behavior earlier in the evening. He turned on more light. There was no mistake. The picture had changed. Then suddenly there flashed across his mind his prayer the day the picture had been finished. He remembered his mad wish that the face on the canvas might bear the burden of his passions and sins, that it might be seared with the lines of age or suffering, and that he might keep the delicate bloom and loveliness of his just, pure manhood. It was incredible, but his wish seemed to have been fulfilled. It seemed monstrous even to think about, and yet there it was on the picture before him. There could be no room for doubt.

Dorian Gray looked in the glass. There was no change in himself; no trace of any wrong could be seen. The picture, not his face, held the secret of his life and told its story. He knew the power of thought upon a living organism, but how could it exercise an influence upon an inorganic thing? It may be that there was some subtle affinity between the chemical atoms that shaped themselves in form and color on the canvas and the soul that was within himself. It may be that some external things vibrate in unison with our moods and passions, atom calling to atom in some strange secret affinity. Or was there some other, more terrible explanation for this change?

But why should he feel sickened or afraid? The reasons for this strange phenomenon were of small importance. The important fact was that it was so. If the picture was to alter, it was to alter—that was that. Why inquire too closely into it? Anyway, who would surrender the chance of remaining always young? If the picture was to change he would have strange pleasure and peculiar advantage in watching it. He would be able to follow his mind into its own secret places and see the transformation brought about by his every thought and deed. This portrait would be a magic mirror; it would reveal to him his soul without hurt to him. And when the winter of age came upon the picture, he would still be standing where spring trembles on the verge of summer. When the blood crept from his face and left behind a pallid mask of chalk with leaden eyes, he would still keep the glamour of boyhood. This was the very thing for which he had promised that he would give his soul. What did it matter what happened to the colored image on the canvas as long as he was safe?

As the days went by, the consciousness of his immunity from consequence encouraged him to investigate life in some of its darker aspects by knowing it firsthand. Why not extend to the limit the advantages of his eternal youth? The picture served as a protective mask over his face and heart. He did not know or greatly care what it is that leads a man to follow an unworthy cause. Dorian Gray made no attempt to understand himself. He wanted only to drain the cup of pleasures of everything it held, good and bad. His picture would keep the sulphurous fumes of each evil experience from troubling him; he held immunity from consequences. Why not take advantage of this unusual protection to know infinite passion, wild pleasure, and wilder sins?

The portrait must bear the burden of his guilt and let him go free.

Perhaps later on, after he had tasted of the things that life had forbidden, he could then teach his real self to yield to some higher influence that could transform him by some noble passion.

For alternating periods Dorian Gray was sad and conscience-stricken. At such times he would mildly reproach himself. There is a certain luxury in self-reproach. When we blame ourselves, we sometimes feel that no one else has a right to blame us. After each of these periods he felt that he had been forgiven. He felt as though his self-censure was equal to a good resolution. And thus, even in his deepest guilt, he was able to keep on good terms with himself.

But there is a fatality about unkept good resolutions. They give us some of those luxurious, though sterile, emotions that go with deceiving ourselves. They are simply checks that men draw on a bank where they have no account. Often our tragedies hurt us mostly because others know about them. We are sorry but not repentant. We are wounded less by great tragedies if they are not known to others. And we can sometimes even hide them from ourselves.

It is often difficult to judge the play in which we have the leading part. But Dorian Gray was not only the actor but also the spectator of his own performance. By means of his portrait he could judge the play as it proceeded. The portrait had received the news of Sibyl's death before he had known of it himself. He would be conscious of all of the events of his life as they occurred. The vicious cruelty that had marred the fine lines of his portrait had no doubt appeared at the very moment of his brutality, just as the features of other men would have been marred at the exact moment of their passion. Like a man seeing his lust or rage in a mirror, Dorian Gray watched himself in every kind of sin, under the reasoning that he was experiencing life.

It is the passions about whose origin we deceive ourselves that tyrannize most strongly over us. Our most destructive motives are those of whose nature we are not conscious.

The picture gradually acquired a corruption distinctly its own, worse than the corruption of death itself. It bred horrors, and yet it would never die. What the worm was to the corpse, his sins would be to the painted image on the canvas. They would mar its beauty and eat away its grace; they would defile it and make it shameful, and yet it would still live on.

Occasionally he shuddered as he thought of the poisonous influences that came from his own temperament. His own soul was looking out at him from the canvas and calling him to judgment. Instead of answering the call, he took the portrait to a little attic room and securely locked it up, so as to keep secure the curious secret of his life and hide his soul from the eyes of men. Why should he watch longer the hideous corruption of his soul? He had his youth; that was enough. If other eyes should never see his shame, why should his?

From time to time there were dark rumors circulated about him. But there was always the purity of the face of Dorian Gray that rebuked any criticism or thought of evil. Often after some of his worst sins, he would creep upstairs to the locked room and open the door with a key which he never let out of his hands. Then he would raise the cover and stand with a mirror in his hand in front of the portrait, looking now at the evil, aging face on the canvas and then at the young, pure face that laughed back at him from the polished glass.

The very sharpness of the contrast served to quicken his sense of pleasure. He grew more and more enamored of his own beauty, less and less interested in the corruption of his own soul. He would examine with minute care, and sometimes with a monstrous and terrible delight, the hideous lines that seared the wrinkling forehead or crawled around the heavy, sensual mouth. He would place his white hands beside the coarse, bloated hands of the picture and smile. He mocked the misshapen body and the failing limbs. There were moments at night when, lying sleepless in his own delicately scented chamber, he would think of the ruin he had brought upon others and upon his own soul. But sensuality increases with gratification. The more he knew, the more he desired to know. He had mad hungers that grew more ravenous as he fed them. He worshiped the senses and smothered the natural instinct to feel terror about passions and sensations that became stronger than their possessor. He felt that manners were more important than morals. He asked himself, "Is insincerity such a terrible thing? It is merely a method by which we can multiply our personalities."

Then one day Basil Hallward called on Dorian Gray. He told him of the rumors that were going around about him. He said, "They say you corrupt everyone with whom you become intimate and that it is quite sufficient for you to enter a house for a shame of some kind to follow after." Hallward was disturbed and wanted to know the basis for the rumors. Dorian Gray asked him for his own opinion, but Hallward said, "Before I could answer that, I would have to see your soul, and only God can do that."

Then Dorian Gray said, "I will show you my soul. You shall see the thing that you fancy only God can see. I have kept a diary of my life from day to day, and it never leaves the room in which it is written." And so he led the way up the stairs to the attic. He seated the artist in his own chair and then uncovered the portrait that Hallward had painted many years ago.

An exclamation of horror arose from the painter's heart, as he saw in the dim light the hideous face grinning from the canvas before him. There was something in the expression that filled him with disgust and loathing. Hallward felt afraid. It was some foul parody, some infamous, ignoble satyr. The idea was monstrous. Still he knew it was the picture he himself had painted long years ago. He prayed that it was only his imagination that had called this vengeance out of the night and set its hideous shapes of punishment before him.

Dorian Gray knew that the soul is a terrible reality, that it can be bought or sold or bartered away. It would have been better for Dorian Gray had each sin of his life brought its sure swift penalty along with it. There is a purification in punishment. We should not pray "Forgive us our sins"; rather, "Smite us immediately for each iniquity," to turn us back from sin. "Each of us has a heaven or hell within himself," cried Dorian Gray, with a wild gesture of despair.

The eyes of the picture were the eyes of the devil. It seemed that from its inside came foulness and horror. Through some quickening of the inner life, the leprosy of sin was slowly eating away his soul. The rotting of a corpse in a watery grave was not more dreadful.

Hallward said, "Good God, Dorian, let us pray. The prayer of your pride has been answered. The prayer of your repentance may be answered also." But Dorian Gray said, "It is too late."

Suddenly an uncontrollable feeling of hatred came over Dorian Gray, as though it had been suggested by the image on the canvas. The mad passions of a hunted animal stirred within him, and he loathed the man who had painted his beautiful portrait. As Hallward sat before the picture with his bowed head resting upon a table, Dorian Gray rushed upon him from behind and plunged a long knife into the great vein behind his ear, crushing the man's head down on the table and stabbing him again and again.

Then when Dorian Gray looked up at his picture, there was a loathsome red hue that now gleamed wet and glistening on the hands of the portrait. How horrible to see the dripping blood of a brother on your hands! As a living thing, tortured and maddened by pain, the picture seemed to dance like some foul puppet on a string.

Dorian Gray suddenly decided that he would destroy the picture. Why had he kept it so long? Once it had given him pleasure to watch it change. Of late he had felt no pleasure in it. When he had been away from this room he had been filled with terror lest other eyes should look upon it. Now he would destroy it. As he had killed the painter, so he would kill the painter's work and all that it meant. He would kill the past, and when that was dead, he would be free. He seized the long knife and, with a vicious blow, stabbed his picture. There was a crash, a thud, a cry. The cry was so horrible in its agony that the frightened servants below awoke from their sleep. They ran upstairs. They knocked upon the door, which they had never seen opened. There was no reply. They called out, but everything was still.

When they entered, they found the splendid portrait of their master, as they had last seen him in all the wonder of his exquisite youth and beauty. Lying on the floor before the portrait, dressed in their master's evening clothes, they found a withered, wrinkled old man of loathsome visage. It was not until they had examined his rings and other effects that they learned who he was.

When Dorian Gray thrust the knife into the picture he had killed himself, and in his death, the great burden of his sins had been transferred back from the picture to his own soul.

And that is where the burden must always finally rest. There are opiates for remorse, drugs that lull the moral senses to sleep, but visibly or invisibly there must always be the sign of degradation that goes with sin. There is a strange affinity between our thoughts and our appearance. And what could be of greater concern to us than the appearance of our own soul when the time shall come for all secret things to be revealed? Then we must stand at last before the mirror of God and, in the bright light of eternal life, find out what we have become.

It is the divinity within that makes the divinity without. "A good appearance is better than all of the letters of reference in the world." In the final test our souls will not be able to keep anything secret, and as the picture of Dorian Gray was its own most accurate letter of reference, so it will be when we come to stand before God. For in a very important way, the story of Dorian Gray is the story of every man.

13

Dr. Jekyll and Mr. Hyde

IN 1855 Robert Louis Stevenson wrote his best-known literary success, entitled *Dr. Jekyll and Mr. Hyde.* Mr. Stevenson first lived this experience in a dream where the plot presented itself. His dream was so real and so startling that he began uttering exclamations of horror in his sleep. Upon being awakened, he immediately wrote down the experiences of his dream.

This interesting and instructive story centers around a kindly and very successful physician by the name of Dr. Henry Jekyll, who at the height of his medical career conducted an exciting but disastrous experiment in which he ventured into the evil possibilities of a split personality. Mr. Stevenson's story spotlights a problem that everyone is confronted with in some degree. Psychiatrists have written much about that duality which exists in human personality. Each of us has a kind of North Pole and South Pole in his character. One is negative, one is positive; one is inclined toward evil, one toward good. Faust said, "Two souls are lodged within my breast that struggle there for undivided reign." If not controlled, this flow of power between opposites tends to cancel the effect of the will and causes frustrations, complexes, and a large number of psychosomatic diseases. Frequently we see the unhappy victims of incessant, unresolved mental and emotional conflicts, "living lives of continual desperation." Sometimes a personality goes to pieces in what we call a nervous breakdown.

One of H. G. Wells' characters might have been speaking for some of us when he said, "I am not a man but a mob." That is, we sometimes develop within ourselves a miscellaneous, heterogeneous personality population consisting of many antagonistic, uncoordinated impulses which waste our energy by fighting another. Mark Twain made reference to this problem when he indicated that "every person is like a moon which has a light side and a dark side." When these opposing forces make war on each other, the resulting internal conflict sometimes attains very serious proportions, depending upon the amount of our integration and control. When left uncontrolled, the casualties of this damaging individual cold war fill the sickbeds, the reform schools, the penal institutions, and the mental hospitals.

In Robert Sherwood's play *Abraham Lincoln,* Lincoln said of himself, "You talk about a Civil War. But there is one going on inside of me all the time." He said, "One of these days I may split asunder and part company with myself."

That was exactly what Dr. Jekyll decided to do on a scientific basis in his medical laboratory. He was endowed with unusual abilities. He was also inclined to vigorous industry with high standards of professional excellence. This combination of virtues and abilities had earned for him a fine reputation supported by a long list of scientific degrees and a large medical practice. Like most conscientious men, Dr. Jekyll was very fond of the respect and sincere good will that he received from his fellowmen. To say the least, his life was fully occupied, interesting, and successful.

Dr. Jekyll felt that his worst fault was a certain natural gaiety of disposition which seemed to be in conflict with his dignity and a need he felt to wear a grave countenance before the public. But in trying to conceal his lightheartedness, he felt that he was developing within himself a kind of duplicity which gave rise to an unpleasant feeling of guilt. This was more especially true because of the exacting nature of his high professional standards. As time passed, it seemed that the split grew larger, further dividing his personality under the two general subdivisions of good and evil.

Both sides of Dr. Jekyll's nature were in dead earnest and each was making a determined effort to win consideration for its own point of view. Dr. Jekyll recognized the claims of each faction, and because he adopted no stern policy of personality integration, the negative influences continually grew in power. To support his high ambition and the religious dedication he gave to his work, Dr. Jekyll labored long and hard in relieving suffering, preventing disease, and promoting the general public welfare. But at other times he felt a strong desire to lay aside restraint and indulge the other elements in his nature. Then, even to himself, he seemed to be another person. Later when he thought of some of the things that he had done, he had an uneasy feeling of regret and guilt. But inasmuch as he seemed not disposed to commit himself wholeheartedly to either side, this disturbing cold war within himself gradually increased in intensity.

He often reflected upon this annoying situation and wondered what should be done about it. It occurred to him how much more simple his situation would be if he were actually two people instead of one. That is, suppose he could split off the undignified and unjust part of himself to go its separate way without enduring the straitjacket of his conscience and the continual accusations of his better self. On the other hand, this separation would leave the just part of himself free of any distraction or guilt to walk steadily and securely along his upward course. Then he would be able to advance his knowledge and enjoy the pure delights of service without embarrassment or the danger of doing any injury to his professional standing.

Dr. Jekyll found this speculation so agreeable that he finally settled himself in his laboratory to try to separate these antagonistic elements and thereby relieve himself of what of late was becoming a rather unbearable conflict. Why should these incongruous elements be thus bound together and both forced to endure an inharmonious, unhappy struggle? He would separate these opposite Siamese twins of personality that had been so unfortunately and, he felt, unjustly bound together. Finally a drug was compounded by means of which he could temporarily dethrone either of his personalities and give complete supremacy to the other. As he seemed to have two characters, why shouldn't he also have two physical identities? He could be the kindly, helpful, highly respected physician by day, living above any thought of wrong or shadow of suspicion. Then when he felt the need to indulge his less worthy self he could go into his laboratory, drink the potion, and completely eliminate Dr. Jekyll so that his reputation would forever remain untarnished.

At first this transformation was brought about only with great difficulty. It was also a rather painful process, resembling a convulsion that shook his entire being. But after the medicine had done its work, something like a new birth occurred, and he stepped out on the other side of the curtain a new man. In his new role he felt much younger. He was lighter of body and happier in his disposition. He was considerably smaller in physical stature, with a completely new physical appearance. He felt a freedom never known before. His double life could now be housed in separate tenements, and he felt that at last he could have peace. His two selves in no way resembled each other. No matter how much evil his unworthy self might be guilty of, he had only to take an opposite kind of drug and he would again be the kindly, faithful Dr. Jekyll beyond the reach of any criticism or punishment. Dr. Jekyll retained his own name for his better personality and gave his new identity the name of Edward Hyde.

The pleasures that he first sought in his new disguise were only undignified. But his strange immunity from punishment soon led him toward the monstrous. The evil within him now operated with a free rein, being no longer restrained by good. Evil braced and delighted Mr. Hyde like new wine. Each personality was soon clearly marked for what it was. As pure goodness shone upon the countenance of Dr. Jekyll, so undiluted evil was broadly and plainly written upon the person of Mr. Hyde. The body of Edward Hyde bore the signature of Satan on its face. Yet when he looked in the glass he was conscious of no repugnance. Rather, he felt a thrill of relief to be free from the continual censure of the disapproving conscience of Dr. Jekyll. Every other human being was a commingling of good and evil. But Edward Hyde alone in all the ranks of mankind was pure evil. He took pleasure only from that which was bad, but after his evil appetite had been fully satiated, he could return from his excursions of depravity, go into his laboratory, take another drug, and again stand forth as the kindly, unblameable Dr. Henry Jekyll.

But appetite grows by what it feeds upon. As his double careers went their unrestrained ways, his hunger for evil increased. When the devil within him was chained up for too long a period, it began to growl for license. He suffered a thousand deaths when confined for long in the fires of abstinence. And each indulgence gave his unbridled evil a more furious propensity to ill. He had been stripped of all of the balancing instincts by which even the worst of mankind may walk with some degree of steadiness among the temptations. But with all restrictions removed, to be tempted, however slightly, was to fall.

He soon noticed that the intervals when he was Dr. Jekyll were growing shorter in duration. This he recognized as the warning handwriting upon the wall, and so he tried to give up his role as Mr. Hyde. He hated and feared the brute that stirred so uneasily within him. But his evil self so long indulged now exercised a kind of control that could not easily be denied. At intervals

more and more frequent, Dr. Jekyll would again find himself
raging and lusting with the passions of Hyde. Hyde was always
burning with anger and lusting to inflict pain, and in the intervals
between, the animal within him sat licking the chops of his
memory.

Finally his evil nature stung him into the frenzied pitch of
murder. In an early morning return from one of his evil expedi-
tions, he clubbed to death a fellow human being. Once his passions were unloosed to commit this capital sin, the spirit of hell
raged within him. With a transport of glee he mauled the un-
resisting body, tasting delight with every blow. A demoniac glee
stimulated his trembling excesses. And it was not until weariness
had begun to set in that his evil passions were satisfied, and he
fled from the scene, in the person of Dr. Jekyll, to conceal himself
from pursuit.

But it was not easy to forget the spilling of a brother's blood.
While Dr. Jekyll had done strange things with his body, he was
unable to put his mind beyond the reach of judgment. He felt
a cold chill of terror run through his heart as he thought about
the murder. In the most earnest prayer mixed with bitter tears
he sought to smother the crowd of hideous sounds and images
that were swarming in his memory against him.

Dr. Jekyll tried to compensate for the evil done by Mr.
Hyde, but the ugly face of sin kept staring into his soul. He felt
nausea and distaste for life accompanied by deep-seated terror.
It was not the terror of death. His soul was hounded by deeper
and more awful dread. As evil had first destroyed the balance of
his personality, so it was now destroying the very foundations of
his soul. He had brought upon himself a punishment so dreadful
that it could not be named. And as he was the chief of sinners, so
he was the chief of sufferers also.

As the change from Dr. Jekyll to Mr. Hyde had become
more frequent, it had also become more easy. Then one night
he went to bed as Dr. Jekyll and awoke as Mr. Hyde. The change
had taken place without the drug. He rushed into his laboratory
and took a double dose of the restorative that recalled Dr. Jekyll.
But six hours later he felt again the automatic pangs that would
change him to Edward Hyde. Again the Dr. Jekyll drug had to
be administered in increased amounts.

In the following weeks it was only under the constant stimulation of the drug that he was able to wear the countenance of Dr. Jekyll. At any hour of the day or night he might be taken with a warning shudder foretelling the change to his dreaded self. If he slept or even dozed for a moment in his chair, it was always as Mr. Hyde that he awakened. Now almost without transition his fancy began swarming with images of terror and his soul would begin to boil with causeless hatreds. His body now seemed too weak to contain the raging energies of his evil self. The power of Hyde had grown with the sickliness of Jekyll. He now knew that his better self was being permanently overthrown, the power to change was being forfeited, and the character of Edward Hyde was becoming irrevocably his.

Dr. Jekyll felt that only those consigned to the deepest hell could ever know the full dreadfulness and horror of the Bible statement that says, "The way of the transgressor is hard." After all, who can understand what it is like to be completely abandoned to evil? Dr. Jekyll's pitiful cry for help and forgiveness was the cry of a lost soul. He had been blasted by a prodigy sufficient to stagger the unbelief of Satan. His was an incurable malady that both tortured and deformed the sufferer. His life was shaken to its very roots. Sleep had become impossible, and the most deadly terror sat by him at all hours of the day and night. He knew that all was lost and that he was approaching the last time that Henry Jekyll would ever be able to think his own thoughts. He had no horror of death. His only horror was of being what he was. And thus the unhappy experiment of Dr. Jekyll and Mr. Hyde came to its mortal end.

And someday when we come to the end of our own lives, how fortunate we will be if we have so integrated our deeds under the direction of our better selves that our lives will have the happy ending that God intended.

14

Paradise Lost

ONE OF the great authors of all time was John Milton. His narrative poem *Paradise Lost* is rated among the first ten of the world's great books. Very early in his life Milton developed an insatiable love of learning. And from the time he was a child he had an ambition to write a world-moving epic poem. He once told a friend that he was pluming his wings for a flight, and he intended that its influence would reach to the highest heaven and to the lowest hell. However, for many years he was plagued by poverty and disturbed by political difficulties. He suffered seriously from family problems and was finally engulfed by blindness at age forty-four. But after some fifteen years of blindness, Milton's great masterpiece was published. Certainly no one could accuse him of picking a subject that was small or unimportant.

Milton's story is centered in "the war in heaven" and its results. Satan's revolt from God not only emptied heaven of one-third of its inhabitants, but it has radically changed the history of this world and the welfare of everybody in it. Most of our life's problems have always involved the influence of Satan. He caused the expulsion of our first parents from their paradise in Eden, and he has also had a hand in most of our difficulties since. It is interesting to imagine what our world would have been like if we had always effectively resisted the devil. The Bible, supplemented by modern revelation, tells us a great deal about Satan and the events that cast him in his present role as the enemy of God and the promoter of evil. To our scriptural information about the war in heaven, Milton has added generously from his own imagination. And while Milton makes some mistakes in theology, our mental powers are greatly stimulated as we become familiar with his tremendous war scenes and the eternal consequences of the enterprises of Satan.

Trying to make a comparison with Milton's theme, I recently looked up the world's ten top news stories for the last several years. But the most important events of this most important age all pale into insignificance when placed alongside the war in heaven. Even our most important present-day events have Satan as one of their chief participants. Among the most important news stories of recent years are the race riots, the war in Vietnam, the assassination of President John F. Kennedy, the Kennecott and Ford Motor Company labor strikes, the disposal of Nikita Khrushchev in Russia, the U.S. Surgeon General's report of the health hazard of cigarettes, and the Chinese Communist nuclear explosions. These and all other events are important or unimportant, depending upon the effect they have on the lives of people. In each of the above listed events someone got hurt. But because of Lucifer's rebellion, one-third of all God's spirit children were forever denied the privileges of mortality and eternal progress. It has been estimated that of the two-thirds of God's children who did not rebel, some 80 billion have already lived upon this earth. This would mean that the corresponding one-third who did rebel would number over 40 billion. But the welfare of the entire 120 billion has been seriously influenced by Satan.

Milton begins his poem with a prayer to God for guidance. He says:

> ... I thence
> Invoke thy aid to my adventurous song,
> That with no middle flight intends to soar
> Above the Aonian mount, while it pursues
> Things unattempted yet in prose or rhyme.
> And chiefly thou, O Spirit, that dost prefer
> Before all earthly temples the upright heart and pure,
> Instruct me, for thou knowest; thou from the first
> Wast present, and with mighty wings outspread,
> Dove-like sat'st brooding on the vast abyss,
> And mad'st it pregnant: what in me is dark
> Illumine, what is low raise and support;
> That to the highth of this great argument
> I may assert Eternal Providence,
> And justify the ways of God to men.
> —Book 1, lines 12-26

The scriptures make it plain that Satan was once Lucifer the light-bearer, the brilliant Son of the Morning. (Isaiah 14: 12.) And he and all of those who followed him were the literal spirit children of God. One of our important religious problems is that we frequently think of eternal beings, including God, as having mysterious influences, whereas Milton shows these spirit participants as the real, tangible people that they are. He makes a kind of catalog of the great generals, statesmen, and warriors on both sides of the war in heaven so that we understand them as real people.

Some of the generals assisting Satan in leading the rebellion are listed as Beelzebub, Molock, Mammon, and Belial. Milton describes Beelzebub as having shoulders like Atlas, capable of bearing the responsibility-weight of the mightiest monarchies. He seemed like a pillar of state; and even after his ruin, his princely face revealed an unmistakable majesty. But dominating the picture of this proud and once noble spirit so highly favored of heaven was his disobedience. He had stood very close to God until his unrighteous ambition had caused him to defy the Almighty. Isaiah quotes him as saying, "I will be like the most High." Satan's program was highly offensive to God, as it was characterized by force. Even Satan himself resorted to arms in challenging the Omnipotent. The forces opposing the rebellion were led by Michael, God's Archangel. According to Milton, he was assisted by Gabriel, Raphael, and other powerful spirits under the general direction of Jehovah. Jehovah is the eldest and most capable son of Elohim, the Eternal Father. The scriptures refer to Jehovah as a man of war (Exodus 15:3); that is, before he was the Prince of Peace, he was Jehovah the Warrior.

Milton knew nothing of nuclear warheads and guided missiles. But even then God had all knowledge, and the most powerful weapons were available to him. However, Milton did talk of "sulphurous hail," "winged thunder," and "red lightning." Because the rebels sought to thwart the work of God and would not repent, and because they could not stand against the superior intelligence and greater power of the Almighty, Satan and his forces were expelled from heaven. What a significant vacancy of emptiness must have been indicated by the statement of John the Revelator when he said, ". . . neither was their place found any more in heaven"! (Revelation 12:8.)

Milton tries to have us feel the importance of this expulsion by having Satan and his followers falling for nine days and nights. Then, for a similar period, their vanquished crew lay rolling on the fiery gulf of hell. And although they were immortal spirits, the confusion and bewilderment of their fall so dulled their minds that for a time they were only partially conscious of their fate. As their senses began to revive, they felt the full torment of their lost happiness, their everlasting humiliation, and their awful suffering. Their horrible dungeon was aflame on every side, and yet the only light was a thick, visible darkness by which they discovered their dismal, wild, and wasted doom. Hell was full of sights of woe, regions of sorrow, and doleful shades, where neither peace, nor rest, nor love could ever dwell. This fiery deluge, causing torture and misery without end, was fed by ever-burning sulphur unconsumed. How unlike was hell to that magnificent place whence they had fallen!

In Milton's story, as Satan's mind began to clear, the baleful eyes he cast around him were still filled with obdurate pride and steadfast hate. As they became accustomed to the scenes of awful affliction and terrible dismay, he discovered that Beelzebub was weltering by his side. This great spirit was Satan's second in command, next only to himself in crime and power. Breaking the horrid silence, Satan said:

> If thou beest he—but O how fallen! how changed
> From him, who in the happy realms of light
> Clothed with transcendent brightness didst outshine
> Myriads, though bright—if he whom mutual league,
> United thoughts and counsels, equal hope
> And hazard in the glorious enterprise,
> Joined with me once, now misery hath joined
> In equal ruin. . . .
> —Book 1, lines 84-91

Then Satan began to think about how the results of their expulsion could be repaired; and with great speeches, Milton puts into the mouths of Satan and his vanquished generals sentiments that under more godly circumstances might have done credit to the grandest enterprises. In spite of being cast out of heaven Satan was still defiant and unrepentant. He said:

> What though the field be lost?
> And is not lost; the unconquerable will,
> And study of revenge, immortal hate,
> And courage never to submit or yield:
> And what is else not to be overcome?
> —Book 1, lines 104-109

Beelzebub suggested that maybe God had permitted them to retain their mental strength and physical vigor that he might

use them in hell for his own purposes. Then the Arch-Fiend said
to Beelzebub:

> Fallen cherub! To be weak is miserable,
> Doing or suffering: but of this be sure,
> To do aught good never will be our task,
> But ever to do ill our sole delight,
> As being the contrary to his high will
> Whom we resist. If then his providence
> Out of our evil seek to bring forth good,
> Our labor must be to pervert that end.
> —Book 1, lines 157-64

Satan then decided to reassemble his afflicted warriors and
plan how to make the most of their situation and to most seriously offend God. He indicated his own attitude when he said:

> . . . this the seat
> That we must change for Heaven, this mournful gloom
> For that celestial light? Be it so. . . .
> Infernal world, and thou, profoundest Hell,
> Receive thy new possessor: one who brings
> A mind not to be changed by place or time.
> The mind is its own place, and in itself
> Can make a Heaven of Hell, a Hell of Heaven.
> What matter where, if I be still the same. . . .
> Better to reign in Hell than serve in Heaven.
> —Book 1, lines 243-45, 251-56, 263

Satan wondered what the reaction of his other followers
would be, and Beelzebub paid a great compliment to Satan's
leadership when he said that they would need only to hear his
voice to fully revive and regain their former courage and united
effort. Then Milton says of Satan:

> . . . on the beach
> Of that inflamed sea, he stood and called
> His legions, angel forms, who lay entranced, . . .
> Under amazement of their hideous change.
> He called so loud, that all the hollow deep
> Of Hell resounded: "Princes, Potentates,
> Warriors, the flower of Heaven, once yours, now lost,
> If such astonishment as this can seize
> Eternal spirits; or have ye chosen this place
> After the toil of battle to repose
> Your wearied virtue . . .?

Awake, arise or be for ever fallen!"
They heard, and were abashed, and up they sprung
Upon the wing, as when men wont to watch
On duty, sleeping found by whom they dread,
Rouse and bestir themselves ere well awake.
Nor did they not perceive the evil plight
In which they were, or the fierce pains not feel;
Yet to their general's voice they soon obeyed Innumera-
ble. . . .
—Book 1, lines 299-301, 313-20, 330-38

In their council it was decided that someone must get out of hell and make his way through the almost impassable chaotic darkness and prepare to take over the earth and destroy those who had helped to banish them from heaven. In making free agency the underlying principle with his children, God is quoted as saying, "I formed men free, and free they must remain till they enthrall themselves. I will not change their natures nor revoke the high decree that hath ordained their freedom. They themselves ordained their fall."

But Satan would still use force, hate, war, and deception. By means fair or foul he would still try to overthrow the work of God. One said:

. . . how wearisome
Eternity so spent in worship paid
To whom we hate. . . .
—Book 2, lines 247-49

Milton tries to indicate the vast power and great ability of Satan by saying:

He above the rest
In shape and gesture proudly eminent
Stood like a tower; his form had not yet lost
All her original brightness. . . .
. . . but his face
Deep scars of thunder had intrenched, and care
Sat on his faded cheek, but under brows
Of dauntless courage, and considerate pride
Writing revenge. Cruel his eye, but cast
Signs of remorse and passion to behold
The fellows of his crime, the followers rather . . .
condemned

> For ever now to have their lot in pain,
> Millions of spirits for his fault amerced
> Of Heaven, and from eternal splendors flung
> For his revolt. . .
> —Book 1, lines 589-92, 600-611

Satan was the only one capable of making this necessary trip to the earth. Milton says:

> Into this wild abyss the wary Fiend
> Stood on the brink of Hell and looked a while
> Pondering his voyage. . . .
> —Book 2, lines 917-19

Then Milton describes that persistence that has always characterized Satan's evil accomplishment:

> . . . so eagerly the Fiend
> O'er bog or steep, through strait, rough, dense, or rare,
> With head, hands, wings, or feet, pursues his way.
> And swims, or sinks, or wades, or crawls, or flies.
> —Book 2, lines 947-50

And when Adam and Eve were placed in the Garden of Eden, Satan was already there waiting, and since that time the battle between good and evil has continued unabated. Satan has had some defeats and many victories. He is now working desperately, with his accomplishment at its zenith, as he knows that the time is near when he will be bound. But in the meantime we should be aware of the ability of our enemy and of the many things that we might do in being valiant soldiers for righteousness to make the cause of our great King victorious.

15

The Odyssey

ONE OF our greatest writers was the blind Greek poet Homer, who lived in the ninth century B.C. His primary works consisted of two great book-length epic poems. The first is known as the *Iliad*. It is the story of the famous Trojan War.

Paris, a Trojan prince, eloped with Helen, the wife of Menelaus, king of Sparta. Menelaus enlisted the aid of his fellow kings of the little Greek states, including his brother Agamemnon, the great Greek fighter who was the king of Mycenae. This aggregation of fighting men sailed a thousand ships across the Aegean Sea and laid siege to Troy, a large and strongly fortified walled city near the Hellspont. The war lasted for ten long years. By a trick the Greeks finally got inside the walls of Troy. They destroyed its fighting power, sacked the city, and burned it to the ground. Then they loaded their ships and sailed for home.

Homer's second book is called the *Odyssey*. It is taken from the name of Odysseus, sometimes called Ulysses, who was king of Ithaca and one of the greatest of the Greek heroes. The *Odyssey* is an account of the experiences of Odysseus as he made his way across the three hundred miles of island-dotted sea lying between the battleground of Troy and his island home of Ithaca off the west coast of Greece.

Odysseus was very happy as he started for home at the head of his fleet of ships. His men were all glad that the war was over and that they would soon be at their own firesides with their families. But in this they were doomed to disappointment, for along the way they met with one difficulty after another, many of which were far more destructive than the war had been. By the time Odysseus finally reached Ithaca, every ship had been destroyed and the life of every man had been lost except that of Odysseus himself.

This great story of the *Odyssey* is the grandfather of all adventure stories. Homer knew every trick of storytelling. The *Odyssey* tells of man-eating giants, bewitching sirens, terrible monsters, frightening ghosts, roaring whirlpools, hair-raising adventures, and romantic interludes, not to mention the interest added by Odysseus himself, who was one of the most courageous and ingratiating heroes in all of our literature.

The *Odyssey* has lived in such fine repute through the ages that the word itself has become a part of our language. "Odyssey" has come to mean any long, wandering, difficult journey. Of course, the greatest of all odysseys is the journey of life itself. We also speak of our strivings for success as an odyssey.

But Homer was not just a great storyteller; he also looked with keen insight into human lives and in a very interesting way described the courage, strategy, and super-strength with which these famous heroes tried to solve their problems. Their errors in judgment are made plain to us, and we are made aware of their moral weaknesses that were so frequently fatal. Homer's skill makes his heroes a mirror by which we can adjust our own lives as we relive their experiences.

As Homer describes their problems, longings, and disappointments and tells of the suffering that they so frequently brought upon themselves, we are stimulated to try to plan our own lives more profitably. This account of what these Greek heroes did and thought thirty centuries ago impresses us that human problems and frailties haven't changed very much in that time. In fact, we might go even further back and read from that interesting stone tablet dug up some time ago which was supposed to have been written fifteen centuries before Troy. It says in part: "Bribery and corruption are common, children no longer obey their parents, the end of the world is at our doors and every man wants to write a book." That tablet might just as well have been written in our own day. In any event, we can learn a great deal from the people of other ages—not only from the challenge of their greatness, but their weaknesses and sins help us, as they point out some of the pitfalls that we should avoid.

Odysseus and his men had scarcely started for home when they were blown off their course by a raging wind which drove them to the island of the Lotus-Eaters. An old legend says that when men ate the magic fruit of the lotus tree, they forgot about their families and responsibilities and lived in dreamy forgetfulness and indolent enjoyment. Only when Odysseus dragged his sailors back aboard their ships were they able to recover enough of their ambition to continue their journey homeward.

But their troubles were not confined to the winds and the lotus fruit. They had many problems, and every one was different. At one time they landed on the island of the one-eyed Cyclops and were captured and held prisoner by the giant Polyphemus. They were able to escape only by blinding the monster with a pole, the end of which had been burned in the fire. Maddened with pain and rage, Polyphemus cried out to his father, Poseidon, god of the sea, and enlisted his help to avenge the wrong. Their ships stopped at an island inhabited by man-eating giants, who destroyed most of the fleet with huge boulders and speared the men like fish. This was a devastating ordeal, and only the men on the ship of Captain Odysseus survived to sail wretchedly onward.

One of their greatest adventures came when they landed on the island of Circe, the enchantress. There some of the men fell into her hands and were turned into swine, but Odysseus obtained the use of a magic power by which he forced her to release her spell and set his men free. This experience kept Odysseus and his men a full year on the island of Circe.

In the course of their journey they were required to pass an island where some bewitching sirens lived. It was known that in times past the song of the sirens had lured many sailors to their deaths. Odysseus had been warned about the hazard of listening to the music of these fascinating, dangerous creatures. When he came near these islands, fearing that his men would not be able to withstand the temptation, he had all of the members of his crew fill their ears with wax so that they would not be able to hear the siren's song. Odysseus himself was overcome by curiosity and did put wax in his own ears. But not quite trusting his own strength, he protected himself against weakness by having his men bind him to the mast. He gave them strict orders that no matter what might happen, they must not release him until they were past the island and out of range of the temptation. When they came within the hypnotic sound of the siren's song, Odysseus weakened and ordered his men to pull their ship onto the shore, but their ears were full of wax and they could not hear his orders. The caution of Odysseus saved the day, and they rowed on past the temptation.

This ten-year odyssey involved many other great dangers. After passing the sirens, the men were required to run the gauntlet down the narrow strait passing between the vast whirlpool of Charybdis, on the one side, and the death-dealing monster Scylla on the other. If the ship went just a little too far to the right, it would be drawn into the deadly whirlpool; if it went too far to the left, it would be within reach of the treacherous Scylla. Even though Odysseus's men barely missed the whirlpool and they rowed with great skill, yet six of them were snatched from the deck as their ship passed the rock of this six-headed female monster.

Odysseus had hoped to avoid the sun god's island, but because of an unfavorable gale his ship was marooned there for weeks. Despite their leader's warning, his men butchered some of the sacred cattle. In revenge their ship was shattered with lightning, and every single man was killed except Odysseus. Clinging to some of the wreckage, he was blown back to the whirlpool, where an overhanging fig tree saved his life. When the timbers again floated up to the surface and out of the whirlpool, Odysseus clung to them and struggled on alone to the island home of the nymph Calypso.

For the next seven years Calypso held Odysseus a prisoner while he longed for his home and his wife Penelope. At last, on orders from Zeus, Odysseus was allowed to sail on. But watchful Poseidon wrecked his home-made boat, and Odysseus, a victim of amnesia, was flung upon the island of the Phaeacians. The king's daughter took him to her father's court. The friendly king entertained Odysseus royally and finally sent him home in one of his ships, so that at last, after ten years of wandering, Odysseus, the sole survivor of the voyage, reached the shores of Ithaca. At home after twenty years of absence, he found about as many troubles as he had encountered along the way.

In this great story, Homer intended to remind us of the odyssey of our lives. We too have problems along life's way. Frequently we too win the great wars of our lives and then lose out while doing some comparatively easy, simple thing. There are times when, to protect ourselves, we should fill our ears with wax and put blinders over our eyes, or have ourselves bound to the mast as a protection against ourselves. If we look and listen intently enough, either the sirens or their songs can sometimes bewitch our greatest powers. Almost daily we are required to sail that straight course between Charybdis and Scylla. Jesus talked a great deal about this same kind of a situation, though he used a different figure of speech. He called this hazardous course "the strait and narrow way." But it is made clear that in either case there isn't much room for meandering or carelessness. Sometimes just one wrong step and we are in serious trouble; sometimes disaster awaits us on both sides. Someone gave expression to this idea by saying that the devil was on one side and the cliff and the deep blue sea on the other. A misstep either way and we are in trouble.

Isn't it interesting that all of these men survived the fierce ten-year Trojan War, but only one survived what was supposed to be a peaceful trip home? They had survived the onslaught of the strongest enemy soldiers and then went down in defeat before the bewitching enchantment of Circe or the languorous appeal of the lotus fruit. They could handle the hard tasks but failed to stand up against the easy, pleasant, beguiling, sweet-smelling sins. As a consequence their loss, which had been small during the ten-year war, was nearly 100 percent during the ten-year odyssey.

This reminds us of the statement of Jesus about the broad road that leads to destruction. It is traveled by so many people even though it leads all who follow it to a place they don't want to go. Our odyssey is often more difficult than that of the Greeks, inasmuch as it usually lasts longer than ten years. But the things that usually bother us most are not the hard, tough battles or the difficult problems; it is the lethargy, the sloth, the little evils, the bad habits, and wrong attitudes. And instead of putting wax in our ears and blinders on our eyes at the right time, we put on our magnifying glasses and turn up our hearing aids as we pay too much attention to the wrong things. Because we don't want to miss anything, we hold too many "foot in the door" conversations with temptation.

Then, like Ulysses, we most often stumble and fall over the trivialities. Plutarch once said, "It is not in the lists that the victors are made, but after the contests are over." The graveyard of success in life is filled with the bones of men who killed all the dragons of the battlefield and then went to their doom during times of peace, because they could not withstand the little pleasant temptations that beckoned them.

Like the problems of Odysseus, all our problems are different, making it more difficult to be prepared against them. We get some wrong ideas and attitudes into our minds and then we allow them either to befog, befoul, belittle, belie, bewitch, benight, becalm, benumb, or betray us until we are lost. Sometimes even the extra courage and self-confidence of the hero lulls him into a false sense of security and makes him careless enough to take unnecessary chances that anyone of lesser ability would avoid. There are also experiences along life's way that, like the enchantress Circe, can cast strange spells over us to make us do strange things, sometimes even turning us into swine. Sometimes we are frightened into discouragement or paralyzed by the soft, warm enchantments that get possession of our imagination.

Ulysses saved himself because he was more wise in devising his strategy and overcoming the hazards that he met along the way, but even he wasted ten years of his life fighting these beguiling, enchanting sins. May God help us to win the great battles, but may we also be successful in solving life's little problems in this all-important odyssey of our own lives.

16

The Divine Comedy

IN THE early part of the fourteenth century, the Italian poet Dante wrote his great literary masterpiece entitled *The Divine Comedy*. In those days a comedy was not something that was funny. A comedy was something with a happy ending. A more understandable title for our day would have been "The Divine Experience" or "The Divine Story." Thomas Carlyle said that in his opinion *The Divine Comedy* was the most remarkable of all books. It was based on the scriptures, to which Dante added generously out of his own imagination.

The book is divided into three parts. Part one is "The Inferno," which tells of an imaginary trip Dante made through hell. In Dante's account, gathered from the scriptures and to which he added generously from his own imagination, hell was the place where departed spirits were consigned who were forever lost. These were the ones whose lives were so warped, twisted, and perverted that there was no hope. Then Dante traveled through a second kingdom, which he called "Purgatory." This was a place of purification, where certain spirits who had not sinned unto death were cleansed through suffering, then educated and made worthy to ascend unto heaven. The Bible refers to this place as the place where Jesus went and preached to the spirits in prison who had been disobedient in the days of Noah some twenty-three centuries earlier. (See 1 Peter 3:19-20.)

Then the happy ending came when Dante concluded his journey in what he refers to as "Paradise," which was that place where the righteous lived forever with God. Dante believed that it was his mission in life to show men hell, and that seems to me to be a necessary and a very important mission. However, it is a pretty difficult assignment, because generally we don't like to think about things that are unpleasant even to avoid them. Think how reluctant we are to think or talk about death or the consequences of sin, and so we bury our heads in the sand, so to speak, to hide from those truths that we do not like. But unpleasant things do not cease to exist just because they are ignored. And a far better way to avoid an unpleasant prospective situation is to do a lot of the right kind of thinking about it in advance.

One of our biggest problems so far as our eternal exaltation is concerned is that we are such incurable optimists. We usually have an overwhelming, unshakeable belief in our own "happy ending," regardless of what we do leading up to it. Jesus talked about many unpleasant possibilities, such as our need for repentance, and the possibility that even some of the elect may be lost. He probably talked as much about hell as he did about heaven. He said, ". . . wide is the gate, and broad is the way, that leadeth to destruction, and many there be that go in thereat." (Matthew 7:13.) Yet comparatively few people ever think of themselves as being in that particular group.

Shakespeare was probably trying to get us to think a little more realistically about our own situation, for over one-half of all of his plays were tragedies. He understood what is very important for us to understand, that unless we do something specific about it, every life may not have a happy ending.

We are reminded of our natural optimism when we say that in our business affairs we work under "the profit system." That is just not true. We work under the profit and loss system, and that is the same system that regulates our eternal welfare.

With the thought in mind of helping ourselves to avoid useless loss, suppose we take a mental journey similar to the one that Dante took. And a good place to begin is where Dante began—in hell.

It was reported that a certain minister once announced that his next Sunday's sermon would be about hell. A newspaperman went to hear him and then commented that the minister was certainly full of his subject. But it is thought to be a very good idea at least to get enough of the ideas about hell into our minds that we may avoid actually going there in person. Hell must be a very exciting place, but there are a great many advantages to first making this trip in the imagination. One advantage is that it is a little easier to get out if we don't want to stay. Another advantage is that we may not want to go there in the first place.

I would like to point out in passing that hell is a divine institution. It was not established by Satan as some of our present-day institutions seem to have been. Hell was established by God for a very important purpose. You remember that in the council of heaven Lucifer rebelled and drew away one-third of all of the hosts of heaven after him. The Lord said, "And they were thrust down, and thus came the devil and his angels; And, behold, there is a place prepared for them from the beginning, which place is hell." (D&C 29:37-38.) There are some people who don't believe in hell. Many others have just never thought about it either one way or the other.

Of course, we have the direct word of God, given on many occasions, that there is a hell. Reason also tells us that there must be a hell. We know that the basic law of the universe is this unchangeable, irrevocable law of the harvest that says "whatsoever a man soweth, that shall he also reap." (Galatians 6:7.) If everyone is going to be judged according to his works, then if there is a heaven there must also be a hell. In the great enterprise of human salvation there must be different places for instruction and reformation, rewards and punishments. Unfortunately Satan and his angels are not going to occupy hell alone. In discussing the outcome of the judgment the Lord said, "And the righteous shall be gathered on my right hand unto eternal life; and the wicked on my left hand will I be ashamed to own before the Father; Wherefore I will say unto them—Depart from me, ye cursed, into everlasting fire, prepared for the devil and his angels." (D&C 29:27-28.)

In spite of its unpleasantness, hell was established for a good purpose, just as penitentiaries are established for a good purpose, and mental hospitals are established for a good purpose, and reform schools and the organizations of Alcoholic Anonymous are established for a good purpose. There is a certain purification that sometimes can best be brought about only through suffering. The members of some religious organizations do what they call "whipping the flesh." They deliberately torture themselves, to help themselves understand the meaning of pain. They believe that a little suffering now may help them to avoid a lot of suffering later on.

One of the most important success factors in life is to settle definitely our minds about the existence of hell. Dr. William E. Orchard, a noted religious leader, was once asked whether or not he thought the concept of hell might now be safely abandoned in

this day of education and enlightenment. With a strange quiet-
ness in his manner Dr. Orchard replied, "I would not bank on it if
I were you."

A student once asked his Sunday School teacher, "Is there a
hell?" The teacher replied, "There is a hell all right, but we won't
go into that now." However, Dante thought it was important
that we should go in occasionally.

The Prophet Joseph Smith once said, "If you could gaze
into heaven for five minutes, you would learn more than by reading all of the books that have ever been written on the subject."
We might also learn a great deal by gazing into hell for five
minutes. That is, human nature is often more effectively motivated by the prospect of pain or loss than by a comparable
promise of reward, but if we go about it right, we can get good
from both the promise of rewards and a foreknowledge of punishments. Of course, no one is ever sent to hell by compulsion. Everyone who goes there goes there voluntarily by his own choice. And
everyone who goes to hell goes there only because he just hasn't
made his mind up definitely not to go there. No one needs to go
to hell who definitely makes up his mind to go some other place.
And if the "picturing power" of our minds is sufficiently effective,
we will be able to make some firm decisions about where we want
to go, if, as Dante did, we visit all three places in advance. Suppose, then, that we first go in imagination and stand before the
gate of Dante's hell and consider its challenging inscription,
which reads as follows:

> Through me you pass into a world of woe,
> Through me you enter into eternal pain;
> Through me you join with souls forever lost,
> All hope abandon, ye who enter here.

Suppose that we become familiar with the real hell by reading the inspired words of the great scriptures and think about the
importance of such messages as those contained in the 40th chapter of Alma, the 76th section of the Doctrine and Covenants, the
16th chapter of Luke, and many others.

It is thought that a thorough understanding of these passages pertaining to hell would forever free us from our difficult
problems in obtaining eternal life. That is, it would not be very
difficult to forsake our sins and get rid of our weaknesses if
occasionally we could clearly see in advance the tragic consequences of our evil.

In trying to show us these kingdoms of hell and purgatory, Dante pictures a series of circles or elevations. The top levels are inhabited by the spirits who have sinned least. Then, as we descend from one layer to another into the depths of hell, the corruption and consequent suffering increase. Dante tries to picture the worst conceivable suffering of which his mind was capable. But the human imagination even at best is very limited in its power and is not capable of giving more than a faint suggestion of the real experience. For example, note the difference between a toothache in your imagination and one in your tooth. For the same reason it is probable that no matter how vivid a description of hell might be, it must of necessity fall far short in its ability to convey to our minds the full impression of those who will actually suffer there. But to see it as clearly as possible in our minds can be a wonderfully helpful experience.

Suppose that we could go as Jesus did and talk with these spirits who had been confined to their prison house for many centuries. Just suppose that we could feel their regret and understand their suffering. Or suppose that we could learn firsthand from them what brought them to this unhappy place. We would probably recognize a great many of our own personal sins. It has been pointed out that there are no new sins—there are only new sinners. As an example, one of hell's prisoners said to Dante, "Not what I did but what I failed to do lost me the right to live with God on high." And then from the point of view of his own hindsight he said, "This desire for God and goodness I knew too late."

One of hell's groups said, "Our lukewarm eagerness for doing good brought us to this place of misery." Another said, "We could not endure the toil unto the end and thereby forever lost the glory of our lives."

As Dante went into the lower regions, he visited with some of those unfortunates who had sinned unto death. These had lived such lives that they could never be redeemed. For them there was no forgiveness. We do not know how intense either mental or physical suffering can be. We know that it can be severe enough to send one insane. And Dante pictures some of hell's inmates as afflicted with madness because some incurable grief had unhinged their minds.

One of hell's spirits said to Dante, "We beg that if ever you escape from these dark places to look again upon the stars of heaven, see that ye speak of us to other men." And then attempting to discharge that obligation in our interests, Dante said, "Reader, as God may grant you reason, gather wisdom from reading this and then take council with yourself."

We should also take council with God and his word, which tells us that there are at least two ways to cleanse ourselves from sin. One is by suffering. A great passage in latter-day scripture says:

"For behold, I, God, have suffered these things for all, that they might not suffer if they would repent;

"But if they would not repent they must suffer even as I;

"Which suffering caused myself, even God, the greatest of all, to tremble because of pain, and to bleed at every pore, and to suffer both body and spirit—and would that I might not drink of the bitter cup, and shrink." (D&C 19:16-18.)

The other way is repentance, as indicated by Walter Malone's poem entitled "Opportunity." He said:

> Art thou a mourner? Rouse thee from thy spell;
> Art thou a sinner? sin may be forgiven;
> Each morning gives thee wings to flee from hell.
> Each night a star to guide thy feet to Heaven.

God has promised us that we may have any blessing that we are willing to live, and we must pay the awful penalty of every sin. This helpful experience of an occasional mental journey beyond the borders of mortality may help us to avoid the suffering of hell and find a happy ending in the celestial kingdom of God.

17

Sohrab and Rustum

IN 1853, Matthew Arnold wrote his great father-and-son poem, entitled "Sohrab and Rustum." Rustum, a powerful young Persian war lord, had met and wed the daughter of the king of the Koords. Before their son Sohrab was born, Rustum was called to a far-away field of battle; and because his wife feared that he might seek out their son to train for war, she sent him word that the child which had been born to them had been a sickly girl.

But Sohrab's warrior inheritance and the stories of his father's heroism and might led him to adopt the profession and develop the abilities of his great father. He was called into the military service of the Tartars among whom he lived, although they were the enemies of Persia. Above everything else Sohrab longed to know his hero father. Everywhere he was sent he was possessed by only one thought, and that was to find Rustum.

One day the Tartars met the Persians by the River Oxus. Sohrab gained consent to challenge the Persians to seek out their greatest champion to be matched with him in a single combat. Because of Sohrab's fame among the Tartars, he hoped that the Persians would not dare to match him with anyone but the mighty Rustum himself. This proved to be the case, and not knowing that young Sohrab was his son, Rustum was persuaded to take the challenge up, though he insisted that he fight unknown. As Rustum watched Sohrab's approach, he felt a strange liking for this heroic young challenger. So slender Sohrab seemed, so softly reared, like some young cypress as in the queen's garden, and Rustum said—

> "Behold me: I am vast, and clad in iron,
> And I have stood on many a field of blood
> And I have fought with many a foe;
> Never was that field lost, nor that foe sav'd.
> O Sohrab, wherefore wilt thou rush on death?
> Quit the Tartars and come

To Iran, and be my son
And fight beneath my banner till I die.
There are no youths in Iran brave as thou."
Sohrab heard his voice,
The mighty voice of Rustum; and he saw
His giant figure planted on the sand,
His temple streaked with the first touch of gray,
And he ran forward and embrac'd his knees,
And clasp'd his hand within his own and said:
"Art thou not Rustum?"

But Rustum feared what the motive of this young man might
be, that maybe he was being tricked into giving up the challenge, and thereby the Persian lords might be shamed through
him. So Rustum turned and sternly spake and said:

"Rise! Wherefore dost thou vainly question thus
Of Rustum? I am here, whom thou hast call'd
By challenge forth;
Is it with Rustum only thou wouldst fight?
Rash boy, men look on Rustum's face and flee,
For well I know, that did great Rustum stand
Before thy face this day
There would be no talk of fighting then,
But I tell thee this;
Either renounce thy vaunt, and yield;
Or else thy bones shall bleach upon the Oxus sands."
He spoke: and Sohrab answer'd, on his feet:—
"Art thou so fierce? Thou wilt not fright me so.
I am no girl, to be made pale by words.
Yet this thou hast said well, did Rustum stand
Upon this field today, there would be no talk of
        fighting then,
But Rustum is far hence, and we stand here.
Begin: thou art more vast, more dread than I,
And thou art prov'd, I know, and I am young—
And though thou thinkest that thou knowest sure
Thy victory, yet thou canst not surely know,
For success sways with the breath of heaven.
And only the event will teach us in its hour."
He spoke and Rustum answer'd not, but hurl'd
His spear: Sohrab saw it come, and quick as a flash
He sprang aside and the spear
Hiss'd, and went quivering down into the sand,
Then Sohrab threw in turn
And his spear struck Rustum's shield;

The iron plates rang sharp, but turn'd the spear.
Then Rustum seized his club, which none but he
Could wield.
He struck one stroke; but again Sohrab sprang aside
And the club leapt from Rustum's hand
And thundered to the earth.
And Rustum follow'd his own blow, and fell
And now might Sohrab have unsheath'd his sword,
And pierc'd the mighty Rustum while he lay dizzy
And on his knees, and chok'd with sand:
But Sohrab smiled nor bar'd his sword,
But courteously drew back and said:
"Thou strik'st too hard.
But rise, and be not wroth; not wroth am I;
No, when I see thee, wrath forsakes my soul.
Thou say'st thou art not Rustum:
Who art thou then, that canst so touch my soul?
Boy as I am, I have seen battles too;
Have waded foremost in their bloody waves,
And heard the hollow roar of dying men;
But never was my heart thus touch'd before.
Old warrior, let us yield to Heaven!
And plant here in the earth our angry spears,
And make a truce, and sit upon the sand,
And pledge each other in red wine, like friends,
And thou shalt talk to me of Rustum's deeds.
There are enough foes in the Persian host
Whom I may meet, and strike, and feel no pang;
Champions enough Afrasiab has, whom thou mayest
    fight
Fight them, when they confront thy spear.
But oh, let there be peace 'twixt thee and me!"
He ceas'd; but while he spake, Rustum had risen,
And stood erect, trembling with rage: his club
He left to lie, but had regain'd his spear,
Whose fiery point now in his mail'd right-hand
Blaz'd bright and baleful
His breast heav'd; his lips foam'd; and twice his
    voice
Was chok'd with rage: at last these words broke forth.
"Girl! Nimble with thy feet, not with thy hands!
Curl'd minion, dancer, coiner of sweet words!
Fight; let me hear thy hateful voice no more!
Thou art not in Afrasiab's gardens now
With Tartar girls, with whom thou art wont to dance;
But on the Oxus sands, and in the dance

Of battle, and with me, who make no play of war;
I fight it out, and hand to hand.
Speak not to me of truce, and pledge, and wine!
Remember all thy valour: try thy feints and cunning
All the pity I had for thee is gone."
He spoke: and Sohrab kindled at his taunts,
And he too drew his sword: at once they rush'd
    together
And crashing blows Rustum and Sohrab on each other
    hail'd
And you might say that the sun took part
In that unnatural conflict; for a cloud
Grew suddenly in Heaven, and dark'd the sun
Over the fighters' heads; and a wind rose
Under their feet, moaning swept the plain,
And in a sandy whirlwind wrapp'd the pair.
The on-looking hosts on either hand
Stood in broad daylight, and the sky was pure,
And the sun sparkled on the Oxus stream.
But in the gloom they twain fought on with bloodshot
    eyes
And labouring breath, first Rustum struck the shield
Which Sohrab held stiff out; the spear
Rent the tough plates, but fail'd to reach the skin,
And Rustum pluck'd it back with angry groan.
Then Sohrab with his sword smote Rustum's helm,
Nor clove its steel quite through; but all the crest
Was shorn away, and that proud horsehair plume,
Never till now defil'd, sank to the dust;
And Rustum bow'd his head; but then the gloom
Grew blacker; thunder tumbled in the air,
And lightnings rent the cloud.
But Sohrab rush'd right on
And struck again; and again Rustum bow'd his head
But this time all the blade, like glass,
Sprang in a thousand shivers on the helm,
And in Sohrab's hand the hilt remain'd alone.
Then Rustum rais'd his head; his dreadful eyes
Glar'd, and he shook on high his menacing spear,
And shouted, "Rustum!" Sohrab heard that shout,
And shrank amaz'd; back he recoil'd one step,
And scann'd with blinking eyes the advancing form:
And as he stood bewilder'd, he dropp'd
His covering shield, and Rustum's spear pierc'd his
    side.
Sohrab reel'd and staggering back, sunk to the ground.

And then the gloom dispers'd and the wind fell,
And the bright sun broke forth, and melted all
The cloud; and the two armies saw the pair;
Saw Rustum standing, safe upon his feet,
And Sohrab wounded, on the bloody sand.
Then with a bitter smile, Rustum began:
"Sohrab, thou thoughtest in thy mind to kill
A Persian Lord this day, and strip his corpse,
And bear thy trophies to Afrasiab's tent.
Or else that the great Rustum would come down
Himself to fight, and that thy wiles would move
His heart to take a gift, and let thee go.
And then that all the Tartar host would praise
Thy courage or thy craft, and spread thy fame.
Fool! Thou art slain, and by an unknown man!"
And, with a fearless mien, Sohrab replied:—
"Unknown thou art; yet thy fierce vaunt is vain.
Thou dost not slay me, proud and boastful man!
No! Rustum slays me, and this filial heart.
For were I match'd with ten such men as thou,
And I were he who until today I was,
They should be lying here, I standing there.
But that beloved name unnerv'd my arm—
That name, and something, I confess, in thee,
Which troubles all my heart, made my shield to fall
And thy spear transfix'd an unarm'd foe.
And hear this, fierce Man, tremble to hear
My father, whom I seek through all the world,
The mighty Rustum shall avenge my death!"
And with a cold, incredulous voice Rustum replied,
"What prate is this of fathers and revenge?
The mighty Rustum never had a son."
And, with a failing voice, Sohrab replied:—
"Ah yes, he had! and that lost son am I."
Sohrab spoke of many things and as he ceas'd he wept
     aloud,
Thinking of her who bore him and his own untimely
     death.
Rustum listen'd, plung'd in thought,
Nor did he yet believe it was his son who spoke
Although he call'd back names he knew;
For he had sure tidings that the babe,
Which was in Aderbaijan born to him,
Had been a puny girl, no boy at all:
And so he deem'd that either Sohrab took,
By a false boast, the style of Rustum's son;

Or that men gave it him, to swell his fame.
So deem'd he; yet he listen'd, plung'd in thought;
Tears gathered in his eyes as he saw
His own youth; saw Sohrab's mother, in her bloom;
And that old King, her father, who lov'd well
His wandering guest, and gave him his fair child
With joy; and all the pleasant life they led,
They three, in that long-distant summer-time—
And Rustum gaz'd on him with grief and said:
"O Sohrab, thou indeed art such a son
Whom Rustum, wert thou his, might well have lov'd!
Yet here thou errest, Sohrab, or else men
Have told thee false;
For Rustum had no son: one child had he,
But one—a girl: who with her mother now
Plies some light female task, nor dreams of us—
Of us she dreams not, nor of wounds, nor war."
But Sohrab answer'd him in wrath; for now
The anguish of the deep fixed spear grew fierce,
And he desired to draw forth the steel,
And let the blood flow free, and so to die;
But first he would convince his stubborn foe—
And, rising sternly on one arm, he said:—
"Who art thou who dost defy my words?
Truth sits upon the lips of dying men,
And falsehood, while I liv'd, was far from mine.
I tell thee, prick'd upon this arm I bear
That seal which Rustum to my mother gave,
That she might prick it on the babe she bore."
He spoke: and all the blood left Rustum's cheeks:
His knees totter'd and he smote his hand
Against his breast
And in a hollow voice he spake, and said:—
"Sohrab, that were a proof which could not lie;
If thou shew this, then art thou Rustum's son."
Then, with weak hasty fingers, Sohrab loos'd
His belt, and near the shoulder bar'd his arm,
And shew'd the sign of Rustum's seal
And then he touch'd it with his hand and said:—
"How say'st thou? is that the proper sign of Rustum's
    son,"
He spoke: and Rustum gaz'd, and gaz'd, and stood
Speechless; and then he utter'd one sharp cry—
"O boy—thy father!"
And then a dark cloud pass'd before his eyes,
And his head swam, and he sank down to earth.

But Sohrab crawl'd to where he lay, and cast
His arms about his neck, and kiss'd his lips,
And with fond faltering fingers strok'd his cheeks,
Trying to call him back to life; and life
Came back to Rustum, and he op'd his eyes,
And they stood wide with horror; and he seiz'd
In both his hands the dust which lay around
And threw it on his head, and smirch'd his hair,
His hair, his face, and beard, and glittering arms;
And strong convulsive groanings shook his breast,
And his sobs chok'd him; and he clutch'd his sword,
To draw it, and forever let life out.
But Sohrab saw his thought, and held his hands,
And with a soothing voice he spoke, and said:—
"Father, forbear.
I meet today the fate which at my birth
Was written down in heaven,
And thou art heaven's unconscious hand,
But let us speak no more of this:
Let me feel that I have found my father.
Come, sit beside me on the sand, and take
My head betwixt thy hands, and kiss my cheeks,
And wash them with thy tears, and say: 'My son!'
Quick! Quick! for number'd are my sands of life."
So said he: and his voice releas'd the heart
Of Rustum, and his tears broke forth; he cast
His arms round his son's neck, and wept aloud,
And kiss'd him. And awe fell on both the hosts
Because of Rustum's grief:
Then Rustum said—"Sohrab my son,
I will burn my tents,
And quit the host, and bear thee hence with me to
        Seistan,
And I will lay thee in that lovely earth,
And heap a stately mound above thy bones,
And plant a far-seen pillar over all;
That men shall not forget thee in thy grave.
And I will spare thy host:
What should I do with slaying any more?
I would that all whom I have ever slain
Might be once more alive; my bitterest foes,
And those through whose death I won the fame I
        have;
That thou mightest live too, my Son, my Son!
Or would that I myself
Might now be lying on this bloody sand,

That I might die, not thou."
He spoke; and Sohrab smil'd on him, and took
The spear, and drew it from his side, and eased
His wound's imperious anguish: but blood
Came welling from the open gash, and life
Flow'd with the stream;
His head droop'd low, his limbs grew slack;
Motionless and white, he lay—
His eyes fix'd lovingly upon his father's face:
Till all his strength had ebb'd, and all
Unwilling his spirit fled away,
So on the bloody sand, Sohrab lay dead.
And the great Rustum drew his horseman's cloak
Down o'er his face
And father and son were left alone upon the Oxus
    sands.

It is thought that the sentiment of this great poem may help to develop our own wonderful father-and-son relationships.

Section

III

Books to Write In

18

Books to Write In

ROBERT LOUIS Stevenson once said that everyone should always have available for his use two sets of books. One of these should be a set of books to read from, and the other should be a set of books to write in. One of the advantages of the books to write in is that before we can put ideas on paper, we must make them definite in our own minds. They are also much more easily remembered after we have gone through the process of writing them out.

Our New Year's resolutions have much greater power to help us if they have been thought through and written down. One man was once asked what he thought about a certain subject and he said, "I don't know. I haven't spoken on it yet." Before we speak on something, we usually think it through on both its positive and its negative sides and make some determinations about it. But we are usually much more sure of our ground when we cast our plans and determinations into written declarations. Someone has said that no plan is a plan at all unless it is on paper. No one would want to employ an architect whose only ideas were in his head.

When the Lord made a disclosure to John the Revelator of his future plans of our world and beyond, even including the final resurrection and the eternal judgment, he said to John, "Write the things which thou hast seen, and the things which are, and the things which shall be hereafter." (Revelation 1:19.)

It has been said that the revelation concerning the three degrees of glory, as given in the 76th section of the Doctrine and Covenants, was the greatest revelation that God had ever given to man in any age. And four times during this revelation the Prophet said the Lord "commanded us to write while we were yet in the Spirit." And that is a great idea for us just as it is for the Lord. Just think what a handicap it would be if we did not have the word of the Lord written down!

The story is told of an explorer in one of the undeveloped

regions of Africa who needed to communicate with an associate working many miles away. It was arranged for a dependable native who knew nothing about the wonders of writing to carry the message. He watched carefully as the explorer took his pen and made certain marks on the piece of paper. He put the letter in an envelope and gave it to the native for delivery. A few weeks later the native had traversed the necessary miles, had found the man for whom the message was intended, and had given him the envelope. While the native watched, the man who had received the letter opened it and looked at the marks on the paper and then, without one word having been spoken, the receiver knew where his friend was, what his needs were, and what should be done about it. The native was so impressed with this magic power of writing that he fell down on his face before the explorer and worshiped the paper.

And what tremendous messages can be conveyed from those books we have to read from and what miracles can be accomplished by those books we have to write in!

One great man gives credit for his success to his book of plans. He starts off each day with a set of written orders from himself to himself and then at night he requires a written summary of his successes and failures as a checkup. Benjamin Franklin accounted for his success by what might be called his "Book of Virtues." He determined that thirteen particular virtues were necessary for the life he contemplated. And so he made a daily chart listing each one, and at the end of each day he made a check mark if he had sufficiently practiced that virtue that day. If not, he set it up as a special order of business for all following days. Benjamin Franklin thought that this procedure would enable him to live without making any mistakes.

Others have had such important books to write in as "A Book of Decisions," "A Book of Dreams," "A Book of Ambitions," Everyone ought to have a diary or a daily journal to write in. Everyone ought to write at least one biography, his own. The word *bible* comes from a Greek word *biblia,* which means a collection of books, and we ought to have a set of books to write in for our own lives.

My most valuable material possessions are my idea books. They have had a tremendous value to me in my business, my family, my religion, and all of my personal affairs. Everyone ought to have some great books to read from and everyone ought to have some great books to write in. It is thought that an effective combination of these books cannot help but add great quality, success, and happiness to our lives.

19

My Idea Books

ONE OF the great experiences of my life began in 1943 when I heard Dr. Adam S. Bennion give a lecture on the values of great literature. It was near the end of World War II, and among other important things Dr. Bennion said, "If you were going to be a prisoner in a concentration camp for the next four years and could take with you the works of any ten authors, which would you take and what would you expect to get out of them?"

It is interesting that everyone believes in the value of great literature and it is easy to sell the values in great books and great ideas to other people. However, most people make this idea inoperative in their own lives and miss the benefit by saying, "I am too busy" or "I don't have time to read." It is interesting that most people do have time to read about the world's crime waves. We know about the violence and sins that are recorded in the newspapers. We do seem to have time to watch television and go go x-rated movies. But we don't have time for the greatest human thought. Most of us excuse ourselves from doing the things that we know should be done merely by telling ourselves that we are too busy with those things that we know we should not do. So in trying to get a favorable consideration of the great literature Dr. Bennion put in the idea of the concentration camp. He said, "Suppose that you didn't have anything but time, what would you do?" He suggested that each person ought to select the ten authors that he would like most to resemble and then exhaust each one in turn by reading everything that he had ever written.

Psychologists tell us that when an idea is run through the mind, it makes a little groove, or engram; and if one runs through his mind enough of the same kind of ideas that went through the minds of Shakespeare, Emerson, the Apostle Paul, or Jesus of Nazareth, his mind will tend to respond as theirs did. That is, each one develops a set of thinking responses that are about as definite and characteristic as his fingerprint, and so Dr. Bennion suggested that we pick out the ten men who in our opinion have the most to give and then read every word that each has ever written. We rethink every idea that he ever thought. We run through our mind every idea that ever went through his mind.

I can easily recognize this as a great idea, but I still have the block of the old mental hazard that I am too busy. At that time I was teaching a class in salesmanship, and I decided to reread the Bible with the idea of getting out of it its salesmanship. The Bible is the world's first book of religion. It is the world's first book of history, it is the world's first book of literature. It is the world's first book of wisdom, and it is also the world's first book of salesmanship. If I were going to try to teach anyone to be a good salesman, I would first try to teach him to be a good man. I would undertake to help him absorb the faith, the convictions, the courage, the enthusiasm, and the righteousness of the Bible.

On trying to be a good salesman, one ought to try to get the spirit of this young man from Nazareth as he went around saying to people such things as, "Be of good cheer. Be not afraid. Why are ye troubled? Why do thoughts arise in your hearts? Rejoice and be exceeding glad." Jesus said to people, "Be ye doers of the word. Be ye therefore perfect. Think no evil. Enter ye in at the strait gate. Be ye clean that bear the vessels of the Lord."

Every time one reads the Bible with a new purpose, it becomes a new book. When we read the Bible for its salesmanship, it is quite a different book than when we read it for its theology or its literature, and I had a tremendous new experience with the Bible. The habits thus formed gave me enough courage to take up Shakespeare.

I suppose that Shakespeare comes close to the top of most people's lists of great authors. Understanding Shakespeare was a little difficult for me at first. I read very slowly and not always too comprehendingly. I had to reread a lot and look up many meanings that I didn't understand. But finally the clouds began to open up a little bit, and the light of understanding started to break through, and I had a wonderful and exciting experience with Shakespeare.

I always read with my pencil in hand, and I took out of Shakespeare what to me were the most meaningful philosophies and the most potent speeches. These I had copied onto 8½-by-11-inch pages to go into three-ring binder notebooks. And my Shakespeare notes amount to 210 pages. Then I have gone back over them and memorized approximately half of them. I select those ideas that fit best in my philosophy and will function best in my mental machinery. I like to read his great speeches involving courage and the attitudes of success.

As an example, when Henry V was king of England, France was one of his vassal nations. Some problems developed that he thought justified his personal attention, and so he took an army and sailed across the channel to correct the situation. The job was a little more difficult than he had imagined, and an early snow cut off escape and he was forced to spend the winter near the little French village of Agincourt. It was a long, hard winter, and some of his soldiers died and many of the twelve thousand survivors were sick and weak.

As the spring began to break so that he could go about his business, Henry found himself confronted with an army of sixty thousand well-trained, well-horsed, well-armored Frenchmen who sought to wipe out the British and obtain their freedom. The normal procedure for ordinary men under these circumstances would have been to surrender. But this was something that Henry was not about to do. Instead, he got his soldiers together and gave them a pep talk about success which might be very usable as some of us attempt to solve our own problems. In Shakespeare's words, which I have edited, Henry said in essence to his soldiers:

"Once more unto the breach, dear friends, once more . . . the blast of war blows in our ears. The French are bravely in their battle set and will with all expedience charge upon us. 'Tis a fearful odds. There's five to one. Besides, they are all fresh. 'Tis true there is great danger. The greater, therefore, must our courage be." Then he said, "O God of battles, steel my soldiers' hearts; possess them not with fear. God be with you, princes all. We may never meet again till we shall meet in heaven. God's arm strike with us! All things are ready if our minds be so. Perish the man whose mind is backward now." And then he said, "On, on you noblest English. I see you stand like greyhounds in the slips, straining upon the start. The game's afoot: follow your spirit. I'll to my task, there's work to be done and throats to be cut."

He didn't tell them this is going to be an easy job. It was one that in all probability would cost them their lives. He said, "We may never meet again till we shall meet in heaven." But regardless of the danger, they must do their duty. He said, "God's arm strike with us! All things are ready, if our minds be so."

After he had finished, a soldier came up and said how wonderful it would be if they had the British army over here to take care of these Frenchmen. There is always someone who wants to solve his problems by having overwhelming odds in his favor. Henry's aide said to this negative-thinking soldier, "God's will! my liege, would you and I alone, without more help, could fight this royal battle!" That may not be good judgment, but that is courage. And that is what many of us need most.

This was one of the places where the English long bow was first used. The British drove stakes into the earth to stop the French horses; and then from behind a protection, they showered the enemy with arrows, knocking the soldiers off their horses. And with their heavy armor, the French became immobile in the mud and were killed or captured by the British, and the British won the battle of Agincourt.

Henry's leadership and his courage give us inspiration to win more of our own battles. And I had a tremendous experience with Shakespeare.

Then in turn I read the works of Emerson. David O. McKay once said that Ralph Waldo Emerson was the greatest thinker that America had ever produced. And I would like to have some of his ideas made negotiable in my own bloodstream.

Then I read twenty-eight volumes of Elbert Hubbard. I read the fifty volumes of the Harvard classics, which is an assembly of what President Elliott and his Harvard scholars consider to be the greatest ideas ever known in the world.

Then I read 19,600 pages of the eloquent and atheistic Robert G. Ingersoll. I have always felt a little bit cheated that my early life has been so devoid of problems or difficulties to be overcome. I have heard a great man say that because he had an atheistic teacher or a wrong-thinking companion, his life had been made very difficult. I have never had from others any serious opposition to my faith, and I have wondered what would have happened if I had been exposed to some serious anti-religion. And so I read 19,600 pages from the man who in my opinion was the greatest atheist in the world. Robert G. Ingersoll was an orator, a salesman, a persuader; and I thought that if anybody could change my faith, it might be Robert G. Ingersoll. And so I read so far as I know every one of his ideas on atheism, which would be the equivalent in volume of some eighty new testaments, and I felt not the slightest problem so far as my faith was concerned. That is, my faith was not shaken in the slightest degree.

In the thirty years that have passed since that time, I have read a total of 983 volumes of some of the world's greatest books. I have built up a rather intimate relationship with Homer, Milton, Dante, Saul of Tarsus, and Jesus of Nazareth. I think of my reading in terms of a combined harvester out on the farm. It sweeps across a field of wheat and cuts everything before it. Then it operates a threshing process by which it throws out all the weeds, the chaff, and the straw, and puts the clean wheat into the sack. I do a similar kind of mental threshing. I mark all of the ideas that I think will be helpful to me. Then I make some decisions about them and prepare myself to utilize them in my own life. These especially selected ideas now fill twenty-five notebooks totaling some 7,500 pages. Then I have gone back and reviewed and memorized the most interesting and exciting of these ideas. The rest I stamp as deeply as possible into my brain cells so that I have an intimate speaking acquaintanceship with those I have not memorized.

Memorization makes it so much easier to retain the flavor, the power, the beauty, the color, and the meaning that these great masters work so hard to obtain. Many have written their ideas in poetic form where they have taken the most appropriate words, which they have measured, metered, weighed, and rhymed. Somebody has said that poetry is language dressed up in its best clothes, and by the proper arrangement, great authors can give our language more striking power.

If I were going on a trip and wanted to take my most exciting reading material, I would not take Shakespeare or Emerson or the Harvard classics or even the Bible. I would take my notes. So far as I am concerned, this is a place where there is no chaff nor waste, as I have selected only the good wheat, or the pure gold that has been fully refined from all of the best sources, including the great scriptures that best suit my needs, and these are the ones that I know best and love the most. And out of my vast paper memory of 7,500 pages, I reap the very profitable income of satisfaction and motivation.

20

A Book of Decisions

F OR MANY years Rudger Clawson served as president of the Council of the Twelve Apostles. One of the duties of this important quorum is to plan for the welfare of the Church and its members. Every Thursday the Twelve meet in the upper room of the Salt Lake Temple where important questions are discussed, problems are solved, and the program of the Church is decided upon.

It is reported that President Clawson always kept what he called "A Book of Decisions." This was a large notebook in which he kept a written record of all official actions taken by the Quorum. After a problem had been considered and a final decision reached, President Clawson made a note of that fact in his "Book of Decisions." Of course, this soon became a rather complete set of rules and regulations to guide future action. It also made it unnecessary to spend any time discussing those matters that had already been settled. It is thought that this procedure is one of the foundation principles of all success.

Emerson once said that nothing puts so much order into one's life as a set of sound principles. And whether one may be an athlete, a businessman, a builder, or a scientist, it is important that he has a dependable and rememberable set of governing rules to go by. An expert builder can erect the most magnificent building that the greatest architect can conceive merely by knowing how to follow a blueprint. A good cook needs a book of recipes. A lawyer increases his ability when he has a usable set of dependable decisions already recorded in the books of law on his library shelves.

Someone has said that science is mostly just a collection of success formulas. It would be a little bit ridiculous for anyone to waste valuable time and money to work out a formula that was already public information. When once it was discovered that strychnine was poison and that electricity could kill, then it would have been foolish for anyone to have personally performed those experiments for himself.

Every wise person, whether he is an inventor, engineer, doctor, lawyer, teacher, parent, or businessman, builds his success largely upon the accomplishments of others. No one can afford to do all of his own discovery and experimentation if it has already been done. And in no field is this principle more applicable to success than in the field of religion.

A friend of mine recently told me that he used to spend a large part of every Sunday morning trying to decide whether or not he would go to church. When he woke up he first considered how he felt. Then he would check whether the weather was too cold or too hot. He would reconsider whether or not he thought the church itself was worthwhile. Then he would lie back in bed for some more consideration until his reluctant mind could come to a decision. Finally he got the great idea that instead of going though this exhausting time-consuming process each week, he would settle these questions in one major decision to last him for the entire year. He knew that his "once and for all" procedure would make his life more pleasant and far less complicated. He also knew that he would be a better man at the end of the year because of his decision. Of course, a cardinal rule of decision making is that the decision must be strong enough to handle the problem. It would be useless to attack a flying fortress problem with a bow-and-arrow solution.

William Ellery Channing once said that "the greatest man is he who chooses the right with invincible resolution; who resists the sorest temptations from within and without; who bears the heaviest burdens cheerfully; who is calmest in storms, and the most fearless under menace and frowns; and whose reliance on truth, on virtue, and on God, is most unfaltering." Of course, if decisions are to stay made, they should be based on facts supported by sound logic and should be thoroughly made. Then the mind is freed for other work.

There is a kind of mental plague that sometimes bothers us, that has been called "the doubting folly." This is the state of mind in which one is insecure in his decisions and unsure of what he has done. Such a one is always returning to see if he turned off the gas and locked the door. He wonders if what he has previously decided is all right and whether or not it was settled in the best way. Such doubters are continually calling their decisions back for review and reconsideration. And one of the most serious causes of failure in both material and spiritual affairs is the inability to make intelligent, firm, correct, once-and-for-all decisions about important fundamental things.

For example, there are many people who haven't yet made up their minds as to whether or not they are going to be honest at all times or just when it is convenient. Each exposure to a choice has to be taken up and decided on an individual basis. Many haven't yet made up their minds whether or not they are going to church next Sunday. Many won't know until the last day of the year whether or not they are going to be full tithe payers. Every time some new temptation presents itself, some people must make up a new mental balance sheet of pros and cons. The pressure of the moment urges them to do one thing, and their conscience tells them to do something else. All of the time their "doubting folly" is shuttling them back and forth, landing them in one place one time and in the opposite place another time, depending upon the circumstances and how they feel at the moment. This is the procedure by which we become vacillators and procrastinators. This is how we develop an unstable character and a mind that has difficulty arriving at a conclusion. It has been said that with some minds nothing is definite but indecision.

A psychiatrist once asked a mental patient if he ever had any trouble making up his mind. The patient said, "Well, yes and no." Because we all have some yes and no inclinations, we need a good Book of Decisions that we ourselves have made up. Just suppose that we make a list of the important as well as the unimportant issues of life, and then make firm decisions about each one of them. Then suppose that as the chairman of the board of directors for our own lives, we keep a written record in our Book of Decisions. We should have a regular procedure for considering and judging any problem when it arises; then when we get an answer, it should be dated and recorded in our Book of Decisions. We would certainly find that a great new strength would be created by this formal businesslike action. This procedure would make it unnecessary for our decisions to be unmade and remade over and over again on several different patterns. If our judgments were all written down where we could review them occasionally, it would make them much easier to remember and more compelling to live by. Even our New Year's resolutions would last longer and be more effective if they were always thought through and then made definite by putting them down in writing.

Some people complain that living the religion of Christ is

for them very difficult. That is only true for those who have never really made up their minds. That is, it is very difficult for one to be a nonsmoker this week if he has always been a smoker previously. It is almost impossible for an alcoholic to be an abstainer. If we get up on time one morning and lay in bed the next morning, we are doing as much to tear down the habit as we are to build it up. It is extremely hard to be honest on all occasions when one has previously been honest only when he felt like it. However, it is just as easy for an honest man to be honest as it is for a dishonest man to be dishonest. It is just as easy for an industrious man to be industrious as it is for a lazy man to be lazy.

Whether it is hard or easy to live the religion of Christ depends upon whether or not we have made any firm decisions about it, around which we have built some solid habits. One man once said that he wanted to live on the perimeter of the Church. He explained that he wanted to live just far enough out that he could do as he pleased, but close enough in that he could go to heaven. He wanted to be just in between, where he was neither one thing nor the other. Of course, that is by far the most difficult place to live. Such a person is like a chameleon that is under the necessity of constantly changing his color to fit every environment and match everyone's mood.

Abraham Lincoln once said that he was just about as happy as he made up his mind to be, and we are just about as successful and just about as righteous as we make up our minds to be. A good Book of Decisions will help us make up our minds and keep them made up. It will solve most of our problems. It will make success easy and pleasant. Then we won't be continually exhausting our strength on problems that have already been previously decided. Of course, we need to get behind our decisions with our full majority support. It would be a very unwise board of directors that allowed its minorities to hold out against the board as a whole. After the vote has been taken and the matter settled, then the decision of the board should be the decision of all of the members of the board. But sometimes we have "minority hold-out elements" in the personality that prevent our decisions from being unanimous. A vote, with a 49 percent reservation, is so weak that it is really no vote at all. Even with a 10 percent reservation, a decision is not a good decision. If we need to do a little self-persuading to bring our minority selves to harmonize and fully support the decision, then by all means that should be done;

for no decision is really a decision that isn't unanimous where we are prepared to go all the way.

It is a well-known psychological fact that many people who complain about their temptations are secretly hoping to be so severely tempted that they will not be able to resist. That is, the minority elements in the personality are frequently hoping for an overthrow of the majority. It is by this process that some people live in a constant state of civil war with themselves. Their opposing factions may be so evenly balanced that any wholehearted action is impossible. To be at one's best, the governing board of one's personality must be able to reach a firm decision about any important issue and then remain solidly united and all in one piece. Jesus once said that a house divided against itself could not stand, and we might add that neither can a personality. Lincoln said that the union could not endure half slave and half free. And how can an individual be at his best, when he is half decided and half undecided?

It is a fatal weakness to be on both sides of an argument at the same time. Anyone who wants to win a victory over temptation and failure must assume the responsibility of taking himself in hand occasionally, and in such a way as to assure his own integration and unity. We must avoid the error of the baseball fan who goes to the ball game to cheer for both sides. Certainly we must not permit the seeds of war and rebellion to maintain their forces inside the citadel of our minds. More often than we would care to admit, it is our own imagination that has paved the way for the sins that we have committed.

It has been pointed out that while we cannot always prevent temptations from knocking at the door of our minds, yet we don't have to invite them in and serve them pie a la mode. If we allow too many "foot-in-the-door flirtations" with temptation, we can hardly expect to prevent the citadel itself from falling eventually. On the other hand, if we are perfectly integrated and follow the rule of "no exceptions," then we are safe. Under these circumstances it won't be very long before every decision will be supported by a habit and reinforced by a character that will make our fortress impregnable.

Now what are some of the issues about which we should make entries in our Book of Decisions? Do we really believe in God? What kind of life do we want to lead? What kind of standards do we want to maintain? It is interesting to remember that a great many of the important questions of life have already been decided for us by an authority much higher and more dependable than our own. It is usually recognized that the most valuable possessions of our world are its books of holy scripture. The Bible is called the Book of Books. It is God's word. It is the world's first book of religion. It is the world's first book of wisdom, it is the world's first book of decisions, and it is the world's first book of answers. The scriptures contain God's answers to life's important questions. They provide us with an answer even before the problem arises. It is very unwise for one to attempt to redo all of the religious experimentation.

When we found out that two parts of hydrogen and one of oxygen can be united to form water, we just accepted the fact. And for the same reasons we should now be ready to accept the Ten Commandments, the Beatitudes, and the Sermon on the Mount, and put them in force in our lives. It is entirely unnecessary for us to make all the mistakes personally. One of the most thrilling things about the life of the Master was that he did not need to commit a single sin to find out that it was wrong. He accepted God's formula and said, "Thy will, not mine, be done." All of the principles of the gospel have been thoroughly tested and proven. And the answers are all recorded in the Lord's Book of Decisions.

Our lives will take on new luster when God's decisions also become our decisions.

21

Your Book of Dreams

BENJAMIN FRANKLIN accounted for his success by what might be called his "Book of Virtues." He determined that thirteen particular virtues were necessary for the life he contemplated. He said, "I wished to live without committing any fault at any time, and I conceived a bold and arduous project for arriving at moral perfection." He said, "I made a little book in which I allotted one page for each of the desired virtues. I ruled each page with red ink. Then at the end of each day I made a black check for every fault that I had committed against that virtue that day. With this constant attention and by a daily practice of these wanted rules, it was not long before they were a permanent part of my character."

There is an endless array of these valuable books to write in. I know of a fairly wealthy man who says that his most valuable possessions are his idea books. He is always on a strenuous idea hunt by reading, thinking, and listening, and he preserves the results in large looseleaf notebooks. Most people have a system for losing notes, but none for preserving and utilizing the ideas they represent.

One great man keeps what he calls a "Book of Accomplishments." This is an especially-made book of heavy paper with plastic binding. Each year is given sufficient space in this book to display a photographic record of certificates received and honors won. All other events that he thinks are important are properly displayed in his book. This visual record stimulates his "accomplishment instincts" much as an accumulation of wealth stimulates the "acquisitive instincts" of a rich man. In one way or another everyone is a collector, and an excellent collection increases the desire for the things being collected, whether they are great paintings or stamps or coins or butterflies or personal accomplishments. Just as eating increases the appetite, so a visual assortment of successful experiences stimulates the ambition.

The other day I found a man with one of the most interesting and valuable of these books to write in. He calls it his "Book of Dreams." Just suppose that you had a special book where you kept a written list of those dreams and ambitions for which you had an unquenchable thirst. A good book of dreams and some well thought-out blueprints for accomplishment will turn ambitions into realities. Among the amazing inventions of man and the miraculous creations of God, nothing can match the human mind, which is the instrument given us by God with which to think, plan, imagine, love, and dream. The Bible tells us of many inspired dreams that have been put into people's minds by Deity himself. The fact that we have been divinely equipped for dreaming indicates that the function is important and that God certainly did not intend to do all of our dreaming for us.

Even when we were young, we dreamed about what we would become later in our lives. As we get older our dreams should get bigger and be better planned. We should make sure that we fully understand the importance of the picturing power of the mind. It was the job of the imagination to show young Wilbur Wright that someday a man could fly, and that he could be that man. It was the office of the imagination to show Thomas A. Edison a world of light, beauty, power, communication, and convenience never known before. It is also the job of the imagination to turn the calendar of our own lives ahead while we preview our success and show ourselves the kind of people that we can become.

An interesting paraphrase says:

> Turn forward, turn forward,
> O time in thy flight;
> And make it tomorrow,
> Just for tonight.

Through the prophet Joel, the Lord said that in the latter days he would pour out his spirit upon all flesh. He said, ". . . your old men shall dream dreams, and your young men shall see visions." (Joel 2:28.) The most successful people are usually those carrying the greatest dreams in their hearts. The Almighty gave us the power to dream as a giant headlight by which we may search the future.

The other night the captain of a new jet airliner explained to me the many uses of his radar system. With this wonderful equipment, the captain can reach out through the sky, across the land, or over the sea, in daylight or darkness, to discover the things that may hurt or help those for whom he has responsibility. He can track down the storm or discover enemy aircraft as if by magic.

Then I thought of the great radar system installed in the human soul that can reach even into eternity. The dreamers are the saviors of the world. And God has also given us an ability to make even our greatest dreams come true.

Columbus cherished the vision of another world and he discovered it. Lincoln dreamed of his countrymen free from bondage and he was able to bring their freedom about. Every great achievement is at first and for a time only a dream. "The oak sleeps in the acorn, the bird awaits in the egg, and in the highest vision of the soul, a wakening angel stirs." "Dreams are the seedlings of reality." And one of our most precious possessions might well be a book of dreams with clear-cut drawings of our ideals and ambitions.

This mental picturing power is God's gift to help us bring about accomplishment. We all live in the embrace of a universal intelligence, and when we dream, we run up our antenna and catch the communication and inspiration from the divine upon the radar screens of our souls.

Inspiration literally means to "put spirit into." That is the function of dreams. Someone said, "Nothing so much convinces me of the boundlessness of the human mind as it operates in dreaming." (William Benton Chulow.) And all of the dreaming has not yet been done. Many worlds are still waiting to be conquered. There are bigger dreams yet to be dreamed than have ever been dreamed.

And dreams never come true by oversleeping. Dreams come true only when we wake up. What a tragedy when we lose our dreams. A story is told of a man who once robbed a large bank of $1,000 and then pleaded insanity. When he was asked why, he said that he must have been insane; otherwise he would have taken $100,000. Someday when we really wake up, we may also feel like pleading insanity because we didn't dream bigger dreams. The doctrine of failure says that we should never cross our bridges before we come to them. But the world is owned and ruled by men and women who have kept ahead of the procession by first crossing life's bridges in their imaginations.

All of the great planners and leaders cross their bridges before they come to them. Before an architect builds a great building, he first dreams about it. Then he puts every detail down on paper. He even builds the walks and does the landscaping. Then he draws a picture of exactly how the building and its surroundings are going to look when they are completed, including the color of the flowers. Certainly that is also good procedure for those of us who are building eternal lives.

Michelangelo once said, "In every block of marble, I see a statue, see it as plainly as though it stood before me shaped and perfect in attitude and action. I have only to hew away the rough walls that imprison the lovely apparition to reveal it to other eyes as mine already see it."

Gutzon Borglum, the sculptor, was once working on a head of Abraham Lincoln. Each day he chipped away the stone and each day it was the task of a Negro cleaning woman to sweep up the pieces and carry them away. Amazed, she watched the head of Lincoln emerge from the stone under the sculptor's hand, until at last the work was finished. When she could hold her wonder no longer, she said, "Mr. Borglum, how did you know that Mr. Lincoln was in that stone?"

The greatest dreamers dream about the most important things. Some see visions of a great character emerging from the rough rock of their unshaped lives. The meaning of success in life is to get the inspired vision of what God intended us to do and to be. Our Christian faith can help us see the possibilities of our lives just as Mr. Borglum could see Lincoln in the stone. We are the children of God, formed in His image and endowed with his attributes and fully capable of realizing the divine destiny that he has marked out for us. We can cross the rivers of doubt and discouragement on the bridge of faith even before we get to them. The architect must first get great ideas in his mind, then on the paper, before he can materialize them in brick and concrete. That is why my friend has his book of dreams.

There is an old saying to the effect that "ideas won't keep." Neither will dreams that are not held onto and materialized.

We remember the interesting account of King Nebuchadnezzar's dream. In a single night the future history of the world was unfolded in his mind. But when the king awoke in the morning, the entire dream had gone from him. He knew that he had had an important idea, but he could not remember what it was or what it meant. Then the prophet Daniel said to King Nebuchadnezzar, ". . . there is a God in heaven that revealeth secrets, and maketh known to King Nebuchadnezzar what shall be in the latter days." (Daniel 2:28.) Only through Daniel did the king and the world get back Nebuchadnezzar's dream. Nebuchadnezzar had his dream while he was asleep, but most worthwhile dreams come while we are awake. We usually lose them if we go to sleep.

H. G. Wells in his *Research Magnificent* describes a young man who lost the righteous dreams of his youth. Then for a period he walked the gay white ways of pleasure, giving vent to the appetites of his body as he felt inclined. But the enjoyments of the flesh soon began to pall on him, and then Mr. Wells pictures him reaching out his arms in the darkness, saying, "Oh, God, give me back my visions."

We should never allow ourselves to become so tired or cynical or sinful that we lose the inspired dreams of either our youth or our age. We may lose our stock certificates, or our real estate, but we must never lose those high expectations that God has given us of ourselves. It is far better to follow the poet who said:

> Dream, O youth, dream nobly and manfully;
> And thy dreams shall be thy prophets.

22

A Book of Remembrance

WE HAVE an interesting custom among us of setting aside special days on which we think about special things. We set aside the second Sunday in May as Mother's Day, and on this day we let our minds reach out and try to understand the purposes for which this day was set apart. We set apart the third Sunday in June as Father's Day for the same purpose. Someone has said that the human mind has some of the qualities of the tendrils of a climbing vine. That is, it tends to attach itself and draw itself upward by what it is put in contact with. We also have some other wonderful days in which we put our minds in contact with great ideas. We have Easter, Christmas, New Year's Day, and the Fourth of July. We set aside the fourth Thursday in November as Thanksgiving, and on this day we recount our blessings and build appreciation and gratitude into our own lives.

And then we have another special day, which we call Memorial Day or Decoration Day. This is a day when we try to remember. Originally this special day in May was appointed as a day for thinking about and honoring the soldier dead who served in the Civil War. But ever since then, its purpose has been steadily expanded. It is a very constructive idea to put flowers on the graves of our departed benefactors and loved ones. It is good to remember what our departed dead have done for us and to cultivate the love that we feel for them.

In several different ways every day ought to be a day of remembering, for without memories, life would not be very important to anyone. There are a great many things that we should retain in our minds and hearts, and because remembering is so important, a number of interesting techniques have been devised to help us. Some people write their finest thoughts and most important goals and ambitions down in journals, plan books, diaries, and idea books, and make other kinds of special memoranda of people, ideas, and things.

Enoch was one of the greatest of the prophets. He records

an interesting line in which he says: "For a book of remembrance we have written among us, according to the pattern given by the finger of God; and it is given in our own language." (Moses 6:46.)

In their book of remembrance some of the ancients kept the lineage of their people. They also kept a record of the divine teachings God had given them. Some of them also kept a written record of what they were doing with their own lives. This must have worked well for them, for the people of Enoch built such a perfect culture that the entire city and all of its people were translated and taken up to heaven.

This very helpful custom of keeping a book of remembrance was also mentioned by the prophet Malachi. He said:

"Then they that feared the Lord spake often one to another: and the Lord hearkened, and heard it, and a book of remembrance was written before him for them that feared the Lord, and that thought upon his name.

"And they shall be mine, saith the Lord of hosts, in that day when I make up my jewels; and I will spare them, as a man spareth his own son that serveth him." (Malachi 3:16-17.)

One of the most important parts of religion, or of success, or of life itself, is that function of remembering. From the top of Mount Sinai the Lord said, "Remember the sabbath day, to keep it holy." (Exodus 20:8.) Those who remember to keep this commandment will be a different kind of people from those who do not. Solomon said, "Remember now thy Creator in the days of thy youth. . . ." (Ecclesiastes 12:1.) That is probably one of our greatest success laws. Many people feel that youth is a time for sowing wild oats. However, most of our failures come because we forget God. So often we forget our relationship to him and what he wants us to do, and when we forget God and fail to identify with him, then to that extent we are lost.

It is likely that one of the finest things that we can do is to have a personal book of remembrance. This could be something to help us to remember the many things that we judge to be helpful. In fact, one might actually have several books of remembrance, for our two biggest problems probably come from not understanding and not remembering. Often we lose our objectives, and even though we are strong on reading, we may be short on remembering. It strengthens our memory to write things down, and we always develop more love because of our greater familiarity. We should encourage ourselves to memorize some of the most potent passages gained from our reading.

Our society itself has done many things to help us to remember. It has written plaques, built monuments, and erected halls of fame to memorialize greatness. We have many ceremonies for helping us to remember great ideas. We write biographies, histories, and philosophies in attempting to build up and enrich our memories. When a great person writes down his plans, his ideals, his motives, and his success formulas, he improves himself.

The dictionary says that a memorial is something to assist the memory in preserving a remembrance. The ancient Romans used to erect memorial arches as a means of memorializing the greatness of particular persons. A memorial arch was a monumental structure that may have been beautified by columns pierced by a passageway and often flanked by smaller arches. It was surmounted and adorned by sculptured figures and made meaningful by inscriptions. A memorial arch was to commemorrate a notable victory of a famous person or a great event.

In a similar way, it might be helpful if we had our minds and personalities richly stored with memorizations and character traits that were preserved by remembrance. One way to do this is to keep a good personal book of remembrance. One book of remembrance might contain one's favorite philosphies, his poems, and those great scriptures that he wants to memorize and live with. One might have another book of remembrance to record the biographies or memories of his heroes. One might be his own personal journal or diary or memoirs. He might have a place to keep his inspiring pictures.

Then he might have another picture book of remembrance that contains some visual recordings of his own life. It would be interesting to have a year-by-year picture of his own goals and accomplishments. He might have some kind of reproduction of his birth certificate, his baptismal certificate, and his marriage certificate. He could have a copy of his patriarchal blessing, his mission call, and those certificates indicating his various ordinations and letters of appointment. There are many other important happenings in one's business life, the memory of which can stimulate his great future accomplishments.

Elbert Hubbard once said that business was the process of ministering to human needs; therefore, said he, business is essentially a divine calling. And many of those who carry on the established work of the world are entitled to think of it in that way and do it in that spirit. And they might have a book of remembrance with space for a year-by-year record to stimulate greater accomplishment. One may vastly increase his future productivity by rerunning the records and refeeling the motivations from the past. Many people get discouraged and depressed because they have forgotten what success feels like, and reliving our past successes can help us to repeat them on a higher level in the future.

One of the most destructive facts of life is that our forgetfulness may become more active than our ability to remember, and we can only change the situation by preventing ourselves from forgetting. One of our problems is that the moment of forgetting is an unconscious moment. It is like the moment of birth. The moment of birth is an unconscious moment, and no one ever realizes that he is being born when the event is actually taking place. In fact, no one ever finds out that he has been born until quite a long time after it has happened.

On the other hand, learning is a conscious moment. One of the great stimulants to learning is that we are usually so highly elated by the joys of discovery. We are greatly motivated when we feel a new idea being born into our minds and personalities. Whereas ideas, ideals, and ambitions that have the greatest values may be allowed to slip away while we ourselves are unaware that we are losing them, ideas never say goodbye, and we don't see them go, and sometimes we never ever discover that they have gone.

We frequently reach a plateau in our education and our ability to accomplish early in life from which we never rise substantially because we tend to forget faster than we learn. Then, in spite of our learning, we may show a steady decline to the end of our lives. This is one of the reasons why we say of people, "He is not the man he used to be." What shocking losses when we lose our knowledge, our abilities, our virtues, and our motivations.

This problem is so important that God himself seems to have given it a great deal of attention, for it is referred to in many scriptures. To prevent forgetfulness is one of the reasons why

God has required that the great scriptures should be written down and rerun in our lives. Whenever nations have gone for very long without the scriptures, their faith and righteousness have soon slipped away from them. Six hundred years B.C. when the people of Lehi were preparing to leave Jerusalem for the western continent, the Lord commanded them to bring with them a copy of the Jewish scriptures. And when Laban would not give them up, the Lord said, ". . . It is better that one man should perish than that a nation should dwindle and perish in unbelief." (1 Nephi 4:13.)

After these people had arrived in their new land, they were split up into two groups. One group had the scriptures and the other did not. The group that had no scripture soon fell completely away from righteousness and from the ways of the Lord. And the biggest problem that presently confronts our world is that of forgetfulness. Because we fail to read the scriptures, we are forgetting the Lord, we are forgetting our duties, we are forgetting our opportunities. We are forgetting the high purpose of our individual and national lives. The great tragedy of our day is that the holy scriptures sit on our shelves unopened, whereas the Lord said:

"And these words, which I command thee this day, shall be in thine heart:

"And thou shalt teach them diligently unto thy children, and thou shalt talk of them when thou sittest in thine house, and when thou walkest by the way, and when thou liest down, and when thou risest up." (Deuteronomy 6:6-7.)

A book of remembrance or a book of our good deeds may solve our greatest problem. The Boy Scouts have a program for doing a good deed each day. And the Scout who keeps score of his activities will make a better record than the one who does not.

A story is told that Whistler once painted a tiny picture of a spray of roses. The artistry involved in the picture was magnificent. Never before, it seemed, had the art of man been able to execute quite so deftly a reproduction of the art of nature. The picture was the envy of the artists who saw it, the despair of the collectors who yearned to buy it. But Whistler refused steadfastly to sell it. "For," he said, "whenever I feel that my hand has lost its cunning, whenever I doubt my ability, I look at the little picture of the spray of roses, and say to myself, 'Whistler, you painted that. Your hand drew it. Your imagination conceived the colors. Your skill put the roses on the canvas.' Then," said he, "I know that what I have done, I can do again."

Then the author said, "Hang on the walls of your mind the memory of your successes. Take counsel of your strength, not your weakness. Think of the good jobs you have done. Think of the times when you rose above your average level of performance and carried out an idea or a dream or a desire for which you had deeply longed. Think of the big moments in your life. Hang those pictures on the walls of your mind and look at them as you travel the roadway of life." Here is a great idea implemented by many of our greatest men. May God help us to remember.

23

Your Book of Heroes

IN 1899 a substantial gift made to New York University was used under the direction of Chancellor Henry M. McCracken to erect a beautiful memorial called "The Hall of Fame for Great Americans." This building is 630 feet long and is located on a beautiful site on University Heights in upper New York overlooking the valleys of the Harlem and the Hudson Rivers. It is a circular terrace in form with a super-imposed columnade connecting the University's Hall of Philosophy with the Hall of Languages. Membership is limited to those who have been dead for at least twenty-five years and who receive a majority vote of the 100 prominent Americans who make up the electoral college. Only ninety-five of the most famous Americans have qualified for membership since 1900, and each of these is represented in the Hall of Fame by a bronze bust and pedestal, accompanied by an explanatory tablet. This represents the most outstanding gathering of greatness in the world and is evidenced by the finest collection of statuary.

Centuries ago the ancient Greeks gave a little different twist to this Hall of Fame idea and put it on an even grander scale. They set aside the most prominent mountain in northern Greece called Mount Olympus, and on its summit, which reaches 10,000 feet into the sky, they created through their mythology a home for their great heroes and national deities. Then around these Olympian personalities they built up a great biographical literature picturing the strength and describing the virtues of these super mortals who in imagination inhabited this sacred mountain top. Poems, songs, and stories were composed about them and written down in heroic scale to match the mountain on which they lived.

The heroic is defined as something that is larger than life. And when we look up to those having heroic ideals and ambitions, we tend to mold our own minds and hearts to heroic deeds. During this golden age Greek culture reached a height that in many ways has never been surpassed even in our day. And the influence from the top of Mount Olympus was an important factor in drawing the Greek nation up to its high place.

What else but strength and greatness could be expected from the people of Sparta, for example, who believed themselves to be descendants of Hercules. They talked about his feats of valor; they breathed his courage and lived his greatness. As a consequence, they became natural heirs to his strength.

Great ambitions can best be formed in a giant mold. Minds can be broadened, hearts can be enlarged, if one has a godly pattern to go by. One cannot long remain small while he is thinking and living big. Through biography greatness can be made to reproduce itself in the lives of others. And one of the outstanding opportunities in any individual life might well be some adaptation of this Hall of Fame idea. We can have a personal Mount Olympus peopled with our own heroes. More than most other things below the actual level of worship, we need someone to look up to, admire, and love, someone with whom we can feel a divine kinship. We need more actual working models of righteous accomplishment formed to heroic specifications.

In his book *Heroes and Hero Worship* Thomas Carlyle said, "Great men taken up in any way are profitable company, for we cannot so much as look upon a great man without gaining something from him." We cannot entertain the great patriots, the great prophets, or the great saints in our minds without bringing ourselves into a more close resemblance. We are automatically lifted up by the love and reverence we hold for those above us. Every human being has a God-given tendency to reach up to those more noble than himself. Carlyle refers to this procedure as heroism or hero worship. Heroism is described as that near divine relationship which unites one great man to other men. He describes worship as "admiration without limitation."

Whatever this relationship may be called or whatever its degree of intensity, there is a powerful attraction involved that may be used for our own uplift and benefit. This idea is very closely related to the second great commandment, that we should love our neighbors as ourselves. This love includes a kind of genuine respect and admiration leading to hero worship, and creation seems to have made special provision in us for effective use of these abilities. That is, in our minds and hearts each of us may have a kind of private Hall of Fame or an individual Mount

Olympus reserved exclusively for those great men and women who have most profitably influenced the direction and extent of our lives. Those admitted to this private sanctuary are the ones who have set our hearts afire with devotion for truth. They have made obedience to duty the essence of manhood and have given us a vision of the kind of people we should aspire to be. Then they themselves serve as our example in personifying faith and fidelity. They repel what is unclean or unfair and strike a direct blow at the painted face of falsehood and deceit. Theirs is the blessed faculty of arousing a desire in us to develop our own talents and aptitudes to their upper limits.

In some degree we are all aware of the tremendous upward pull that one personality may have upon another. It might be compared to the attraction of the planets as they hold each other in their orbits.

We see examples in the influence that Socrates exerted upon the life of Plato, or the effect that Jesus had upon Simon Peter, or Beatrice upon Dante, or Nancy Hanks upon Abraham Lincoln. The Greeks set their idols upon the top of Mount Olympus. In the American Hall of Fame we have eighty-five of our greatest men and ten of our greatest women assembled together. As individuals we may use our own adaptation of this very helpful idea to bring about our own improvement. But before those we hold up as ideals can have maximum power, we must put ourselves within their magnetic range. We might imagine how greatly Carl Sandburg has added to his own life by becoming the biographer and admirer of Abraham Lincoln. It is easy to become great in the company of great men when we are familiar with their lives and have a Carl Sandburg love of their virtues. Greatness feeds upon itself, and men absorb other men.

There is an interesting account in the Old Testament explaining how young King Saul qualified as King of Israel. The record says, "... and there went with [Saul] a band of men, whose hearts God had touched." (1 Samuel 10:26.) That is, Saul had his own Hall of Fame. James Preston Burke has written a stimulating poem based on this passage of scripture which he has entitled "Bands of Men." He said:

> Lord, don't send us out to battle alone
> Amid the entanglements of life's unknown,
> But support and cheer us, thou guardian friend,
> In bonds of fellowship with bands of men.

Much is perplexing in life's every day
With great complications obscuring the way;
Because we are anxious to reach the end,
Accompany us, Lord, with bands of men.

Men with compassion, men with zeal,
Men who can think, men who can feel,
Men whose hearts are touched by thee,
Noble men, strong men, men who are free.

Of course we need to be very careful that those who are
admitted into the sanctuary of our lives have been proven and
tried in the fire.

We might apply the interesting selection procedure used
by one man in buying an oil painting which he expected to
bring inspiration and delight into the inner sanctum of his home.
When he was attracted to a particular piece of art, he sat down
before it and studied it thoroughly. He thought about it and tried
to fully understand its message. Then after the lapse of a few
days he went back and looked at it again to determine whether
or not his feeling for the picture had diminished or increased in
power. After a few visits with the painting he tried to forget it.
If it was easy to forget, the relationship was ended; but if the
picture had grown in his mind to a point where he felt that he
could not get along without it, if it had assumed an importance
to him that he could *not* forget, then he bought the painting to be
uplifted by it.

It is a natural principle that Abraham Lincoln would have
greater power to lift up Carl Sandburg than he would someone
who was unsympathetic with the principles to which Lincoln
gave his life. Only those who love liberty, integrity, and right receive power from Lincoln. Lincoln is one of *our* heroes "whose
heart God had touched." All of his days he fought for freedom,
righteousness, and truth. What a wonderful thing it would be for
our world if the Russians had a Mount Olympus peopled with
men like Abraham Lincoln.

Lincoln, of course, is unique. There never has been and never
will be another man like him. But every man is unique. Creation
makes no duplicates, and no one can ever be replaced. It is interesting to try to imagine what it would mean to Americans if
by some unfortunate magic the memory of Abraham Lincoln was
completely erased from our minds and literature. That is, suppose

that the unswerving honesty, the stimulating humility, the love of freedom as represented in his life were totally expunged from our memories as though they had never existed. Then imagine that the same thing happened to our memory of George Washington, Benjamin Franklin, and the ninety-two other great Americans making up our Hall of Fame membership. What a void, what lonesomeness, what a sense of lessening we would feel. We thank God more fervently for these great men when we think what our lives might have been if we had been brought up at the feet of such men as Karl Marx, Joseph Stalin, Adolph Hitler, and Nikita Khrushchev.

Abraham Lincoln met his death in 1865, but in our memories he will never die. During the last hundred years there have always been statesmen in Washington, D.C., to whom Abraham Lincoln was a living presence. His spirit not only helps to direct the decisions on Capitol Hill, but his principles flourish in our hearts. We may give his influence greater lifting power by reading about his work, quoting his wisdom, loving his honor, and feeling his spirit. The history of our world is very rich in the lives of great men who are available to serve our most personal needs.

On one pedestal in my private Hall of Fame I have placed my high school principal. Close by him is an early-day Sunday School teacher. The man who molded my business life has a prominent place and will remain close by forever, always ready to help even as Lincoln helps those who love him. Lincoln also occupies a place of honor in my gallery of great men. With him are Socrates, Emerson, Moses, Mahatma Gandhi, and Antonio Stradivari. I have included Booker T. Washington, George Washington Carver, Marie Curie, Edith Cavel, and Joan of Arc. My own mother and father are prominently pedestaled in my council of great lives.

The chief place, a little apart from the others, is reserved for the greatest life that ever lived—the Master of all men, the Savior and Redeemer of the world, Jesus of Nazareth. His was the only life that was ever lived that did not need to make a single mistake to find out that it was wrong. Surrounding him are some of the great prophets who over the centuries on two continents have been commissioned to speak and write in God's name for my benefit. I have searched the scriptures and I have studied the individual lives of the great men and women selected for my gallery. I have personally written up a tablet for each containing those qualities that I want to stamp indelibly into my memory. Each of the ninety-five persons in the American Hall of Fame was selected for a particular purpose, and each of the 102 making up my gallery were chosen because of some unique ability they possessed to help me. That is, my father serves in a different place than does Abraham Lincoln, but each is indispensible in his sphere, and none of them can ever be replaced. To each of these special advisers has been turned over a particular part of the responsibility for my success.

In my imagination I like to go into my private hall of Fame to draw strength and satisfaction from my own band of men whose hearts God has touched. And from each I receive a power in my soul from the wonderful gifts that God has bestowed upon those heroic individuals who are now so willing to spend their strength to lift me upward.

Through this Hall of Fame philosophy each of us may receive a maximum of enrichment from those wonderful gifts that God has lavished upon his chosen children and thus once again we may fulfill the grateful prayer of Harry Kemp wherein he said,

> Chief of all thy wondrous works, O God,
> Supreme of all thy plan,
> Thou hast put an upward reach
> Into the heart of man.

24

Promise Books

RECENTLY A story appeared in the newspaper about a newly married young woman who gave an overworked mother next door a small notebook containing forty perforated slips of paper. On each slip this young woman had written: "I promise to give to Mrs. John Jones any time during the next year one evening of free baby sitting—date to be arranged." She then signed her name.

This interesting example of helpfulness inspired a Girl Scout to make up her own version of what she called her "Promise Book." It contained a great number of slips that she had made out to her mother and on which she had promised her mother to give certain services, such as washing the dishes, making the beds, and doing a lot of other helpful things. This would not only greatly please her mother, but it would be of even greater benefit to the daughter herself. To this young Girl Scout these promise slips were all sacred pledges, and they were backed up by the character and integrity of a very responsible maker. They were guaranteed by her firm determination that in no case would she ever fail to honor them in full. I do not know what anyone else may think about this situation, but if I know a great idea when I see it, this is it.

In the world around us, there are a great many promise books containing important promises to pay. For services received, the government has accumulated a vast debt of approximately five hundred billion dollars, which it has an obligation to pay. The government currency is made up of slips of green paper on each of which has been written a promise to pay the bearer a certain sum of money. On the bills themselves are shown the pictures of some great men, most of whom are American presidents. On the other sides of these slips of paper are emblems and significant insignia. A one-dollar bill has the picture of George Washington; two dollars—Thomas Jefferson; five dollars—Abraham Lincoln; ten dollars—Alexander Hamilton; twenty dollars—Andrew Jackson; fifty dollars—Ulysses S. Grant; one hundred dollars—

Benjamin Franklin; five hundred dollars—William McKinley; one thousand dollars—Grover Cleveland; five thousand dollars— James Madison; ten thousand dollars—Salmon P. Chase; and one hundred thousand dollars—Woodrow Wilson. A great amount of our energy and a large portion of our time are spent in earning the right to possess these slips of green paper. And of all of those mentioned above, we seem to prefer the ones having the likeness of Woodrow Wilson.

The greatest promises that have ever been made are not on the faces of $100,000 government bills nor even the promise book of a wonderful Girl Scout, but the greatest promises have been made by the God of creation himself. And our holy scriptures are the most magnificent of our great promise books. In fact, someone has compared the sacred scripture to a great collection of promissory notes. God has never given a commandment to which he did not attach the promise of a blessing. The value of this blessing always far exceeds the amount of the service given. For example, through Malachi he said that we ought to pay our tithing. He said: "Bring ye all the tithes into the storehouse." That is the command. Then the blessing was attached when he said, ". . . and prove me now herewith, saith the Lord of hosts, if I will not open you the windows of heaven, and pour you out a blessing, that there shall not be room enough to receive it." (Malachi 3:10.) That is, if we keep his commandments, the blessings will be so great that we will be unable to contain them.

From the top of Mount Sinai, God said, "Honour thy father and thy mother." That is the command. Then the blessing is attached, which says, "that thy days may be long upon the land which the Lord thy God giveth thee." (Exodus 20:12.) He has said that if we obey the Word of Wisdom, we will receive the invaluable blessings of health. He referred to the Word of Wisdom as "a principle with promise," but all of his principles have promises attached. And if we live the celestial law, we will receive all of the blessings of the celestial kingdom, including the privilege of resurrecting celestial bodies and having celestial minds and celestial personalities.

Isn't it interesting that we can't even keep the Sabbath day holy without receiving a reward. We can't even think a good thought without being paid. And we can't think an evil thought without suffering a penalty. That just is not possible.

In one of his greatest promises, he has indicated that the success and welfare of our eternal lives are based on what we do in these few years of mortality. That is, the basic law of the universe is this immutable, inexorable, irrevocable, unchangeable law of the harvest that says, ". . . whatsoever a man soweth, that shall he also reap" (Galatians 6:7), multiplied. It is one of the fundamental laws of our existence that everyone will be judged according to his works.

It is very interesting to try to place a figure on the number of God's commandments. It is even more exciting to try to place a value or a number on his promised blessings. And so far as I know, these numbers will be about the same. What an inspiring thought to know that we can build up the most tremendous eternal estate and bind the great God of heaven, the Creator of the universe, to the most magnificent promises possible. He himself has said: "I, the Lord, am bound when ye do what I say; but when ye do not what I say, ye have no promise." (D&C 82:10.)

One of the great characteristics of God is his desire to be bound in our service. In every age and with every people he has desired to make contracts or covenants of behavior through which it is possible for us to bind him to the most fantastic agreements in our interests. As a natural corollary to this idea, just think how profitable it can be for us to make out some promise books to God.

Abraham Lincoln said: "I am not bound to win, but I am bound to be true. I am not bound to succeed, but I am bound to live by the best light that I have. I will stand with anyone who stands right and I will part with anybody when he goes wrong." There are many wonderful promises that we may make and keep. We make some sacred promises to God at the waters of baptism. We make others when we are ordained to the priesthood or called to any important divine service. We go into the holy temples and make God a party to our sacred marriage promises. We promise God that we will be righteous. We give some promise books to our wives that we will make them happy. We give some promise books to our children that they will be loved and educated.

Governments were instituted by God for the benefit of man, and he holds each of us personally responsible for our acts in relation thereto. We reaffirm those promises when we sing our national anthem and take our pledge of allegiance to the flag. Each of us who lives under the stars and stripes has inherited a responsibility for our country's safety, and one of our greatest opportunities is to make our nation greater and better than it would have been. Nathan Hale gave a promise book to his country, and just before he was hanged by his government's enemies, he made the last entry in which he said, "I only regret that I have but one life to lose for my country."

Martin Treptow was also a great soldier and was killed in the battle of Chateau Thierry in 1918 in World War I. In the diary found on his body were written these words: "I will work, I will save, I will sacrifice, I will endure, I will fight cheerfully and do my utmost as though the entire conflict depended upon me alone." Such patriotism should inspire us as the young wife did the Girl Scout.

In 1852, John Ruskin wrote in his diary, "Today I promise God that I will live as though every doctrine contained in the holy scriptures was true." And if each one of us were inspired to emulate his example and with great integrity and character back up our promise that we would live by His every word, this earth would soon be God's paradise, and we would be the greatest generation that has ever lived upon it. And why not?

To begin with, God created us. He has granted unto us our lives, for which we will be forever indebted to him. But when we do any righteous thing, he does immediately bless us with manifold blessings, and our debt is increased. He has told us the sure way to eternal exaltation and eternal happiness, and if we make our covenants and keep our promises, no blessings will be withheld from us. In one of the greatest of all his promises the Lord said:

"For he that receiveth my servants receiveth me;

"And he that receiveth me receiveth my Father;

"And he that receiveth my Father receiveth my Father's kingdom; therefore all that my Father hath shall be given unto him.

"And this is according to the oath and covenant which belongeth to the priesthood.

"Therefore, all those who receive the priesthood, receive

this oath and covenant of my Father, which he cannot break, neither can it be moved." (D&C 84:36-40.)

Try to think of something more exciting or worthwhile than to be a part of that great enterprise in which God himself spends his entire time. How much better it is for us to be great human beings, to obey the law, to keep the commandments, to build up our balances with God, and to qualify for his promises. Before we can keep his commandments, we need to know what they are and have strong convictions about them. The kind of promises we make to God will not only determine the kind of people we will become, but they will also determine his promises that will be fulfilled in our behalf.

Section

IV

The How Books

25

The How Books

ONE OF the greatest wonders of our day is our books. For a few cents we can have the greatest books, even though they may have taken a lifetime for the wisest men to produce.

Among our most important books are those that deal with telling us how to do things. So many of the serious problems of the world come because of our lack of know-how. We don't know how to do the right things well enough. This is a reason we may fall down in our objectives, fail in our relationships with others, and miss our own objectives for happiness. We haven't yet discovered how to close the generation gap, how to cure the drug plague, or even how to govern ourselves effectively.

Recently I heard a young woman accuse her father of being unfriendly to her boyfriend. I think I understand her father a great deal better than she does, and I am sure that more than anything else in the world, her father wants to be friendly. The problem comes from the fact that he just doesn't know how to be friendly. He has never practiced being friendly and he is so preoccupied with her welfare that he fails to do those things that she interprets as evidences of friendliness.

But being friendly may not be as simple as it sounds. Suppose that someone asked you to write out the directions on how to be friendly. Where would you begin and how would you suggest that we go about it? Is friendly something that we say or feel or do? And specifically, what are these things? Why do so many children feel that their parents don't love them? Why is it that the biggest problem that many husbands and wives have is to convince the other of their love? Why is it that so many people are united in marriage who are not united as friends? What makes the nations so antagonistic to each other? Dale Carnegie once wrote a great book entitled *How to Win Friends and Influence People*. That is a book that a lot of people, including husbands, wives, children, and national leaders, should read and then add a few chapters of their own.

We also have a lot of other bothersome questions such as "How can I maintain my health? "How do I develop the right kind of personality?" "How do I go about acquiring a good character or building a godly spirituality?"

As a result of this pressing human need for understanding, a great segment of our literature is made up of the "how" books that we should be more familiar with. Many people who feel that they have special know-how in some particular field have written their best ideas down in some how-to-do-it books. Frank Betcher once wrote a best seller entitled *How I Raised Myself from Failure to Success in Selling.* The salesmen who do as he has directed will immediately become more successful. You can get books on how to make more money. There are books about how to lose weight. Centuries ago, Aristotle wrote out his famous sixteen laws of oratory, which are still available and right up-to-date. If you want to be a great orator, all you need to do is to follow Aristotle's sixteen laws. Or if you'd like to become a great cook, get a good cookbook and learn to follow it. Any builder can erect the most magnificent building that the greatest architect can conceive if he just learns how to follow the blueprint. A dressmaker follows the pattern. Someone has said that all science is just a collection of success formulas.

The United States was the only nation that knew how to make an atomic bomb until Klaus Fuchs sold our formula to the Russians. Then, without the necessity of spending billions of dollars in trial and error research or wasting valuable years in costly experimentation, the Russians could make just as many bombs as they wanted to, merely by following our formula. But even since the original discovery, we have learned how to make atomic bombs many times more destructive.

And there are so many different ways to do most things, and some are so much more effective than others. Therefore, it becomes important to keep ourselves informed about the best ways to do things. Recently I heard a discussion about how to shake hands. That seems very simple, and yet think how many different ways there are of doing it. To shake hands with one person gives you the impression that you may have a dead fish by the tail. When you shake with someone else, you think you may have put your hand into a bone crusher. Some handshakers seem to be trying to pull your arm out of its socket. Some people shake hands at ninety miles per hour on a hit-and-run basis.

I know a man who can shake hands with a dozen people in about that many seconds while he is talking to someone else. He shakes hands like he takes steps, without actually realizing what he is doing. This does not put the people he shakes with in a very congenial frame of mind. When some people shake hands, there is little or no favorable exchange that takes place between themselves and the one they are shaking with. On the other hand, there are some people who have real know-how in this important area of human communication. When you shake hands with some people you feel the warmth of their greeting, the integrity of their purpose, and the greatness of their souls. Some people shake hands just with their hands, but others shake with a twinkle in their eyes, the warmth that comes from their hearts, and the radioactivity that comes from their spirits, their good will, and their friendly hearts.

There are many ways to communicate with people. Our spirits frequently talk to each other, and everyone is radioactive. To shake hands with certain people can be a very uplifting, spiritualizing, socializing, heartwarming experience. To shake hands with others makes you feel that you have been used or that you have been made the object of some cheap kind of charity. A handshake can be clammy, depressing, painful, disagreeable, and even horrifying in its consequences.

If such a simple activity may run between such a wide range of failure and success, what might be expected in more complicated situations? To help us solve many of our problems, we have a great many good how-to-do-it books. The good ideas, effective methods, proven procedures, motivating attitudes, and helpful techniques of the best people may be made negotiable in our own success. There are good books on almost every subject that explain, compare, illustrate, demonstrate, and motivate. And if we are careful in selecting our authors, the quality of our excellence may be greatly increased in almost any field of endeavor.

There are so many places where we need assistance, and no one has enough time to learn everything by his own experience. From books we can get excellent help in our occupations. We can get help in our marriages. We can get help in improving our citizenship, our leadership, our intellectuality, and our morality. Probably our greatest need for help is for someone to show us how to live.

Thomas Carlyle once said that a man's religion is the most important thing about him. That is what he believes in and thinks about and works at and fights for and lives by. And fortunately for us, this is where some of the most expert help has been given.

The most important of all the how books are the holy scriptures. It would probably be conceded by most people that the Bible is the world's most valuable possession. And yet we don't use it very effectively. Actually, we don't know very much about the holy scriptures; and yet if we would resolve to practice what they teach us, we could very quickly and substantially upgrade our individual lives and make this earth God's paradise. And a few such resolutions would guarantee the highest type of happiness for us, for too frequently we fail to definitely make up our minds between right and wrong, success and failure, excellence and mediocrity.

That would also be a profitable resolve for any criminal, any atheist, or even for one who is uninformed. For everyone would be improved, and how could anyone be hurt by it? That is, if one should err in supposing that the gospel of Jesus Christ is true, he could not possibly be the loser by the mistake. But how irreparable would be his loss if he should err in supposing the gospel of Jesus Christ to be false. Or what a tragedy would take place if one should fail to live the gospel principles and then someday discover that they were true. And if one doesn't have time to personally do all of the research, investigation, and decision-making about gospel principles, he ought to live them anyway.

When one is about to begin any important enterprise, such as a business or a marriage or a life, there are certain rules to follow if he would be successful. First, he must know where he wants to go; second, he should make a written list of those things that he just must not do under any circumstances; and third, he can then devote himself fully to doing the things that will make him successful. But in marriage or in business or in any other success, there are also some things that one just cannot do if his enterprise is to succeed.

In this procedure the Lord has set us a good example when he undertook to make the new nation of ancient Israel the greatest nation on the earth. He first liberated the people from their Egyptian bondage. Then almost immediately he gathered them together at Mount Sinai and gave them the stern "thou shalt nots" of the Ten Commandments. Anyone who obeys any of the Ten Commandments will be a different kind of person from one who does not. The scriptures also furnish us with one of the finest sets of human objectives ever known. To begin with, we are the literal spirit children of God. Then we were added upon when out of the dust of this earth God formed our physical bodies in his own image to match our spirits. He also endowed us with a set of his attributes and potentialities.

And just as the life of God is eternal, so he has ordained that our lives should be eternal also. Our possible destiny is that the offspring of God might someday become like our eternal parents. No one could ask for greater possibilities or finer opportunities than these. If we become celestial people, we may qualify for celestial glory, and we may bring both of these about merely by living as we should.

A salesman once asked his sales manager to help him to become more successful financially. The sales manager said, "I can guarantee to quadruple your income in one year if you will obey two simple rules." The salesman was delighted and quickly promised that he would carefully follow all of the directions. The sales manager said, "Rule number one is, You are to immediately stop doing all of the things that you are now doing that you know that you should not do. Rule number two is, You are to immediately start doing all of the things that you are not now doing that you know that you should do." The salesman was very disappointed, as he had not expected anything quite so difficult. This is also the reason why we fail in most of our spiritual enterprises.

In our Bible "how-to-do-it book," Jesus gave the greatest public relations procedure ever given when he said, "Therefore all things whatsoever ye would that men should do to you, do ye even so unto them. . . ." (Matthew 7:12.) However, we don't seem to know how to treat other people the way that we would like them to treat us. Just think how we would prosper if we obeyed God's laws of honesty, industry, sobriety, righteousness, responsibility, and obedience.

Jesus organized his church and taught that everyone should belong to it. The gateway to membership is faith, repentance, baptism, and the gift of the Holy Ghost. And we can keep ourselves in good standing merely by behaving ourselves and following directions. Jesus told us how to get to heaven. He said to his apostles: "Go ye into all the world, and preach the gospel to every creature. He that believeth and is baptized shall be saved; but he that believeth not shall be damned." (Mark 16:15-16.) And there we have it. It is as simple as that, but so frequently we don't want to do it. Jesus not only taught that people should do right, but that they should also love doing it. He said, "Blessed are those who do hunger and thirst after righteousness." He also taught that we should get along with each other. He said, "Blessed are the peacemakers."

In this great how-to-live book, the Master glorified the family. He taught us the value of love and truth and harmony. He blessed the children. He taught us how to pray, how to be good neighbors, how to worship, and how to honor God. He gave us some great leadership formulas, in one of which he said: "Wherefore, now let every man learn his duty, and to act in the office in which he is appointed, in all diligence. He that is slothful shall not be counted worthy to stand, and he that learns not his duty and shows himself not approved shall not be counted worthy to stand." (D&C 107:99-100.)

He taught us how to live, how to die, and how to get into the celestial kingdom. He said, "Believe in God and do the works of righteousness." He discouraged hate, selfishness, greed, and sin. He was the greatest teacher, but of what value are his teachings if we don't know what they are or if we do nothing about them? It is thought that one of the greatest of all benefits can come to our lives if we but learn how to effectively use our greatest how-to-do-it scriptures.

26

How Readest Thou?

ON ONE occasion Jesus was discussing the importance of the ministry of John the Baptist with some Pharisees and lawyers who had been out into the desert to hear John's message. He said to them, "What went ye out into the desert for to see?" That is a very important question, because we usually find about what we are looking for. Jesus bore a strong testimony to the Pharisees and lawyers of the divinity of John's mission. He said to them, "Among those that are born of women, there is not a greater prophet than John the Baptist." (Luke 7:24, 28.)

But neither the importance of John's message nor the testimony of Jesus helped the Pharisees and lawyers very much, because that was not what they were looking for. We don't always interpret our experiences as they are, but as we are. "But the Pharisees and lawyers rejected the counsel of God against themselves," not because the counsel was unwise, but because they were unwise. It is thought that we might also make substantial use of Jesus' question to ask ourselves what we are looking for. How do the important issues of life appear to us. What do we conceive our duty to be? What are the opportunities that we are most pleased to take advantage of? Do we see beyond the material values in life? What are our reactions to the Lord's messengers, and how well do we live the sacred messages given for our benefit?

In discussing the scriptures with another lawyer, Jesus said, ". . . how readest thou?" (Luke 10:26.) He wasn't trying to find out what the scriptures meant; he merely wanted to know what they meant to the lawyer. Unfortunately the great scriptures don't tell some people as much as they do others. Some people never rise above the low and unimportant in life because their hearts are not set upon anything higher. Why is it that we don't govern our lives more fully by the word of the Lord as found in the Holy Bible? Is there a possibility that like the Pharisees and lawyers we may be more interested in less worthy goals?

The Church is trying to encourage all of its members as well as all nonmembers to read the Book of Mormon. This book is the world's most important witness to the truth and divine origin of the Holy Bible. If understood, this message could have as much significance to us as the message of John the Baptist would have had to the Pharisees and lawyers if they had only listened to it. Assuming that you are going to read this book very carefully, what will you be looking for? If you find the book's most important values, what will they be? In other words, "how readest thou?"

We should find out in advance what some of the important benefits are that may be had from reading this great volume of scripture. One of the most important is probably the one mentioned by the Prophet Joseph Smith when he said, "I told the brethren that the Book of Mormon was the most correct of any book on earth, and the keystone of our religion, and a man would get nearer to God by abiding by its precepts, than by any other book." (*History of the Church,* vol. 4, p. 461.)

If we are looking for eternal exaltation, we might find exactly what we are looking for, as this great volume of scripture was written by divine command. If we desire to reach the celestial kingdom, this book will show us the way. If we want more testimony of the truth of the Bible, it can be found in this book. The book itself says that its purpose is that men may be persuaded that Jesus is the Christ, the Son of the living God. (Mormon 5:14.) Just think what it would mean if everyone in the world understood that above the dictators, and above chance, and above circumstances, there is God, to whom every individual must finally render an account of his life.

There are many other values in the Book of Mormon. Without this book, we are strangers in our own land. We live in a land unbelievably rich in tradition and promised blessings for the future. This land is a divinely appointed sanctuary of freedom. The mission of our nation is to extend and preserve free agency and righteousness in the world. The center of gravity so far as both spiritual and material things are concerned has long since passed from Asia to America. Blessings beyond the power of imagination await us if we will serve the God of this land, who is Jesus Christ. (Ether 2:12.)

We are not the only group of God's children who have lived

upon this land. Four other groups were destroyed here because they failed to follow the divine decrees concerning this land. These decrees are still in full force, and we can no more escape the consequences of sin than did our pre-Columbus predecessor nations. But if we are looking for the secret of American greatness, individually or collectively, past or future, we may find it in this book. Much of America's destined accomplishment is still in the future. We can find how that greatness can be best served if we become familiar with this great volume of scripture that speaks to us out of the dust of America.

As another specific value of the Book of Mormon, look for the uplifting effect of its philosophy. Millions who have read and loved the Holy Bible have automatically brought about a great improvement in their lives. For example, young Joseph Smith read from St. James one stimulating verse that took him to his knees in the Sacred Grove, where he asked God for direction and guidance. This one experience not only changed his life, but it has and will also change the history of the world. As many have turned to God by reading the account of God's dealings with his people in the East, so others are being turned to God by reading of his dealings with the people of our own hemisphere.

We have often been reminded that as a man thinketh in his heart, so is he. A great philosophy or a great faith put into operation in a human life can be one of the most stimulating of all uplifting influences. What would happen if we actually learned to put the Golden Rule into operation, or lived by the Ten Commandments, or practiced the Beatitudes. If that is what we are looking for, there is a way to really make use of the principles of repentance, forgiveness, and love of each other that was taught by the Master. How it would tone up our lives if we would read the last thrilling discourse of King Benjamin in the spirit in which it was given, or share the enthusiasm of Alma for the word of the Lord. We will also be able to learn correct Christian doctrines as they were given by the Master himself to the people who once lived upon our land.

Another value of the Book of Mormon is found in the personal inspiration that comes from the lives of the great prophets. We frequently express one of our most common needs by saying, "If only I had someone to give me a lift once in a while, someone to stir up my faith and wind up my enthusiasm, someone to talk to me and give me encouragement." When you feel such a need, suppose you get down from the shelf one of these great volumes of scripture, which has been called "God's Who's Who." The scriptures tell of the men who are important to God, and they are the ones that we ought to know much more about, particularly those who lived on our own continent. It was specifically for us and to us that this great book was written. Each of the great prophets is unique, and each may serve some special need existing in us.

Carlyle once said, "We cannot look upon a great man without gaining something from him." You cannot look upon Moroni or Helaman or the brother of Jared without being made better. You cannot feel their faith or hear their testimony or be instructed by their example without being stimulated and uplifted.

We never think of George Washington or Abraham Lincoln without improving our own lives. On February 12 I reread one of Lincoln's anti-slavery debates. His opponent had said in substance, "You can't afford to free the southern slaves, because there are some four million of them. Each has a value to his owner of approximately a thousand dollars. To free the slaves would upset the economy of this little group of southern people by some four billion dollars, which they can't afford. In addition, who would take care of the corn, the cotton, and the tobacco crops?" From his point of view these arguments were unanswerable, but when Lincoln came to the platform he brushed all of these considerations aside as immaterial. He said, "There is only one question to be answered in solving the problem of slavery, and that is, is slavery right or is it wrong? Is it right for some men to hold other men in bondage?"

When we have a problem to solve in the future, suppose that we remember Lincoln's formula and ask ourselves, "Is it right or is it wrong?" Once that is settled, all other considerations will more or less solve themselves. As we hold this picture of "Honest Abe" in our minds and as we love him for his unswerving devotion to right, a productive cross-pollinization takes place in us that raises the quality of our own lives.

How grateful we ought to be that we have our founding fathers to stand in the forefront of our civilization and give our nation its start toward its destiny! We are very proud of Washington and Lincoln, who were great Americans and serve among our finest benefactors. We also have some great pre-Columbus

Americans who can make an equal contribution to us. In about the same way that we can benefit from Washington and Lincoln, we can borrow the best in the lives of Lehi, Mosiah, Alma, Abinadi, and Samuel the Lamanite.

Think how many of the benefits that enrich our lives were borrowed from this great scriptural gallery of ideals and inspiration. President Heber J. Grant used to tell how as a boy he fell in love with Nephi, and how advantageously his life was influenced by his predecessor of 2,500 years. Of course, one of the greatest powers in the world is the power of example. What effect does it have upon us when we feel the devotion that made young Nephi say, ". . . I, Nephi, said unto my father: I will go and do the things which the Lord hath commanded, for I know that the Lord giveth no commandments unto the children of men, save he shall prepare a way for them that they may accomplish the thing which he commandeth them." The Book of Mormon is full of great men who are ideally suited to serve us in this important field of inspiration and example.

It is stimulating to think of the interesting relationship existing between Mormon and the Savior of the world. So far as I know, Mormon is the only man whose name has been used as a substitute name by which the Church of Jesus Christ has been called. We remember something very similar when in the days of Melchizedek, in order to avoid the too-frequent repetition of the sacred name of Deity, the Holy Priesthood was called after the name of Melchizedek. If for the same reason a substitute name is needed to avoid the too-frequent repetition of the name of Deity in our day, I can think of no one that suits me quite so well as this great man who was such a perfect instrument in God's hands in getting the Book of Mormon to us.

There is also a very interesting relationship existing between Mormon and every member of the Church, inasmuch as we are also called by his name. The prophet Helaman, in explaining to his sons Lehi and Nephi why he gave them their particular names, said, ". . . I have given you the names of our first parents . . . [that] ye may remember them; and when ye remember them ye may remember their works. . . ." (Helaman 5:6.)

Now suppose that when we are called Mormons, we remember Mormon's works, what he stood for, how he thought, what he did, and the kind of man he was. President George Albert Smith used to tell of an interesting experience of his young manhood. On one occasion he had a dream in which he saw his grandfather, whose name was also George Albert Smith, approach him and, without taking time to greet him or ask him how he was, say to his grandson, "What are you doing with my name?" President Smith indicated that this experience had always been a source of great strength to him, because he knew that someday when he actually went to meet his grandfather, one of the things that his grandfather was going to want to know was what he had done with the name of George Albert Smith.

Mormon has promised that he will meet us before the judgment bar of God, and one of the things that he may want to know from us is what we have done with his name.

Sometimes we hear one referred to as a "jack Mormon." I am not certain what the term means, though I am sure that it is not a title of honor. But when I meet Mormon before the judgment bar of God, I would not like to have him think of me as a "jack Mormon."

The final point that I would like to hold up for your consideration is that in one of the most earnest voices of modern scripture, the Lord himself has said, "Seek ye out of the best books words of wisdom." And one of those "best books" about which he has given specific command is the Book of Mormon. If he thinks it is so important, we had better know what it says. This can best be found out first by reading it and then by thinking about what we should get out of it. How much will we get by way of doctrine, how much inspiration, how much devotion, how much will our lives actually be changed for the better? All of this will be determined by how well we answer that great question asked by the Master, "How readest thou?" This will determine every other condition in our lives.

27

The Book of Instructions

W E HAVE developed a number of interesting procedures to assist us in solving some of the complexities of our present-day affairs. To help us with some of the problems incident to our knowledge explosion, the people who manufacture our appliances now usually send along with their product a book of instructions for their use.

For example, our family recently came into possession of a color television set. This miraculous instrument is one of the wonders of our day. It has taken our world nearly six thousand years to produce it. And it might take another six thousand years for some of us to learn to operate it if we first had to understand it. It performs miracles that if I didn't actually see, I wouldn't believe. The sights and sounds of the world's scenery, music, gunfire, and tornadoes are all hurled through the air in every direction by hundreds of telecasting stations. But they all find their way to quietly assemble in my living room. The book of instructions that came with the television set tells me which knobs to pull and which dials to turn to get any program onto my television screen in color with sound effects to my heart's content.

Because of this modern-day wonder, our family was able to watch the astronauts land on the moon. We also saw President Richard M. Nixon in Washington as he was talking with astronauts Neil Armstrong and Buzz Aldrin out in space. We could hear both ends of the conversation that went back and forth between the White House and the moon.

I don't even try to understand how it was that these identical pictures and sounds were in ten billion other locations on every part of the earth's surface at the same time. Once when we tired of waiting for action on the moon we turned the television knob and watched some elephants stampede in Africa. When that was over we paid a short visit to Queen Elizabeth in Buckingham Palace and then went back to finish our program on the moon.

The thing that impresses me most is the fact that in order to benefit from all of these miracles, I don't even need to understand them. Neither do I need to pay for any part of the billions of dollars worth of scientific equipment necessary to produce them. All I need to do is to read my book of instructions. Then by pulling the right knobs and turning the proper dials, I can bring into my living room the finest symphonies, the greatest stage plays, the most constructive movies, the biggest tidal waves, the hottest wars, and all of the other wonders that make up our age.

We are also beneficiaries of a lot of other miraculous events. I have a daily newspaper laid on my front porch that tells me what is going on in every part of the world during every hour of the day and night. I could not gather the news and print my single paper for a million dollars. And yet I get the news gathered, the paper printed, and the delivery made for less than the cost of the paper used. I don't need to become a reporter or a printer or a news analyst to get all of these facts with the most expert opinions about them. Nor do I need to understand the millions of other miracles in order to receive their blessings. I can attend school in my own home, or go sightseeing in Europe, or fly over the north pole, or do a million other wonderful things merely by keeping on good terms with my book of instructions.

Our family recently transacted some business with General Motors, and as a result we acquired an automobile. It will go fast or slow, uphill or downhill, backward or forward as I manipulate the gadgets. I can have almost any desirable temperature inside the car no matter what the climate may be on the outside. If I pull the right buttons even on the darkest night, two giant headlamps throw great beams of light down the roadway ahead of me. This car has some little mechanical hands that keep the snow wiped off the windshield. Other devices will wash the front window, tell me the time of day, how warm the engine is, or how much gasoline remains in the gas tank. My automobile has puncture-proof tires, push-button windows, six directional seats, turn blinkers, tail lights, radio, and power-steering. With a little pressure from my right foot the 350-horses under the hood will fly across the earth at 70 miles an hour and keep up the pace day after day, without complaining about being tired. As long as I follow the book of instructions, everything performs miraculously, whether I understand it or not.

However, the most complicated of all our machines is the human machine. In great admiration David exclaimed, "We are fearfully and wonderfully made." (Psalms 139:14.) And certainly we can all say that again! For example, I have a personal fuel tank called a stomach. Into it I can put all sorts of herbs, grains, meats, sweets, and liquids, and the most fantastic of all manufacturing devices will turn them into energy, vision, heat, light, and understanding. This digestive system can take proteins, carbohydrates, and fats and turn them into flesh and blood, bones and tissues, brains and personality. I also have a wonderful pair of lungs. They automatically draw into themselves a mysterious substance called air that I can't see or understand. My lungs not only understand what they are doing, but they are also fully automatic. They work while I am asleep or awake, sick or well, and while I am running or standing still. In the field of their activity my lungs are far more intelligent than I am. And every other organ of my body also has an intelligence that far surpasses mine.

My bloodstream contains trillions of microscopic red corpuscles that carry oxygen and nutrition to every part of my system. I have other trillions of white corpuscles that serve my body as its medical men. My white corpuscles fight disease, kill infection, and keep me in good health without my knowing what is happening. Billions of these wonderful little corpuscles are automatically manufactured in the marrow of my bones every day. Yet if I had all of the intelligence of the wisest combination of medical men, I would not know how to manufacture even one red corpuscle. And I wouldn't have the slightest guess about how to supply the oxygen to nourish even one brain cell. I know very little about estimating the needs of my liver, thyroid gland, or spirit. I don't even know where the self-starter is located that enables me to get myself going every morning. Every human being has some wonderful abilities to move and speak and laugh and think without knowing how it is done. There are millions of ideas filed away in my brain any one of which can be flashed upon an invisible screen by pushing the right mental buttons.

I also have an inaudible voice speaking to me that I have never heard, and yet it is telling me things every minute of every day in a language that is clearer than any audible voice. It lets me know when I am hungry or tired or cold or when I feel guilty or inferior or lazy.

The other day someone asked me to give them my opinion about two possible book covers. After I had looked at each one for a few seconds, something told me several reasons why I liked one very much and why I liked the other one not at all. In this interesting combination that I call myself I have many aptitudes and abilities that are as mysterious to me and even more wonderful than those miracles on my television set. And if I touch the right buttons I can laugh, love, think, repent, breathe, sleep, eat, work, and worship. And if I turn the dial to the right place an unmistakable voice will tell me when I am doing wrong and when I am being unwise.

I have some tremendous assets that even my television set or automobile doesn't have. Somewhere within myself I have a wonderful thing called life, which is the most valuable of all commodities. I also have a brain, a personality, and a will. I have a marvelous physical body equipped with a lot of helpful emotions. I also have a spirit, and while no one, including me, knows very much about it, yet I wouldn't sell it for a trillion dollars. It is an interesting fact that I have never so much as even seen my own spirit, and yet it is very close to me. I live with it every day. I can feel its presence and I can recognize some of its abilities and attitudes.

I also have a whole collection of miraculous instincts, abilities, character traits, and ambitions. I have a conscience, a voice, a will, a set of emotions, and access to the use of the still small voice. But probably my greatest good fortune is that the omnipotent Creator who is my manufacturer and the inventor of all of these wonderful installations has prepared some instructions as to how I should most effectively operate myself.

Over 3,400 years ago God came down onto the top of Mount Sinai and, to the accompaniment of the lightning and thunders of that holy mountain, gave us some important rules to make us function more effectively. And as a safeguard against ruining ourselves, he gave us some stern "thou shalt nots." The first step toward any success is to get clearly in mind and make some decisions about those things that we must not do. From the top of Mount Sinai God placed these flashing red lights of warning on such things as murder, adultery, dishonesty, profanity, Sabbath day violations, and the practice of identifying with false gods.

In 1832 the Lord placed some "thou shalt not" signs on

alcohol, nicotine, and caffeine to emphatically warn us against them. Then in January 1964 the Surgeon General of the United States gave us a kind of progress report picturing the devastation that was taking place in our magnificent human machinery because we were not following instructions but were taking these poisonous substances into our lungs, tissues, and bloodstream.

A prominent doctor recently attended the birth of a baby whose mother was a user of morphine. When the baby was born it looked more like a tiny Egyptian mummy than the proverbial "bouncing baby" described in the book of instructions. The baby's skin was an unhealthy blue-gray color, and within a few moments after birth he began to twitch and jerk with an increasing violence. The doctor knew that the baby was responding to his mother's craving for dope. He also knew that unless the baby received an immediate injection of morphine, he would have a convulsion from which he might never recover. The doctor injected the dope, which produced only a very short tranquillity. And in less than an hour the baby was again twitching his way toward a convulsion.

The nurse said, "The poor little guy is hooked just like his mom." She said, "What did he ever do to deserve a rotten deal like this?" When the mother was questioned about her habit she said, "Okay, okay, I am on the needle, so what? That is nobody's business but my own." The doctor said to her, "You don't believe that any more than I do." Then he went on to comment on the tragic life this poor little human being has to look forward to in living with a mother who is out of control of herself and who is trying to make herself believe that what she does is nobody's business but her own. When she saw the pathetic-looking little son that she had produced, she closed her eyes and began to cry.

What a tragedy that she didn't give her son the kind of start in life that he would have had if she had followed the Lord's book of instructions. From it we learn that our immoralities, our venereal diseases, our venereal attitudes, our atheisms, and our crimes can have devastating effects, and they are the business of a lot of other people, including God.

I might claim that my automobile belongs to me, but it is still the business of a lot of other people if I drive it down the wrong side of the street at a hundred miles per hour. But who are we ourselves responsible to?

The apostle Paul says, ". . . ye are not your own, For ye are bought with a price. . . ." (1 Corinthians 6:19-20.) Christ redeemed us from death by sacrificing his own life. Even the earth on which we live belongs to him. And only by his grace are we permitted to live here and to work out our eternal salvation. The most important part of our success is to pay particular attention to the direction given in our book of instructions. It says that we should take maximum care of our bodies, our minds, our spirits, and our personalities.

We start out our lives here with a father's blessing given under the power of the priesthood. We are directed that at the age of accountability we should be baptized, receive the gift of the Holy Ghost, and join the Church. At that time we are asked to make some covenants of faithfulness and not to take poisonous ideas into our minds.

Then as we develop our abilities we may receive the priesthood and by the quality of our service and obedience we may demonstrate our worthiness for increased blessings. We are instructed to be married in the temple where the sacred family relationships are formed for eternity. The book of instructions says that these covenants must be kept.

We are privileged to take upon ourselves the name of Christ and live by every word that proceedeth forth from the mouth of an all-wise Heavenly Father. And one of his greatest commands has to do with having children and rearing them according to his rules. The correct answer to every problem in our lives is found in the great books of instruction that God has caused to be written to teach us how to live. And may we make certain that we follow them.

28

Ballistics

THERE IS a very interesting science called *ballistics*. It deals with the motion and impact of projectiles, especially those discharged from firearms. One part of this science is very important in crime detection. Because each gun barrel is different, those bullets shot through it will be given a set of characteristic markings that may lead to the criminal.

But this science is not limited to the motion and impact of projectiles. It also has an application to the motion and impact of ideas and ideals. Out of this fact is born a kind of science that we might call "mental ballistics," or "spiritual ballistics." Minds are like guns and fingerprints in that they also have a set of characteristic markings. Whenever an idea is passed through the mind, the idea is marked by the mind, but the mind is also marked by the idea. Someone has said that "the mind, like the dyer's hand, is colored by what it holds." That is, if I hold in my hand a sponge full of purple dye, my hand becomes purple, and if I hold in my mind and heart great ideas of faith, devotion, and righteousness, my whole personality is colored accordingly. On the other hand, if I hold in my mind thoughts of spite, dishonesty, idleness, and lust, my personality will take the color of what it holds.

In the operation of this law we see some of our worst dangers as well as some of our greatest opportunities. The one who practices this science of ballistics is called a ballistician. An expert mental ballistician might be described as one skilled in devising effective programs of mind development by regularly passing the right kind of ideas through his own brain. The results of this science are certain. One cannot think big and be little. One cannot think righteously and be evil. When good ideas are run through the mind, the person will soon be distinguished for his goodness. Even when we rethink the great ideas of someone else, we will soon resemble the greatness of the man whose thoughts we are rethinking. The mind of a student tends to assume the characteristics of the mind of the teacher. Socrates left his marks upon Plato. Jesus stamped his impress upon Simon

Peter. The operation of this law not only makes people think alike, but it can even make them sound alike in their talk or even look alike. Children develop the family characteristics of speech and behavior. A mother and father who live together harmoniously may grow to resemble each other physically.

We know of no greater rewards than those received by an expert ballistician whose program of reading, thinking, and action makes the right kind of engrams in his mind. Therefore, to help ourselves become expert in this important field, suppose that in our mind's eye we place ourselves on an elevated balcony from which we can get a good view and exercise a firm control of everything that comes into our minds. Suppose that we not only carefully select the kinds of ideas that will be admitted, but rigidly control their use thereafter. Our idea supply should come only from books, people, and other sources of the highest quality, and there is plenty of raw material, for all of the ideas that have been well thought are our property. And the best mind is not necessarily the one that first discovers the greatest truth, but rather the one that puts it to its most effective use. Truth shows itself in its best form only when it is being lived.

An expert ballistician first acquires truth and then makes it a part of his bloodstream by thoroughly memorizing and practicing it. Thus the pathway of uplifting ideals and powerful ideas becomes so easy to follow that a characteristic response on the highest level is more or less automatic. Solomon referred to this law when he said, "As a man thinketh, so is he." However, that is not true of those thoughts that touch our minds so lightly as to leave no imprint. Some ideas wear a kind of snowshoe and leave a trail too indistinct for other ideas to follow.

One way to give our ideas greater influence by getting good, deep engrams into our brains is to put our plans and thoughts down on paper. Before we write our ideas down, we must think them through and get them more definitely organized in some usable form. Francis Bacon pointed out that "reading makes a full man, but writing makes an exact man." Too much of our thinking is done on the same level that we use for our New Year's resolutions. They are usually so poorly prepared that only a few hazy ideas skate lightly across our polished brains, making almost no impression. If we would thoroughly work out the details of our plans, then make a permanent written record with an accomplishment timetable attached, we would find our New Year's resolutions and all other resolutions assuming far greater importance. When we write our ideas down, it is like putting a bridle on them and making their intelligent guidance and direction possible.

We can also greatly increase our thought control by memorizing. The constructive ideas, uplifting philosophies, and great scriptural passages that we memorize make up our mental substance just as bricks make up the substance of a wall. And if we become effective in this important construction process, we can build our lives to any desired specification.

Action always follows the trail of a thought, and when we have a regular program of right thinking in sufficient depth, we can control the result of our lives. But when even the best ideas are allowed to skim too lightly over our minds, no path is left and confusion reigns. Without a good bridle, even the best ideas may go in several directions. Then there is no central path to establish a main purpose in life. To bring the highest price, ideas, like anything else, must be sorted, graded, organized, harnessed, and utilized. Even good ideas need direction, for while they may all start out with good intentions, they are bound to cross the scent of some conflicting thoughts going in another direction, and any idea can be misled. Unbridled thoughts are like the molecular action in nature, going in all directions. When we fail to hold a tight rein on our thoughts, they may easily jump the track or go in circles or go down a dead-end street. Sometimes one impulse tries to follow the scent of a half-dozen ideas at once.

An interesting study in thought direction is illustrated when a number of people get together for a group conversation. The course of the discussion may run smoothly for a time, but soon it may be jumping rapidly from one subject to another so that no particular progress is being made. Lacking thought guidance, a kind of barbed-wire entanglement of our engrams results and we get nowhere.

It is very important that our ideas themselves are not indefinite, fractional, immature, infirm, or unrighteous. But by constant planning and good mind management, we may become more and more effective in the development and control of our thoughts. This can be brought about by a definite regular program of reading, writing, memorizing, and practicing so that we get the pathways through our minds clear enough and definite enough that our lives can be brought under our control.

Of course, a good ballistician should make sure that the mind does not shirk its responsibility or engage in the questionable practices of rationalizing, offering excuses, or indulging in negative thinking. At the first sign of any mental trickery the reins should be tightened and the whip should be brought into play, if necessary.

As a young man on the farm I had a kind of demonstration of this ballistics idea in irrigating a field of tomato plants where the furrows ran from east to west with the gradual slope of the land. But the field had its greatest grade from north to south. And because water always seeks out the path of least resistance, the water in one row would sometimes find a weak place in the banks of its furrow and run down to join the water in the row next to it on its downhill side. The double amount of water thus accumulated in the second row could then more easily break its banks and both run into the third row. If someone were not on hand with a shovel to keep the ditch banks repaired and insist on each stream of water remaining in its proper channel, the individual small streams would soon gang up and run at right angles down through the field, washing a gully as they went. Of course, this downhill channel would make it impossible to get the water to do its assigned job in the rows, and consequently the plants beyond the gully would die for lack of nourishment.

Our minds also have some of these same characteristics. When they are not given proper attention and supervision, they frequently center on the wrong things, and soon the gullies caused by wrong thinking habits cut off all nourishment from the important areas that should be served by the mind. When the mind is short-circuited by a surge of contrary thoughts, it soon gets out of control. Then instead of resembling a well-irrigated, productive field, the irresponsible gullies use the mind's power for destructive ends.

What a wonderful thing it would be if we could get the same control over our thoughts and feelings that we have over our body members. That is, if I tell my finger to bend, it bends. If I tell my foot to move, it moves. My legs can be depended upon to carry me to almost any destination almost automatically. But I don't have that kind of control over my will or my enthusiasm or my faith. I have a great deal more trouble managing my thoughts than I do managing my fingers. One of the probable reasons for this lack of mental control is that we improperly humor our minds and gratify those thoughts that clamor most loudly for attention rather than those that serve the most important ends. Too often our thoughts are subject to the destructive cross-currents of our fears, doubts, negative thinking, and evil imaginations. Then when too many of these harmful gullies are running in the wrong direction, we lose control of the personality. An effective ballistician, like a good irrigator, should keep things under sufficient control that he can use his thoughts to vitalize the useful plants at the very end of the mental row.

Food can be purchased at the grocery store, but there is no central marketplace for self-control or the attainment of effective idea management. Of course, the right kinds of ideas do not come easily or automatically. They have to be ensnared, impounded, and preserved. Then each good idea that we capture and domesticate will introduce us to its friends and relatives. If you examine one idea closely, you will usually find that it is holding another idea by the hand, and thus through one idea you may get acquainted with a whole family of interesting thoughts.

One gold mine for great ideas is the holy scriptures. These are the ideas that an all-wise Heavenly Father has prescribed to serve our best interests. These especially should be loved, memorized, kept in good working condition, and practiced. God wants us to become as he is. This requires that we should think as he thinks, and do as he does. We should live by every word that proceeds from the mouth of God. We should never allow doubts and fears to stampede our ideas out of their proper channels. But by organizing our thinking and by putting our ideas to work, we may get the same discipline over our minds that we get our body organs.

Then week after week as we sit on our mental balconies and direct our thoughts in the right kind of mental grooves, we may give our lives purpose as we stamp them with the characteristics of godliness.

29

Memorizing With Success

I T IS a very interesting fact that everyone complains of a poor memory. We can't remember names, we can't remember faces, we can't remember ideas, and therefore many people feel that success is out of their hands because they were short-changed when the mental equipment was handed out. However, in almost every case the only thing that is wrong with our mental machinery is that we don't use it properly.

Our brain is one of the greatest wonders of creation. It is about the size of our two hands. It is composed of fourteen billion cells. It can contain more information than can be stored in a dozen libraries. It is the most wonderful problem solver. It is the greatest inventor. It has the most remarkable powers of creation. Thomas A. Edison was expelled from school at age fourteen because he couldn't learn. And yet out of his brain came a long string of wonders, including electric lights, phonographs, refrigerators, and hundreds of other things that had never been known before.

Robert Updegraff, a prominent success counselor, says that it is not lack of brain power or business capacity that holds men back from their objectives; rather, far more failure occurs because people take only about one-fifth of their minds with them into their work. It is the contention of those who are supposed to know that about four-fifths of the mind lies below the level of consciousness. In fact, the mind has frequently been compared to an iceberg, about four-fifths of which lies below the surface of the water. And psychologists maintain that it is what we do with the subconscious four-fifths that lies below the surface of the water that largely determines our success.

Our knowledge, attitudes, skills, habits, and personality traits must first be learned on the conscious level, and then the responsibility for our success is largely turned over to that part of the mind that lies below the level of consciousness. For example, we learn to walk, talk, feed ourselves, etc., by our conscious effort. But once these abilities are developed, their operation is performed more or less automatically. Then we walk, speak, breathe, and eat with very little help from the conscious mind.

We can also accomplish about any other success in the same way. We fill the subconscious mind with the knowledge, attitudes, feelings, and techniques of success by memorizing them in the conscious mind and then storing them up in the subconscious mind. Later on men show themselves as industrious, faithful, courageous, and enthusiastic without always knowing the reason why. We store all of these success characteristics in this great subterranean region; then, like a giant artesian spring, they gush up more or less automatically to feed our success.

Or, we might use a little different figure and say that the subconscious mind is like a field of good soil. With care and attention we can grow whatever crop we desire. But if we leave the field uncultivated and uncared for, it will produce only troublesome weeds. That is, we can grow success only by design, whereas we get failure primarily by default.

Many people use their subconscious minds as dumping grounds for doubts, fears, sins, inferiority complexes, and negative attitudes. Then when the mind puts our success together, it uses only the materials previously made available to it. It should be easy to understand why we don't get a higher grade of success when we make so many inferior materials available to the subconscious mind. The reason that so many people are inclined toward sinfulness, have bad tempers, or get discouraged so easily, or get down in the dumps on the slightest provocation, or are continually doing the very things that reason tells them they shouldn't do, is that these traits have been made so easily available to their subconscious minds. We may read bad literature and see many bad movies about violence, sin, and crime and then wonder why we respond as we do. Sometimes we let our problems become so acute that we have to pay a psychiatrist to dig down into our subconscious minds and burn out the harmful experiences that we ourselves have previously stored there. Before we can change ourselves, we must change the kind of mental building material hidden below the level of consciousness.

This great subconscious mind is always at work. It never forgets; it never rests. It works while we sleep and almost automatically determines our failure or success based on the kind of material it has to work with.

Some time ago a friend of mine told about something his father had said to him when he was just a young man. The idea had stuck in his subconscious mind and had gone all through his system. It had become so much a part of his philosophy of life that it influenced his very reaction. We are all subject to this same kind of influence.

There is an old adage that says, "Beware of what you want, for you will get it." What we want determines the kind of power we supply to the engine rooms of our lives. If we are careless in our screening and store a mixture of Dr. Jekyll and Mr. Hyde inclinations in our subconscious mind, these same harmful influences will appear in the future pattern of our performance in the same proprotions in which they have been stored. We also tend to produce inferiority when we store up only fragments of thoughts, or when we store up incomplete motives or ideas that are immature or partially forgotten. Then nothing can prevent confusion and irresponsibility in our accomplishment program.

Now if we would like to greatly increase the probability of our personal success, we should start our conscious minds on a program of memorizing plenty of the highest quality of ideas and emotions. Certainly we should never allow evil or fear or doubt to be sitting around the workbench when our success is being put together. Some people who have never practiced self-control say that they have to "blow their tops" occasionally. But if we permit ourselves this indulgence, then the next thing we know we are blowing our blood vessels and our nervous systems. Think how much our strength could be increased if we would control our output of emotion and had a regular, well-planned program for furnishing our subconscious mind with ideas of faith, industry, courage, positive thinking, and righteousness. Then suppose that we made sure that every idea was whole, definite, specific, clean-cut, crystal clear, of top quality, and in a good state of preservation.

We see this principle at work in the experience of all great men. During his years of preparation Abraham Lincoln spent his evenings lying before the fire memorizing the Bible and other good books. He went over these ideas again and again until they were firmly established in his soul. The reason that Lincoln did not practice deceit, force, or murder like some of our present-day dictators was because none of these things had ever been a part of him. It was easy to predict what Lincoln would do if you knew the kinds of things he had stored in his subconscious mind.

There are some people who give themselves over to failure by saying that they can't memorize, and they feel that there is nothing they can do about it. But everyone will find that if he fails to memorize the right things consciously, he will soon be memorizing a lot of the wrong things subconsciously. The most important reason that we fail to memorize is the same reason that one who never throws a baseball fails to become a great baseball pitcher. An inexperienced arm never performs like a champion's arm, because it hasn't stored up enough of the right kind of pitching muscle. Every one of us would be amazed if he could just comprehend the tremendous possibilities that lie buried within him that can be released by a lot of good hard drill.

The second largest university in the world is the Moslem University in Cairo, Egypt. One of its entrance requirements is that every student must memorize the Koran, word for word. The Koran is only slightly smaller than the New Testament. If someone asked us to memorize the New Testament, we would probably say that we couldn't do it. But we would be mistaken. We could do it and we can do just about anything else that we really set our hearts on, train for, and work at in the right way.

The one who really desires success should always be on the look-out for good ideas, just as a good prospector is always watching for signs of gold. When found, these good ideas should be stored away just as the squirrel stores up his acorns for the winter. That is, everyone should have some kind of an idea bank where valuable ideas can be deposited for safekeeping, so that they are easily available for rerun to revitalize our thinking. When this helpful information and these motivating ideas, important bits of philosophy, and inspirational poems are carefully memorized and lived with, they become a part of us and constitute our most valuable property. We may be sure that the time will come when all of these nuggets of thought will find their place in our jigsaw of success.

We might also type these ideas onto cards so that they can be carried with us and memorized while we are waiting or walking or traveling. Ideas are like people; they attain their maximum influence only when we get intimately acquainted with them. The statement made by the father to the son has great power because the son loves the father. He also understands and believes the idea. He first accepts it in his conscious mind and then sends it down to the engine room below with a high recommendation. There it will remain to influence every future action of his life forever.

These instruments of motive power embedded in our lives determine what we think, do, and feel, and we should adopt an effective technique for memorizing and upgrading them.

Someone has said that our first investment should be made in a pair of scissors and a pot of glue. Then we have the beginning of an idea book or a motivation bank, and we can read and cut and paste and develop the most powerful ideas and motives. When these are cast into exactly the right words, memorized, and lived with, they get into our bloodstream and determine the power and direction of our lives.

There is a peculiar sight sometimes seen at sea where the winds, the waves, and the surface ice are going in one direction. And in the very center of this movement, an iceberg is seen sailing serenely along in exactly the opposite direction. The explanation is that the bulk of the iceberg is based in the powerful subcurrents prevailing at the bottom of the ocean. Thus, the iceberg pays little attention to which way the wind is blowing or what the surface ice may be doing. We have a similar possibility when we effectively train and motivate the subconscious mind with the right kind of ideas and ideals. Then we get a "success in depth" that is not controlled by the superficialities on the surface of life.

Jesus pointed out that man does not live by bread alone. Rather, he said that man should live by every word that proceedeth forth from the mouth of God. The easiest way to live this commandment is to fill our subconscious minds with the word of the Lord. The word of the Lord is good for us, and when we get it into the depths of our souls, we develop a righteousness and a stability of character that will guide us straight toward the celestial kingdom.

Thinking in depth makes hypocrisy and surface living impossible. It is in the heart that issues are decided. The heart is the composing room for our most important success. The scripture says, "Keep thy heart with all diligence; for out of it are the issues of life." (Proverbs 4:23.)

We have a phrase in which we say something is "learned by heart." When we learn honesty, industry, and faith in God by heart, then we begin living in depth. What a thrilling privilege to memorize the great scriptures. These ideas come from God himself, and when we develop a love for his ideas and an ambition to live accordingly, our strength is greatly increased. Then we will have a philosophy of life and a depth of character that can guarantee any success by always keeping us moving in the right direction no matter which winds may be blowing on the surface of life.

30

The Book of Acts

THE FIFTH book of the New Testament is one of the world's most important books. It is called the book of Acts, or the Acts of the Apostles. Before the time had arrived for the book of Acts to begin its account, Jesus had already established the church and had chosen and instructed the twelve apostles in their responsibility for carrying on its work. They had been commissioned with divine authority and assigned to the important task direction concerned with the eternal salvation of all members of the human family.

To connect up the book with the related events that had preceded it, the opening chapter gives a brief account of the resurrected Christ's postmortal ministry. Then just prior to his departure he gave his final instructions. He said to the apostles, ". . . ye shall be witnesses unto me both in Jerusalem, and in all Judaea, and in Samaria, and unto the uttermost parts of the earth." (Acts 1:8.) Then as two angels dressed in white apparel stood by him, he was taken up, and a cloud received him out of mortal sight. Thus the earthly ministry of Jesus came to its end, and the leadership of the church was transferred to those shoulders that Jesus had assigned to receive it.

Up to this point the members of the Twelve had been primarily concerned with listening, learning, asking questions, and following instructions. They had always had Jesus to lean upon and to help with their problems, but now he was gone and the problems were up to them. The authority as well as the full responsibility was now in their hands. They held the center of the stage, and the book of the Acts of the Apostles was about to be written.

The holy scriptures include many kinds of books. One book is devoted to the psalms and one to the proverbs. Some scriptural books deal with biography, some with doctrine, and some with philosophy. The Bible speaks of a book of remembrance. There are books of wisdom and books of covenants. Some books have to do primarily with history and some with poetry. Some speak of faith and miracles and blessings. We have the books of the prophets. There is a book of Isaiah and a book of Jeremiah and a book of John. But probably the greatest title in the scriptures is the book of Acts. It tells the story of what some human beings actually did. What people think and believe and plan are all very important, but what they do is the thing that counts most.

Brigham Young once said that "anyone can preach, but it takes a good man to practice." The truly great man is the one who can put ideas, ideals, and ambitions into actual operation. The mission of Jesus was not merely to find or to develop idea men. There are millions of books and millions of heads filled with good ideas. Jesus didn't come seeking new ideas. He already had the greatest ideas, and what he wanted was people who could follow them.

Throughout his ministry, he stressed the importance of doing things. He was continually pointing out that mere belief by itself was of small consequence. Even Satan believes. Satan knows beyond a shadow of any doubt that God lives. He knows the kind of being God is. He knows without question that the gospel of Jesus Christ is true. But this is not enough. Even the greatest faith, without works, is dead. It was the "doers of the word," not merely the hearers, that incited the admiration and favor of the Redeemer of the world. Jesus tried to develop workers. He sought for people who could translate ideas into action. As we might say, he wanted someone who could "get the ship into port."

The most serious blasphemy in the world is not profanity but lip service. And one of the biggest problems of our personal lives is that while we pay homage to the idea of the gospel, we frequently trifle with its actual practice.

Jesus poured out his most severe condemnation upon the heads of those who believed one thing and practiced something else. He said to them, "But woe unto you, scribes and pharisees, hypocrites! for ye shut up the kingdom of heaven against men: for ye neither go in yourselves, neither suffer ye them that are entering to go in." (Matthew 23:13.)

To the vinedresser's son who said, "I go, sir, and went not," Jesus said, "That the publicans and harlots go into the kingdom of God before you." (Matthew 21:30-31.) The central theme of the entire ministry of Jesus was that great line in which he said,

"Wherefore by their fruits ye shall know them." This one state- ment pretty well sums up the religion of Christ. It is the standard of judgment for both here and hereafter. The apostle James dis- approves of that kind of verbal Christianity that says, "Depart in peace, be ye warmed and filled" (James 2:16), yet gives not those things that the need requires. This still tends to be our problem. We are still willing to pray about our religion, to die for our reli- gion and do everything for our religion except live for it.

But Christianity is not merely an idea; it is an activity. The religion of Christ is not merely something that we think about, or discuss, or argue over. It is something that we do. It is some- thing that we put in force in our lives by which to live and for which to work.

The scripture speaks about "saviors upon Mount Zion." The only way that I know of to be a savior is to save someone. On that basis, how much religion can we personally take credit for? How many people have we saved personally? What could we think of one who spent his entire life in the practice of medicine and yet had never saved anyone? Suppose that you were a doctor who had never seen anyone get well under your hands. The same standard of judgment might be applied to those of us who claim to be followers of the Great Physician.

The only way anyone has of proving his worth is by his works. That does not discount the ability of those who are won- derful conversationalists, or who have a head full of ideas and a heart full of good intentions. There are some people who are good to look at; some have pleasing personalities and are delight- ful companions. But after all has been said and done and we have arrived at the great day of judgment, the thing that will then be of primary importance will be what we have actually done.

Jesus gave some emphasis to the negative side of this situa- tion when he foretold that at the day of judgment many people would say to him, "Lord, Lord, have we not prophesied in thy name? . . . and in thy name done many wonderful works?" But the Lord will then say unto them, "I never knew you: depart from me, ye that work iniquity." (Matthew 7:22-23.)

It may not even change the situation very much, then, to speak of the books we have read and the wisdom we have acquired or even the great precepts that we have believed in.

So far as we know, no books have ever been written called "The Resolutions of the Apostles," or "The Good Intentions of the Apostles," or even "The Faith of the Apostles." The book of books, the title that will stand out above all others, will be the "Book of Acts."

But the scripture gives us the interesting information that the book of Acts will not be confined to describing the deeds of the apostles. On the day of reckoning the book that will probably have the greatest challenge for us will be the one telling of our own acts. John the Revelator saw such a book when in his great vision he was permitted to look a few thousand years ahead of his own day when all people should be assembled for the final judgment. John said, "And I saw the dead, small and great, stand before God; and the books were opened: and another book was opened, which is the book of life: and the dead were judged out of those things which were written in the books, according to their works." (Revelation 20:12.)

That sounds as if each of us will have his own book of acts. The acts of the apostles are important and are recorded. But someone is also keeping track of the acts of Satan, the acts of Hitler, and our own acts. When Josef Stalin stands before the judgment bar of God, he may find that there will be a volume bearing his name and giving an account of his blood purges, his lying, and his trouble-making. Every one of his evil deeds will be recorded in all of its ghastly detail. In this life, Mr. Stalin was able to shift much of the blame for his own evil acts onto someone else. But in the judgment that system may not work very well, either for Mr. Stalin or for us. And when that great day arrives, the most important of all the books may be that book of acts that has our name written on its title page. It will give an accurate and detailed account of what we have actually done. It will tell what we have done with our time, what we have done with our talents, what we have done with our opportunities, and what we have done with our temptations.

What a great idea it would be if each of us would take over the responsibility for keeping a written record of our own acts similar to the written daily journal kept by many people. Suppose that every night before going to bed we wrote down an account of the things that we had done during that day. It might be very profitable to write down our failures as well as our successes. We should include our sins as well as our good deeds. If we did it as

God would do it, then our conversations and even our thoughts would go into the record. Then we could see ourselves as nearly as possible as God may see us and as we may see ourselves at a later date.

Paul Goebbels, the German propaganda minister under Hitler, was engaged in an evil cause, but he had a very constructive system for developing effectiveness in himself. Each morning he wrote down in his diary his objectives and plans for that day; then each night before going to bed he analyzed what he had done. If he had succeeded, he wrote down the reasons for his success and tried to identify and further develop those factors that had been responsible. By this process he could make his good ideas even more effective the next time he had opportunity to use them. In the places where he had fallen down he tried to determine the reasons for his failure so that he could avoid making the same mistake again. When any principle was proven unsound, it was discarded; when some particular technique worked, it could be still further perfected and prepared to serve some greater future need.

While Mr. Goebbels was evil, this idea itself is excellent. Therefore, just suppose that we actually kept a book of acts for our own lives. Then instead of being surprised on judgment day, we would have the advantage of having known what the score was as we went along. No one likes to meet his own evil face to face, and if we made every day a judgment day, then our lives would take an immediate sharp turn upward. Any game loses its interest, its effectiveness, as well as its motivation when we fail to keep score. Keeping the score of our lives would not only stimulate a more intense interest, but it would also motivate a more faithful performance.

We wouldn't want to drive an automobile without a fuel gauge or do extensive banking business without a record of deposits and withdrawals. Then why shouldn't we keep a current record of the solvency and insolvency of our own lives? If we had 365 judgment days every year, based on the daily record of our dishonesties, our disloyalties, and our immoralities, they would work like a powerful antitoxin and would soon destroy the diseases that produced them.

One of our biggest problems is in checking our spiritual diseases on time. In fact, someone has said that "hell is just truth seen too late." When we stand before God in judgment, every individual will then want to be a devoted, faithful, hard-working, full tithe-paying member of God's kingdom. But we must not wait until that time to develop our righteous impulses. Judgment day will be our day of greatest joy if we have made a good score. But whether or not we keep the record, each of us is writing his own book of acts—we are writing an eternal record, and may God help us to write it well.

31

A Paper Memory

A GREAT PSYCHOLOGIST challenges us with a very provocative thought when he asks, "How would you like to create your own mind?" At first thought that idea may seem a little strange, and yet it has the most substantial possibilities. Actually, the mind is made up of what it feeds upon. The mind, like the dyer's hand, is colored by what it holds.

But the mind was never intended primarily as a baggage room or a storehouse. Its greatest service comes from its possibilities as a mental machine or as a great spiritual workshop. The mind's chief functions are to think, to make decisions, to motivate, and to take action.

A prominent British neurophysicist recently said that you couldn't build an electronic computer for three billion dollars that would be the equivalent of a human mind. But even so, who could endow an electronic computer with reason, discernment, kindness, logic, or judgment? The memory function of the mind is also important, but this is one of the departments where it most needs assistance. If anyone plans to reap the most profitable harvest, he will need to supplement his powers of recall. However, this fault may be corrected by supplementing our mental powers with a paper memory.

To illustrate, just imagine that you were to attend some kind of a three-day educational convention. Suppose that during that period you heard one hundred ideas that you wanted to remember. Without the aid of some kind of paper memory, the average person would have lost 60 percent of his ideas by the time the meeting closed. The ideas may still be in the mind and they could be recognized if someone else reminded you of them, but they have passed beyond your ability to recall them, and as time passes they sink deeper and deeper into oblivion and take many others with them. That is, if you wait for another six months, many of these other ideas will join them in regions of forgetfulness. In time a large majority of our ideas will have slipped below the level of our consciousness.

One of the difficult things about this situation is that the moment of forgetting, like the moment of birth, is an unconscious moment. The moment of learning is a conscious moment but the moment of forgetting is an unconscious moment, and we can sometimes lose our finest ideas without actually realizing our losses.

However, when these ideas are made a part of our marvelous paper memory, they become our permanent possession. Many people are capable of extensive reading and straight thinking, but they are weak in remembering. In fact, everyone complains of a poor memory. One man once said, "There are three things that I can't remember. The first thing that I can't remember is names; the second thing that I can't remember is faces, and I have forgotten the third thing I can't remember." Writing an idea down helps you to retain possession of it, but it can also be a helpful aid to understanding. That is, before we write a thing down we usually think it through and make decisions about those points that are not clear or about which we have doubts. The act of writing an idea down stamps it more indelibly in our mental memory; it also makes an imperishable paper record that can be used as an aid to the mental memory. In fact, it has been said that so far as memory is concerned, one dull pencil is worth five sharp minds.

It can be very helpful for one to get in the habit of reading with a pencil in his hand. Then he can underline, make notes, and add any ideas of his own that may occur to him in the process. It has been pointed out that there is a way to get more out of a book or a lecture than there is in it. By absorbing each thought as we read it, we can get everything out of the book that is in it; in addition, as our mind pursues the content of the book, it will occasionally strike an idea that will send a thought ricocheting out into space. It is suggested that frequently we should let our minds follow the new thoughts and make notes about those ideas that we come in contact with along the way. We will find that some of our best ideas will be those that we ourselves think during one of these mental excursions. By this process our thoughts will lead us to a lot of its friends and relatives that we didn't know before. Ideas almost always come in chains or clusters or in family groups. Following ideas is one of the best ways to learn things. Then when our exploring effort has exhausted itself, we may come back and take up our reading again at the place where we left off.

We will certainly also want to write down these flashes of inspiration that sometimes seem to come from nowhere. It has been said that we sit in the lap of an immense intelligence, and some of our most outstanding ideas will be those things that we ourselves think. In trying to connect up the human race, the evolutionists have talked a great deal about "missing links." But there are also a lot of missing links in our philosophies, our morals, our inventions, our business successes, as well as in our religion.

Most people's ideas come in fragments, and if we keep the pieces, the missing links will soon show up so that the jigsaw will be complete. Sometimes we must discover the key idea that makes the whole meaningful, or sometimes we get the materials that will purge the impurities out of the mixture that has been causing our philosophy or our lives to malfunction. A reading process can be like a mining operation where we burn out the dross, eliminate the slag, and keep the pure gold.

Frequently ideas deteriorate in our mental memory. They sometimes disappear as they come in fragments. We may have the general idea but a missing key word or a missing punch line or a supporting phrase makes the whole weak and unproductive. But if an idea is transferred to our paper memory while we have the spirit of it, it can be recorded in all its vigor and beauty. Its cheeks can be painted, its attire can be made spotless, and its hair arranged at its best, and that is the way it will always remain. We can preserve our memory, our culture, our spirituality, and our occupational know-how by an acquisition of the right combination of ideas that are properly preserved in our paper memory, ready to be applied whenever the need arises.

Of course, any book from which we get ideas can't do the job by itself. That is, every inspired book needs an inspired reader. And an inspired reader is one who already has some parts of the ideas. He is one who thinks, meditates, makes notes, joins ideas together, decides questions, and makes applications. Then he is in a position to write them down and prepare to take action. Some people may read and listen endlessly to the thoughts of others only to have them go in one ear and out the other without any gain or profit being left to the one concerned. The reason that the teacher always learns more than the student is that the teacher must get a better possession of the facts.

An idea collector should walk around an idea a few times so that he knows it on both its positive and negative sides. He should make a personal examination of both the pros and cons of the matter. Both the teacher and the student should have done their homework and have researched the subject in such a way that they are capable of a written report. But one is only able to get the clearest ownership title after he has put the idea into action. Neither the giver nor the receiver should sit back and expect the other to do all of the work. And whether one is reading for enjoyment or for profit, it is necessary for him to use his powers of understanding, concentration, conviction, and action.

Pretty words and high-sounding philosophies may by themselves be useless. There may be little value in ideas about culture, education, and success unless we link with the actual industry that must always be present in any success; that is, we learn to do by doing. As part of one man's New Year's resolutions, he decided to stop smoking, but he said, "Don't tell anyone about it, because I may not want to go through with it." This man would do better with his resolutions if he first made some strong decisions about them. Then his determination could have been strengthened by writing them down. Someone has said that no plan is really a plan until it is on paper. No architect would amount to much without a good set of paper drawings.

One of the most important parts of our religion is memory. From the top of Mount Sinai the Lord said, "Remember the sabbath day to keep it holy." Those who violate the Sabbath day are those who can't remember that the people who properly honor the Sabbath day will be a different kind of people from those who don't. The entire scriptures should be a part of our paper memory. To strengthen this part of our lives is also the purpose of books of remembrance and diaries.

A written memory helped Ralph Waldo Emerson's moods to believe in each other. He said it was as difficult to manage his mind as it was to manage thunderbolts. Emerson's chief business was thinking, writing, and speaking for the benefit of others, yet he says that at times his brain would become a blank and his mind would be left in a state of barrenness. Life seemed to him like an occasional flash of light followed by long periods of darkness. As one of his most profitable moves, Emerson decided to keep a journal. And once begun, he kept it up faithfully.

In his journal he wrote down his every thought and made many helpful written suggestions to himself. Each day he collected in his journal his disjointed dreams, his mental reveries, and the fragments of all of those ideas that his mind was able to conceive. He found that the act of writing an idea down improved both his idea and his mind. His journal became the hive in which he stored the honey of his mind as the bees of his brain distilled it. When once his thoughts were written down, he could come back and review them again and again and make all needed improvements.

As he visited with great ideas, every day he grew accustomed to their faces. After he improved their dress and brightened their eyes and increased their muscle power, he was able to join them together in a more effective order. And once Mr. Emerson snared an idea, he never allowed it to get away. He not only wrote it down immediately but he also put it in his mental incubator. He knew that ideas have a natural tendency to propagate and every idea has the possibilities for a large posterity. Emerson worked incessantly. He said, "Of all the tonics, work is the most effective."

There was a great inspiration for Mr. Emerson in every assertion of his will. He knew that every personality needs an emotional generator to set industry in motion, and there are many of these stimulators that should be made a part of our paper memory. Sometimes a song or a phrase or a poem has the power to set our greatest impulses in motion. But left in our mental memory alone, they can soon grow dim, indistinct, and unusable. If left in the mental memory alone, ideas can deteriorate very quickly. And when a particular word is misplaced or the spirit of the idea is lost or its rhythm is forgotten, the idea loses both its punch and its beauty. But when we keep our poems, our philosophies, and other spiritual motivators in our paper memory, they always remain as fresh as when they were written down, and they can be used to revitalize our entire personality.

Mind is the master power that builds and molds, and mind is man. Ever more he takes the tools of thought and fashions what he wills, bringing forth a thousand joys, a thousand ills. We think in secret and it comes to pass; environment is but a looking glass. May the Lord help us to use all of our resources in order to live most effectively.

32

Your Book of Proverbs

ONE OF the important books in the
in the Bible is the book of
Proverbs. It is a collection of profound truths and thought-
provoking maxims intended to bring about a betterment in human conduct. It includes some of the most pungent statements in
the scriptures with many motivating ideas from the wisest men.
Under the title of the book of Proverbs have been assembled several thousand of the most noble axioms and finest adages that
have ever come from human minds.

It is an interesting thought that all important things are
made up of parts. A molecule is composed of atoms. An atom is
a collection of electrons and protons. Books are made up of chapters. Chapters are assembled from paragraphs, and paragraphs are
constructed from sentences, words, and letters.

Our greatest building responsibility is that of putting together our own personalities in such a way as to make the best
and the most of our own possibilities. The wise man Solomon
gave us the key to this success when he said that as a man thinketh, so is he. (See Proverbs 23:7.) That is, we build our lives with
ideas; and the quality of the individual thoughts that make up
our philosophies, attitudes, and ambitions will determine what we
ourselves will become. Bible wisdom reminds us that we always
get out of life about what we put into it. And when we get good
ideas into our minds, they soon start operating in our hearts, activities, and accomplishments. Of course, there are many excellent proverbs that may be had from sources outside the Bible.

The claim has been made that Benjamin Franklin was the
wisest man ever produced in America. And he is remembered
primarily for his proverbs. He made his living as a printer and sent
out in his newspaper short, pithy statements to enlarge the minds
of people. And as Oliver Wendell Holmes once said, "A mind once
stretched by a new idea never returns to its original dimensions."

Because of the proverbial truth that "the teacher always
learns more than the student," it is suggested that each of us

should write down some proverbs of his own. Solomon and Franklin prepared these capsules of wisdom to benefit other people, but their proverbs reacted inwardly to make their authors the wisest men of their time. We may also literally lift ourselves up by the bootstraps of our own wisdom after it has been made a part of us.

This principle of learning by teaching was once illustrated by a nationally famous life insurance salesman. Someone asked him how he got out of a sales slump. He replied that he usually took three or four of his fellow salesmen friends out to lunch. Then he gave them an enthusiastic discussion about how to sell life insurance. He didn't say what the discussion did to his friends, but after he had finished instructing them, he had so greatly enlightened and motivated himself that thereafter any accomplishment seemed easy. Most worthwhile success begins with us. Success does not so much resemble pouring water into a cistern; it is more like opening a spring. When we give an idea its life and charge it with power, it always cuts a deeper pathway through our minds and makes a greater alteration in our personalities than those ideas do that we get from others.

Solomon prayed for wisdom to lead his people more effectively. Then by going to work thinking up and writing down the wisest thoughts, he helped to answer his own prayers. Just suppose that you undertook a similar project of writing down over three thousand proverbs, covering every subject, to be loved, memorized, and lived by thousands of people in all future generations. If we prayed for wisdom and then worked as hard and as long as Solomon did in thinking, composing, testing, discarding, improving, and memorizing, we would also be wise men.

Of course, we do not need to invent every good idea personally. There are thousands of old ideas of excellent quality that we haven't yet used. These can be memorized, practiced, and made an integral part of us. If we effectively used each Bible proverb and each of those that made Benjamin Franklin great, our lives would also blossom with the same kind of success that distinguished theirs.

What an exciting thought that everything that has been well said belongs to us personally! The Apostle Paul said, ". . . whatsoever things are true, whatsoever things are honest, whatsoever things are just, whatsoever things are pure, whatsoever things are lovely, whatsoever things are of good report; . . . think on these things." (Philippians 4:8.) In this thinking process we may even use the ideas of God himself in making our mental grooves so broad and deep that all future ideas will want to follow them.

Proverbs may also be used to correct our faults. If this seems too difficult, we might try to find proverbs to correct the faults of other people. Then it is comparatively easy to incorporate our readymade solutions into our own program. Or when we see someone else demonstrating some special virtues or helpful abilities, we may adopt them for our own use. Any abilities may be made to grow in our lives by filling our minds with their particular thought seeds. Even by helping others, we help ourselves. One proverb says, "Tow your brother's boat across and lo, your own has reached the shore." As soon as Solomon and Benjamin Franklin set out to solve the problems of others, they began solving their own more or less automatically. All great events first take place as thoughts in the mind. The problems of idleness, fear, immorality, and dishonesty that we can definitely solve in our minds even for other people can then be more easily solved in our own lives.

And many millions of people have changed their lives for good by reading, loving, and memorizing the great Bible proverbs. Just think how we might tone up our own lives by living the following. In the first chapter (verse 7) of Proverbs, it is written, "The fear of the Lord is the beginning of knowledge: but fools despise wisdom and instruction." The second chapter (verse 20) says to "walk in the way of good men, and keep the paths of the righteous."

Here are some others: "My son, despise not the chastening of the Lord; neither be weary of his correction." (3:11.) "Keep thy heart with all diligence; for out of it are the issues of life." (4:23.) "A wise son maketh a glad father: but a foolish son is the heaviness of his mother." (10:1.) ". . . the way of transgressors is hard." (13:15.) These lessons are all less expensive when learned from the book rather than from actual experience.

"He that walketh with wise men shall be wise: but a companion of fools shall be destroyed." (13:20.) "A soft answer turneth away wrath: but grievous words stir up anger." (15:1.) "He that refuseth instruction despiseth his own soul: but he that heareth reproof getteth understanding." (15:32.) Pride goeth before destruction, and an haughty spirit before a fall." (16:18.) "He that answereth a matter before he heareth it, it is folly and shame unto him." (18:13.) "A good name is rather to be chosen than great riches, and loving favour rather than silver and gold." (22:1.) "Train up a child in the way he should go: and when he is old, he will not depart from it." (22:6.) "A man that flattereth his neighbour spreadeth a net for his feet." (29:5.)

Of course we are not limited to those proverbs recorded in the Bible. Some of the proverbs best suited to our need will frequently come either out of our own experience or from the experiences of others near us. But they need to be given definiteness and importance by writing them down and memorizing them.

Suppose therefore that we make up our own collection of those well-expressed principles that we expect to govern our lives. Every day most people meet up with enough good ideas to completely transform their success, but if these ideas are not impounded, most of them will get away. If we wrote all of our own best ideas down, we would soon have a good answer for every need. Then they could be sharpened, polished, and given power through activity. Jesus himself made great use of proverbs, many of which he took out of the Old Testament and some he distilled from his own experience. He illustrated the greatest truths with everyday experiences and taught people wisdom from the things that they already understood.

In building our great, modern freeways, we have found it profitable to protect them with fences and illuminated markers. Delays and accidents are prevented by having some underpasses, overpasses, and interchanges. We no longer permit stray horses or other animals to wander across our highways to slow down our speed or cause us damage. In like manner, we should also create some spiritual safeguards to make that straight and narrow highway leading to eternal life safe for our souls to travel. Our lives can be guarded against evil and failure by erecting some good strong mental and moral fences out of those great ideas that we have memorized and made commitments to live by. When we are in danger of being injured by pride, we may flash upon the screen of our minds that great truth that says, "Pride goeth before a fall." When the foolishness of others attracts us, we can recite to ourselves the proverb that says, "The companion of fools shall be destroyed." In hundreds of great Bible proverbs we are urged to seek knowledge, "develop wisdom," "love righteousness," and "fear God." These should be made as solid as reinforcing steel in our lives. Our daily activities are made up of hundreds of problems, and we need hundreds of firmly made, ready-to-use answers. It is not always easy to do accurate, safe, and original on-the-spot thinking; therefore, we frequently let our problems go unresolved unless we have on hand some prefabricated, pretested solutions ready for immediate use. For these purposes, we may use the best thinking already done by the wisest men, the greatest prophets, and even God himself.

Our own book of proverbs will also serve us as a book of inspiration. Most of the problems of our lives can be anticipated. We can tell in advance that sometimes we will meet with discouragement. We know that there will be moments of weakness and temptation, hours of fear, and days of loneliness. To have our fortifications already erected and the solution previously worked out is the most valuable kind of wisdom. There are certain ideas that, if used, never fail to cheer us up. By proper preparation we may flood our minds with courage and infuse strength into our hearts at a moment's notice. We may develop some ready-made antidotes for loneliness, and they provide such a reserve supply of virtues that we will never be at the mercy of temptation or fall to defeat's most dangerous ally, which is known as surprise.

Abraham Lincoln once said that when he was preparing for a debate, he spent three-fourths of his time thinking about what his opponent was going to say and one-fourth thinking of what he was going to say. Good hindsight is a common quality, but by thoroughly exploring all of the possibilities in advance, Lincoln was able to develop a foresight comparable to his handsight. By advance planning and advance organizing, he could plug up every loophole and stop every possibility of his opponent's escape. We can also greatly reduce the chances of our own failure by having a sufficient supply of these proverbial success elements readily at hand. Almost always we lose our contests with evil because we are not prepared. But we can inoculate ourselves against weakness and error by the use of these powerful little maxims just as a good doctor can immunize us against the measles. Properly used, good proverbs may guide our success and enable us to score a victory in every play of life.

Each member of a great football team is drilled in advance so that he knows where he should be in any given situation, without taking the day off to figure it out at the time it occurs. Even the substitute sitting on the bench is never idle. In his imagination he is always in the game. He knows that the same situations that are calling for answers now will be coming up again when he is carrying the responsibility for victory. If he can develop the strategy to solve the problems while he is sitting on the bench, he will be able to solve them more or less automatically when he is in the spotlight. It is the same in life. History repeats itself, and no one is allowed time out to solve his problems after the play has been called.

However, if solutions are worked out in advance, we may develop enough foresight to handle the hardest problems with ease and assurance, and thereby we may help God to answer some of our own prayers for wisdom. And that will help us and greatly please him.

33

Here's How by Who's Who

THE OTHER day a friend of mine sent me a book entitled *Here's How by Who's Who*. This is a compilation of fifty-six great messages about how to be successful in the important business of life. They were written by fifty-six men especially selected from *Who's Who in America*. It is an important fact that everyone wants to succeed, and yet so frequently most of us just don't know how.

So many people never learn how to be friendly, or ambitious, or courageous, or industrious, or honest, or happy. We can't always depend on other people to show us the way, because they themselves are also frequently in the dark. Over and over again we see the fulfillment of the parable of Jesus, in which the blind lead the blind and all fall into the ditch together.

In addition to having a formula, we also need to know who gave it. That is, we need to know who says a thing is right or wrong, good or bad. Success in every field is governed by definite laws; and unless others have proven the laws in their own lives, they may not be safe guides for us. It is far too expensive for us to learn success by the hard, wasteful process of personal experience. Life is much too short for us to make all of the mistakes personally. When it was discovered that strychnine would kill, it became forever unnecessary for anyone else to have an actual experience in that field. For many centuries it has been completely unnecessary for anyone to put his hand on a red hot stove to discover what the effect would be.

One of the fifty-six great men chosen for this special job was Howard E. Kershner, president of the Christian Freedom Foundation, Inc. He says, "There is no need or time for my son to relearn by experience that which I have already learned. He should not start out from the ground, but from my shoulders." The compiler of this book is Jesse G. Bell, chairman of the board of Bonne-Bell Incorporated. He is a very successful businessman, and he made his own contribution under the title of "Developing Success Habits." He said:

Always keep your promises.

Always be on time.

Never forsake right, to follow the line of least resistance.

It is far better to do things the right way than the easy way.

It is smart to be honest; it is stupid to be dishonest. You will never have much standing with other people if they always discount what you say.

I read each of these fifty-six important success articles very carefully, trying to understand why these men had become what they were. Although this book was published after the death of General Douglas MacArthur, his prayer for his son was included. The great general said:

"Build me a son, O Lord, who will be strong enough to know when he is weak, and brave enough to face himself when he is afraid; one who will be proud and unbending in honest defeat, and humble and gentle in victory.

"Build me a son whose wishes will not take the place of deeds; a son who will know that to know Thee and to know himself are the foundation-stones of knowledge.

"Lead him, I pray thee, not in the path of ease and comfort, but under the stress and spur of difficulties and challenge. Let him learn to stand up in the storm and to feel compassion for those who fail.

"Build me a son whose heart will be clean, whose goal will be high, a son who will master himself before he seeks to master other men, one who can see into the future, yet never forget the past.

"And after all these things are his, give him, I pray, enough of a sense of humor so that he may always be serious, yet never take himself too seriously. Give him humility so that he may always remember the simplicity of true greatness, the open mindedness of true wisdom, and the meekness of true strength.

"Then I, his father, will dare to whisper, 'I have not lived in vain.' "

I was impressed by how certain it would be for any ambitious, aspiring young man to fully answer this great prayer in his own behalf. Each can make of himself the magnificent person that the great general desired his own son to become.

Some of these fifty-six men were former United States Presidents, some were generals, some were great businessmen, some were important educators and religious leaders. Some of their contributions were made under the following headings:

> "The Making of a Man"
> "The Art of Growing Up"
> "The Planned Objective"
> "Friends"
> "The Inner Light"
> "The Best Within You"
> "Guidelines to Success"
> "Accepting Your Role"
> "The Life Abundant"

In reading these articles, I thought what a great thing it would be if every person everywhere could learn these success laws and then follow them enthusiastically. One of our biggest difficulties comes from the fact that we have never learned very much about following instructions. Someone has said that the most important thing that we learn from history is that we never learn very much. Charles Edison, former governor of Pennsylvania and son of the late Thomas A. Edison, was selected as one of those to contribute to *Here's How by Who's Who*. He was asked to give his best advice to the young people of America. He told the compiler that many years ago this same request had been made of his famous father, and his father had merely said, "Young people never take advice," and had gone on about his business. We have a great deal of evidence certifying to the truth of this statement. Not only do young people not take advice very well—neither do older people.

We have no shortage of good advice in the world; it is in not using what we have that causes our problems. To allow ourselves to go on making the same mistakes is producing most of the trouble, heartbreak, and disaster of our world. That is, despite the counsel from our great leaders, despite the work of our educational institutions and the help from religious organizations, despite our laws and enforcement agencies, we still insist on delinquency, crime, nervous breakdowns, sin, and failure. There are many people who could easily become successful, happy people if they could learn to follow a few simple rules. And it is unfortunately true that the people who need counsel most are usually the very ones who accept it least.

Recently I talked with a brokenhearted father who had tried very hard to help his daughter prepare to live a successful, useful, and happy life. He had talked with her at great length about the advantages of a good education, a sound character, and a wholesome morality. But as Mr. Edison has pointed out, some young people not only don't take advice—the best way to get them to put their hands on a red hot stove is to tell them not to do it. Despite this father's teaching, his daughter became a dropout from school and while still unmarried is going to have a baby at age seventeen. One of the most outstanding things that she seems to have learned from her good home and wise, loving parents is a certain quality of perverseness that classifies her as a delinquent and problem child among her friends and before God. Now she blames her troubles on her father. She says that he tried too hard to help her.

Some children have parents who are so afraid of them that the parents dare not offer a suggestion for fear of touching off this streak of contrariness that would set their children going in the wrong direction. To some young people the suggestions from their parents that nicotine, alcoholism, immorality, or dishonesty are not good might arouse their desire to indulge. I am certainly not an expert in this field of behavior, and I am aware of the advantages that kindness usually has in people's lives; but on the other hand there are those among both young and old who ought to be turned over someone's knee occasionally for a good old-fashioned spanking. As Thomas A. Edison has inferred, it is unfortunately true that frequently ideas don't make a very effective entrance into our minds. However, we do have some notable exceptions to this situation.

One of the world's greatest success stories centers in the life of Abraham Lincoln. As Nancy Hanks lay on her deathbed, she said to her nine-year-old son, "Abe, go out there and amount to something." The idea was accepted and Abe spent all of the rest of his life trying to fulfill the ambition of his mother. And one of the strongest influences contributing to his success was that he never forgot his mother. Later he said of her, "All that I am or ever hope to be I owe to my angel mother." After his mother's death, Abe helped his father put together a pine box that would serve as her coffin; then he walked thirty miles to secure the services of a minister that she might have a Christian burial. And then he enrolled in a "night school" of his own, conducted before an open fire with a Bible and such other books as he was able to attain. He said, "My best friend is the one who will get me a book I haven't read."

Each time I remember Lincoln, I offer a prayer for our present-day "dropouts" and those who so vigorously resist the efforts and prayers of their own parents that they will someday amount to something. Lincoln was successful because he was able to get those great biblical qualities of honesty, integrity, righteousness, and faith into actual operation in his life. This ability is in contrast to those people who can read the entire Bible from one end to the other without any change taking place in them.

But success didn't come easily to Lincoln. He was not one of those who might be called a natural-born success. In 1831 he failed in business. In 1832 he was defeated for the legislature. Then he tried to get an appointment to the United States Land Office but was rejected as unfit. In 1833 he failed in business again and spent the next seventeen years not only paying off his own debts, but he also assumed the debts of his irresponsible partner. In 1834 he was elected to the legislature. In 1835 his sweetheart, Ann Rutledge, died. Later he married a woman who was a constant burden to him all of his days. In 1836 he suffered a nervous breakdown. In 1838 he was defeated for Speaker of the House. In 1840 he was defeated for elector. In 1843 he was defeated for the vice presidency. In 1858 he was defeated for the Senate again, and in that year he also lost the great debate with Stephen A. Douglas. But in 1860 he was elected the President of the United States. His desire to fulfill the ambition of his mother was stronger than any discouragement or inclination to quit. And today he stands out as one of the greatest men who ever lived.

Life is also offering to us some equally great challenges. Life is presently saying to us, "You go out there and amount to something." Jesus used different and even stronger words when he said, "Be ye therefore perfect, even as your Father which is in heaven is perfect." We can all succeed merely by following a good "here's how" formula. Of course we are not dependent on this particular compilation made up by these fifty-six men selected from *Who's Who in America*. We may want to use the compilation that made such a great contribution to Lincoln's life. The Holy Bible has sixty-six books. It is a collection of the success formulas written by the men found in God's "Who's Who." These are men who are not only important to God: they are men whom God has inspired and whose lives he has approved. The Bible is the greatest of all "Here's How" books. From the top of Mount Sinai God gave us the Ten Commandments, one of the greatest formulas for success.

What a great civilization we would have if we followed this direction. Someone has complained that these commands from Sinai are too harsh for our delicate minds and that instead of calling them commandments, the Lord should have called them by some such softer term as "suggestions" or "directions." Like the seventeen-year-old girl who became immoral to show her father that she could do as she pleased, many people violate God's laws in the desire to show him "who's who." But we make ourselves dangerously vulnerable when we resent God's commands or disregard his advice. In just two words Jesus also gave us the greatest "Here's How" formula when he said, "Follow me."

Our problem is that we don't follow. We don't follow him in his faith or in his self-discipline or in his righteousness. Jesus didn't come looking for some great brain who could figure out how to save the world; that had already been done in the council in heaven before the earth was created. What Jesus sought was followers. He wants someone who can carry out a program that has already been approved as the best. There are too many people who know what everyone else should do except themselves. Jesus, not us, was appointed and ordained as the Savior of the world and the Redeemer of men. And in carrying out that assignment, he has given us the holy scriptures as a set of detailed specifications of "Here's How." To implement this program, he has also given us a wonderful creation called a "brain" with which to put his program into operation.

Yet we don't always follow either the scripture or our reason or our conscience. We even turn off the still small voice of the Spirit so that frequently nothing gets through to us. Then in our blindness we are soon piled up in a ditch. If we make the best of our directions and our faculties, we can learn how to repent and be baptized. We can also get the entire gospel of Jesus Christ in operation in our lives. We might do well to remember, then, that his name is the most important one listed in the "Who's Who of the Universe." And he will help us to master this greatest "Here's How from Who's Who" program.

34

The Paper Man

MANY YEARS ago, Mao Tse-tung, the chairman of the People's Republic of China, referred to the United States as a paper tiger. He was trying to convey the idea that the military power of the United States looked good only on paper. His thought was that the United States may be a great power in theory, but in an actual demonstration of strength he felt that it would not stand up very well. While he believed that his own country might not have done as well in some places of actual accomplishments, yet it would be a veritable tiger in any test of actual performance. Mao used this particular figure because in his part of the world a tiger is thought of as the strongest of animals, and a tiger is frequently used as the symbol of the greatest strength.

There are many individual people who feel about this same way as they compare themselves with others. They feel that while they may not have many tangible favorable facts that they could put down on paper, yet when the need arises they will be able to perform like a tiger. But if one wants to be a tiger in any actual accomplishment, it is a pretty good idea to be a tiger on the paper first.

Recently I met with a group of church leaders where some of the statistics of their church activities were being discussed. Some of them seemed to show a considerable amount of resentment toward the records of their own work. One of them said, "We are not interested in the statistics; it's the people that count." They were saying to themselves, "Our statistics are terrible, but we are wonderful."

This human attitude of resenting our own statistics is all too common. Because our statistics are the best way of representing what we are, it might be a pretty good idea for us to pay a little more attention to how we look on the paper, especially in the bright light of day. How we feel in our hopes and ambitions or what our wishes and dreams are is very important, but we should also give some consideration to the facts.

We usually have more power for the actual contest when we have a strong reflection coming from the paper. It would be pretty difficult to develop an athletic program if we left out the paperwork. In football, every kick, every pass, every run, every down, and every penalty is measured and timed and counted and recorded. It is also interesting that we always add up the score. It is the score that makes the game. If the score is 6 to 7, and we are on the one-yard line with a minute and a half to play, everyone is excited. If the score is 50 to 0, most of the crowd will have gone home.

Everyone wants to know who won the game and what the score was. The statistics are a kind of itemized statement of the accomplishments. It is from the statistics that we get the final score. A football team's morale and a football team's prestige go up and down with its statistics. The team that looks the best on paper is usually the one that stays up at the top of the league.

In baseball we keep an accurate record of the hits, runs, and errors of each individual player. Life is also a great game, and in life the statistics are much more important than they are in a ball game. One of our human weaknesses in life is that when we are losing the game, we don't always like to keep track of the score. Certainly we are not very enthusiastic about putting the errors down on the paper, and most people don't even know what their individual batting average is. This makes our success much more difficult both to figure out and to attain.

If you bat .350 in the big leagues, you may receive a salary of a hundred thousand dollars a year. If you bat .250, you may get ten thousand per year. This is quite a difference in pay when the difference in effectiveness is only one additional hit in ten times at bat. That is, the .350 batter gets on first base three and a half times out of ten tries, whereas the .250 batter gets on first base two and a half times out of ten.

The greater success is not always because of how frequently or how hard you hit the ball. The .250 man may be held back because he can't run. There are enough photo finishes at first base to indicate that if you had been half a step faster in 90 feet you would have been safe, but because you were half a step too slow, you were called out. It would not even have been necessary for the unsuccessful man to have been faster every time. He was fast enough two and a half times out of ten; all he needed was a little more speed in one out of ten tries.

However, it is far more important that we know our batting average in life than it is in athletics. We cannot separate our success from our statistics. That is, a banker may not be very favorably impressed if we say, "Our financial statistics are terrible but we are wonderful." The banker might want to know about such prosaic things as our assets and liabilities, our income and our outgo, our bank balances and our overdrafts. Planning and record keeping are so closely related in our success that they cannot be discussed separately.

Someone has said, "You cannot effectively increase accomplishment without some accurate measurement of the progress made." That is, you can learn to be a high-jumper much more quickly by laying a bamboo pole across two measured uprights and then jumping over it than you can by merely going out onto the field and jumping up in the air without any knowledge of your effectiveness. It has been said that when accomplishment is measured, accomplishment improves, and when accomplishment is recorded and reported back, the improvement is accelerated. But when accomplishment is also publicized, our motivation is given gigantic power. If you want to help your son, don't give him an assignment and then fail to check up; and while your own planning, goal-setting, and motivation are good to watch, never fail to keep an accurate score on yourself.

It is an interesting fact that God is the creator of, and the greatest believer in, statistics. He not only keeps records, but he also advises us to do the same. He said to John the Revelator: "What thou seest, write in a book. . . ." (Revelation 1:11.) He also might have said, "What thou doest, write in a book."

If each day we could see what God writes in his book about our works for that day, it would certainly motivate us to make better scores. We can most surely reach any goal by putting our results down on the paper every day. When our statistics are low, it is more important than ever that we keep them. How stimulating it would be to see our personal errors published every day on the front page of the newspaper. With this kind of situation, our errors would be much fewer. This would also help us prepare for that great day when all of our present secret acts shall be revealed. Of course, there are some things about ourselves that we can't get on the paper.

Many years ago Clarence E. McCartney compiled an important book entitled *The Great Sermons of the World*. After an exhaustive amount of research and selecting, Mr. McCartney collected in one book the greatest human utterances that had ever been made. He included two sermons by an old preacher named Whitefield who used to live in New England a couple of hundred years ago, and as kind of an apology, Mr. McCartney said, "No one can read the sermons of Whitefield and understand why thousands of people were always flocking out to hear him." Then by way of explanation, he added, "You can't get the man on the paper. You can get his words and his paragraphs and his questions, but you can't get the man." What he meant was that you can't get the light in his eye or the music of his voice or the love vibrations that come out of his heart. You can't get the fire of his personality or the warmth of his soul on the paper.

One famous minister was once approached by an admiring listener who had just heard what he thought was a magnificent sermon. The listener said, "I would like your permission to publish and distribute that sermon." The minister said, "You may print and distribute the sermon if you will also print and distribute the thunder and lightning that go with it." It is pretty difficult to get human thunder and lightning on paper. It is very hard to get real love, personality, and faith on paper.

On the other hand, we can get on paper many of the things that cause love, personality, growth, and faith. And there are some things that must be put down on the paper. If a man's biography is not written down, the story of his life is soon lost, frequently even to himself. If one's plans are not put down on paper, they are soon forgotten. It has been properly said that "no plan is a plan until it is on paper." You wouldn't employ an architect who didn't know how to get ideas out of his head onto the paper. If the bishop tries to keep the records of all of his ward members in his head, he is doomed to fail.

Suppose you take any group of even fifty people, no matter how well they may be known to you, and see how many of them you can remember without hesitation. You will be shocked at how ineffective are your powers of recall. But your brain was never intended to be a baggage room or a storehouse; it much more resembles a machine shop or a workbench. One of our greatest opportunities is that each of us may increase his total mental equipment by building a great paper memory. A good bookkeeper with an ordinary brain can have a fantastic paper memory. A lawyer sits in his library where he has on paper all of the legal experience of the greatest legal minds, and they are more readily available to him than if he had to depend on some kind of magic recall from his own mind.

We may make the greatest literature a part of our paper memories. You can't judge a man by watching him live or a baseball player by seeing him bat. I personally watched Babe Ruth at bat three times, and he struck out every time. But at the very time that I was watching him strike out, the record said that he was the greatest home-run king who ever lived.

What a great thrill it would have been to have studied at the feet of the great thinkers and leaders of the past, and yet we have many of them down on the paper verbatim. Written expression can be much clearer as more care is taken in its preparation. We can hear the words and feel the ideas of Shakespeare, Washington, and Lincoln even better now than if we had lived in their own day. Through books we may know the greatest men and women with an intimacy and completeness that was perhaps not even enjoyed by those who lived in their own time or in their own household.

Recently a woman came to talk about some of her emotional and moral problems. She said that her boyfriend liked to go to x-rated, sex-oriented movies. She pointed out that when she went to any kind of a movie, she lived the events as they took place on the screen; and while she felt that she had high moral standards, when she came out of this particular kind of movie she felt like a different person than she had been when she went in. The people on the screen were actually getting over to her. The people in great books can, with real power, get over to us also, because every contact that we ever make, either good or bad, modifies us. Some people make us feel like we are ten feet tall, and some can make us feel small, dirty, and sick.

We have detailed editions of Shakespeare, Moses, and the Apostle Paul all arranged on paper. We can be with them at our leisure and enjoy their inspiration to our heart's content, and, like the girl at the movies, we can absorb their spirits and breathe the atmosphere of those things that were in their minds and souls.

One of our greatest blessings is that even God has made himself available to us in a very real way on paper. We may spend a lifetime waiting for some sign or revelation from him, but on paper we may feel his inspiration immediately and listen to his words at will. At our pleasure we may witness the thunders and lightnings of Mount Sinai and be present in spirit while God gives again those fundamental laws. With Moses we may go and spend those memorable forty days and nights in God's presence. But that is not all. We may make ourselves a part of those other important conversations that God has had over the centuries with Adam, Enoch, Noah, and Abraham. We may read at our pleasure the revelations of his mind and will to all of the holy prophets and understand again his words that "whatever principle of intelligence we attain unto in this life, it will rise with us in the resurrection." (D&C 130:18.) One of the great opportunities of our lives is to learn to do the paper work on which a most happy and successful eternal life can be built.

35

Semantics

THERE IS a rather high-toned, fancy-sounding word called *semantics* that everyone should get better acquainted with. It has to do with the meaning of words and the development of our abilities to use them effectively. The dictionary says that semantics is the science of sounds. It has to do with the evolution of our language. It involves the continual expansion in word meanings and the effectiveness of our expression.

The 140,000 words that we had in Shakespeare's day have greatly grown in number, and many changes in their usage have also taken place in recent years. It has been said that if some contemporary Rip Van Winkle should wake up today after sleeping for twenty years, he would have to go back to school before he could intelligently read the morning paper or clearly understand an ordinary conversation.

Semantics is closely related to some other fancy-sounding words called *semasiology* and *philology*. Semasiology has to do with the significance of words and the development of their meanings. Philology signifies a love of learning and a devotion to literature. When we put all of these twenty-dollar words together, we have one of the most productive of ideas, meaning a satisfying expression, a fondness for communication, and a skill in fitting into a constructive whole the best of these important instruments called words. Think what would happen to our business or to our happiness or even to our lives themselves if we lost our words. We remember the calamity of the builders of the Tower of Babel. When their words could not be understood, all building immediately ceased and confusion reigned.

The human intellect itself with all of its powers manifests itself primarily through words. In various combinations, words make up our ideas, give form to our ambitions, inspire our wisdom, shape our emotions, direct our actions, and build our Towers of Babel.

Words are the means by which our minds are enriched and

our enthusiasms are given power. They are like sacred ships that are designed to carry cargoes of meanings. Words are the chief tools of the teacher, the salesman, the parent, the lover, the preacher, and the empire builder. By the proper use of words we may increase our occupational skill, multiply our social satisfactions, establish higher standards of thinking, and even help to bring about the eternal exaltation of our souls. Words also enable us to increase the happiness and success of many other people.

Therefore, whether we are operating in the areas of romance, patriotism, finance, religion, or any other area of human experience, we need a good supply of the right kind of words and the ability to use them effectively. In fact, the skill that we are able to develop in the use of words can probably give us greater power than any other thing, either to bless our lives or to make them wretched. Except by his own choice, no one should be handicapped for lack of words, as we have the tremendous array of 450,000 different ones in the dictionary that are all placed at our disposal free of charge. These become our property just as fast as we learn to use them.

Suppose that we make and absorb a list of great key words, such as faith, works, ambition, leadership, love, knowledge, success, and fairness, or we might profitably catalog some of the famous expressions and then capture the spirit that goes with them as one of our personal possessions.

Nathan Hale said, "I regret that I have but one life to give for my country." Patrick Henry said, "Give me liberty or give me death." Joshua said, "As for me and my house, we will serve the Lord." In speaking of God Job said, "Though he slay me, yet will I trust in him." And Jesus said, "Father, not my will, but thine be done." What tremendous values these words would represent if we had a full personal possession of the words and what they stand for. Of course, we live in a world of opposites, and we should be aware of the fact that some words bear a poison fruit. Judas Iscariot said, "What will ye give me, and I will deliver him into your hands." Richard B. Speck, who cut the throats of eight nurses in Chicago, had the words of death tattooed on his arm and impressed into his soul. They said, "Born to raise hell." Everyone's success or failure, happiness or misery, will be determined by the words and meanings that we have tattooed into our lives. It is with them that we construct our oaths of office, take our pledges of allegiance, feel the meaning of the Lord's Prayer, live our marriage vows, and make our covenants of devotion to God.

The other day a young father of three children asked me to read a letter that he had just received at his place of business from his wife. She told him how much she loved him and how she appreciated all of the wonderful, thoughtful things that he did for her and their children. She also expressed the great confidence she felt in him and in his ability. These few simple, heartfelt words had stirred up something in this man's soul that was wonderful to see. With his wife's words of love and appreciation in his heart, he felt that he could conquer the world. Unfortunately, there are many cases of husbands and wives where these magic words are not to be found in their vocabulary. Neither are the emotions that go with them lodged very solidly in their hearts.

Sometimes our vocabulary is made up primarily of critical words that nag, irritate, belittle, and destroy. We sometimes use great words for profane or immoral purposes, and some of the most profound words don't mean very much to some people. There are those who could read the entire Bible from beginning to end without being very greatly changed. To some people, even the most meaningful words seem hollow and empty.

Shakespeare's Polonius said to Hamlet, "What readest thou, my Lord?" Hamlet replied, "Words, words, words." Hamlet's state of mind had destroyed the significance of these great words so that they were now empty and meaningless. One of the big problems mentioned by Jesus was our natural inclination to separate words from their meanings. Entire creeds become meaningless when a faith loses its works. Quicker than about anything else, empty words can give institutions and men split personalities and cause a life to lose its meaning.

The Holy Bible makes use of 773,693 words to effectively tell the story of God's plan of salvation, including the atonement of Christ, the ugliness of sin, the possibility of eternal progression, and the horror of eternal damnation. We commit grave sins when we debase God's words or use them to give ourselves or others wrong meanings. We sometimes deceive ourselves by referring to "the new morality" in order to cover up our immorality or our lack of morality. Sometimes by a change in word meanings we impoverish our own character, and every place we turn we find the apostate forces of evil twisting the finest words out of shape and depriving them of their Christian meanings. We say, "God is dead," that "revelations from God have ceased," and that "it doesn't matter any more what we believe or what we do." We say that the great Christian doctrines are mere allegories or stories for our amusement. Therefore, one of our most serious sins is our debasement of good words by subtracting from their real meaning. Words are also used sometimes to belittle faith and make fun of the doctrines of Christ.

We have a distortion of words, a misuse of words, and sometimes we just don't use them at all. It is probable that the most serious marital sin is lack of communication. We so severely restrict our words and meanings that understanding is destroyed and happiness breaks down. By failure in semantics, we frequently build massive "Berlin walls" between ourselves over which very little information or love or understanding is ever allowed to pass. We have a kind of Tower of Babel situation where wives do not understand their husbands, and husbands do not understand their wives. Many parents don't communicate with their children, and the ideas of many children are not very well integrated with the ambitions of their parents. Our greatest success is impoverished when we fall down in the science and art of semantics. Then life itself loses much of its purpose and meaning.

Socrates once said that "a philosopher should never speak until his words have been steeped in meaning." And we can more effectively carry on the business of our lives when we learn how to fashion the most worthwhile ambitions and objectives and get them over to the right people.

Sometimes one's entire existence may turn on the use of a single word. A discouraged man once called his minister in the middle of the night and asked him to come to him at once. Later the caller said, "Had you said 'no' instead of 'yes,' I was prepared to take my own life."

Far more frequently we injure ourselves when we say "no" to God, or "no" to ambition, or "no" to enthusiasm, or our lives may be lost if we say "yes" to alcohol or nicotine or immorality. Likewise, we can ruin the reputations of others and destroy their morale, kill their faith, and seduce them into sin with words. Many people have actually been killed physically, socially, and spiritually by words. The news of some great tragedy can sufficiently shock one's constitution as to bring about his death. Many parents have lost their health and sometimes their lives worrying over their children.

On the other hand, we can establish faith and build ambition, courage, and righteousness with words. In fact, we can almost bring people back to life with the right kind of words. The night before Robert E. Lee surrendered his army to end the Civil War, Ulysses S. Grant had been sick all night. He had been sitting up doctoring himself in preparation for the following day. But early in the morning a messenger rode up to General Grant's tent to tell him that General Lee was waiting to surrender his sword. General Grant's pains and aches immediately left him, and he never felt them again. He quickly dressed, and as a completely well man he mounted his horse and rode to take charge of the surrender. Words of success, praise, love, and appreciation have cured many serious aches and pains in the hearts of people. Words of bitterness, quarreling, and hate will bring sickness to the mind, the body, and the spirit, whereas those who live on words of faith, courage, happiness, and love will tend to be well and strong.

We sing a song in which we say:

> O holy words of truth and love
> We hear from day to day,
> Revealed to Saints from God above,
> To guide in heaven's way.
>
> (*Chorus*)
> Beautiful words of love
> Coming from God above,
> How sweet, how dear the words we hear!
> They're beautiful words of love.
>
> They're from Apostles full and true,
> Whose names we all revere,
> Who daily teach us what to do,
> In words of love and cheer.
>
> They're from the Prophets God inspires,
> In counsels oft withstood,
> Reproving all our ill desires,
> Commending all that's good.
>
> As gems of wisdom, pure and bright,
> That glow with lustrous ray,
> We'll seek to gain these words of light,
> Their counsels to obey.

We can greatly improve our lives by watching our words and vitalizing our semantics with the right meanings.

We frequently hear someone complain that he doesn't have the words to express how he feels. And many people have spent an entire lifetime stumbling in their speech. This fault can be corrected if we firmly connect up our words with our works. It has been said that Christianity is not just an idea; it is an activity. Dr. P. W. Bridgeman, the noted physicist and Nobel prize winner, once said, "The true meaning of a word in a man's mind is to be found by observing what he does with it, not by what he says about it."

We can also get some idea of a word's value by what it does to us. Words that we love and that represent ideas that we believe in can quickly change our lives. Then, followed by appropriate actions, we paint a beautiful picture on our mental canvasses. Great acts help us steep our words in better meanings. And if we desire to be architects of speech, we must also be masters of emotion and feeling.

There is a very important phrase frequently used in the scriptures called "the word of the Lord." That is the most important word. The word of the Lord is the standard by which our eternal lives and our eternal success will be determined. We should make sure that we understand his word and why it was given. We should also make sure that we have used the right words with the right meanings in making our covenants with him and that he can depend on our word.

36

The Idea Supermarket

IT HAS always been a source of great delight to me to walk through a well-ordered supermarket and see the attractive array of fruits and vegetables in every variety and color. While on the farm I learned something about the thrill involved in bringing various kinds of products out of the raw soil. With the right kind of planning, industry, irrigation, fertilizer, cultivation, sunshine, and soil, one may literally accomplish miracles in producing beauty, taste, and vitamins. It is by this miracle that life is maintained, giving pleasure and strength to the body, the mind, and the personality. I suppose that because my taste buds have been developed above the average, my supermarket appreciation has grown accordingly.

I am confident that these beautiful supermarket products were designed by a Creator who loved color and taste. He knew how to best pack the nutritious ingredients into them to form strength, vision, personality, love, and joy in human beings. Good food supports the best there is in the mental and spiritual characteristics of people. And if God had lacked the ability to manufacture these wonder products out of elements in the sunshine, air, water, and soil, everything in human life would wither and die. The light would go out of our eyes, our minds would cease to function, our personalities would no longer operate, and the greatest of all of God's creations would come to a halt. As I walk through a giant supermarket literally filled with thousands of God's wonder inventions, I feel as though I were witnessing some kind of an eternal life process. These foods are sent to us from every corner of the globe all beautifully arrayed and packaged for our benefit and pleasure. And as I think about them I am uplifted and made to feel grateful to God.

However, I frequently have a related experience that is even more exciting, when I spend an hour or so in a bookstore. I see the great volumes that have been wonderfully written and packaged to bring me another kind of nourishment, from the more fertile minds in the universe. I read the challenging titles and imagine their pleasant taste as well as contemplate the faith, strength, personality, and vision they contain. Abraham Lincoln fed on his books as he lay on the cabin floor before the open fire in the evenings. He gained his unusual strength as he digested the Bible and transferred to himself the valuable things that were stored away therein. To understand the difficulty Lincoln had in getting books should help us to appreciate our own situation when thousands of excellent volumes are published each year on every conceivable subject by the greatest minds, and they are all made available to us for just a few pennies.

"A good book is the very essence of a good man wherein his virtues survive while his faults and failings are forgotten." T. G. Cuyler said, "All the goodly company of the excellent and great sit around my table, or look down upon me from my shelves. A precious book can be a kind of foretaste of immortality." In a way books are embalmed minds. "The world's greatest men can put themselves down on paper and give themselves a kind of immortality for our benefit." I never cease to marvel at this great invention where the most delicate or profound meanings can be preserved and conveyed by the marks that are made on paper, parchment, the bark of trees, or even cut into stone building. Then, centuries after the buildings have become ruins and the parchment has faded, these magic marks made by those long since dead can still make us weep or laugh or move us to the most profound thoughts.

In some primitive places in the past only the priest could read and write, and others have looked upon him as though he were the agent of Deity, the very mouthpiece of God. It was not very long ago that a book was so treasured that sometimes it was bound between oak boards, riveted in bands of iron, locked with a ponderous key, and carried with slow steps to the altar by a solemn procession of priests. Then the book was unlocked and opened, and the priest read from it while the people listened in breathless awe to the words that Deity himself had dictated in order that men might save their souls.

And yet even the grandest books don't help us very much unless we are familiar with what they say. In the midst of the knowledge explosion, which makes us the beneficiaries of the greatest miracles of enlightenment that the world has ever known, we may still be living in the mental and spiritual dark ages. As a consequence of such an unfortunate situation, the Lord once said about another group of people, "They who are not chosen have sinned a very grievous sin, in that they are walking in darkness at noon-day." (D&C 95:6.) It is this darkness in human souls that makes our world sick. Woodrow Wilson was referring to this general problem when he said, "The greatest ability of the American people is their ability to resist instruction." And I suppose that most of us have our share of that unfortunate talent. Sometimes even the most significant happenings leave us unchanged. A prophet speaks, or the gospel is restored, or even the Savior visits the earth, but like the antediluvians to whom Jesus compared us, we frequently go along relatively unconcerned, insisting upon our puny business affairs proceeding as usual.

Thomas A. Edison indicated a related difficulty when he said, "There is no limit to which a man will not go to avoid thinking." Thinking is often the most disagreeable, unpleasant exercise that most of us ever undertake, and yet as Solomon said, as a man thinketh in his heart, so is he. Now I don't know exactly where that leaves us, if we are what we think—and if we don't think—but it indicates that we have a problem.

It might help us to remind ourselves of the experience that Goliath had when he met David with his slingshot. After the whole affair was over, someone commented that such a thing had never entered Goliath's head before. In a little different way, the experiences that most of us need more than nearly anything else is to get more things into our heads, and into our hearts, and into our activities.

Upon the cross, Jesus said, "Father, forgive them; for they know not what they do." (Luke 23:34.) The people referred to were committing the greatest possible sin, but they didn't even know what they were doing. Almost all of the sins in our world are the sins of ignorance. The people who involve themselves with alcohol, nicotine, and caffeine don't realize what they are doing. Those who absent themselves from church or engage in other kinds of evil don't understand that they are changing themselves and that in some degree they are destroying their own eternal possibilities.

The scriptures say that no man can be saved in ignorance. But neither can anyone make himself happy or successful in ignorance, and even most of our satisfactions in life come from the way that we ourselves think. People with negative minds think negative thoughts. Depraved, unhappy thoughts are produced in depraved, unhappy minds. When we feed our minds out of poison books, we produce poisoned minds. There is a deadly fall-out that comes from the violence, hate, and immorality of certain movies, newspapers, and magazines. But some good treatments from the right kinds of books can build minds capable of thinking the most pleasant, happy, constructive thoughts.

Sir Edward Dyer says:

> My mind to me a kingdom is,
> Such present joys therein I find,
> That it excels all other bliss
> That earth affords or grows by kind. . . .
> —"MY MIND TO ME A KINGDOM IS"

In times of old, many books had an influence almost equal to divine authority. But as the number of books has been increased, the appreciation of their value has diminished in the minds of some people to the point that they have little importance. However, suppose that we go into one of these great supermarkets of the mind and think about their various titles. We will find books of poetry that can start feelings of love and metered rhythm moving through our hearts. There are many books of useful fiction, books of history, books of biography, and books of religion.

Charles Lamb said, "I love to lose myself in other men's minds." Through books we can see into the minds of great men. It is much easier to make our lives productive if we have some good books to help us. Erasmus said, "When I get a little money I buy books, and if any is left over, I buy food and clothes." Fenelon said, "If all of the crowns of Europe were placed at my disposal on condition that I should abandon my books and studies, I should turn away from the crowns and stand by my books."

But books are only waste paper unless we can translate into action the wisdom that their thought stimulates. We make a serious mistake when we spend more money for beer than for books, and life's most critical danger comes from full stomachs and empty minds. Empty minds are like deserted houses that attract the haunting stay of base spirits, whereas the love of knowledge is a warrant for the excitement of superior passions and virtues. We learn to read in the presence of books, and the love of knowledge not only comes from reading, but also grows upon it.

May God help us to eat wholeheartedly from those great books growing on the tree of knowledge.

37

The Magnificent Obsession

ONE OF the popular books of the past century was written by Lloyd C. Douglas, entitled *The Magnificent Obsession*. This story has a unique and very interesting plot telling how a young man by the name of Robert Merrick learned the secret of great personal growth and happiness. Heir of a wealthy manufacturer, he had plenty of money and no real motive for personal accomplishment. He lived a reckless, useless, and empty life and had something of a reputation for corrupting his friends.

Then one day while maneuvering his sailboat, young Merrick was knocked unconscious and pushed into the water by a swinging yardarm. His life was saved by a pulmotor and an oxygen tank borrowed from the nearby summer cottage of Dr. Wayne Hudson, a world famous brain surgeon.

The village physician, thinking that Merrick's head injury should have the most skillful treatment, sent him by ambulance to Dr. Hudson's hospital. After Merrick had regained consciousness he learned that the famous brain surgeon himself had drowned because his equipment was being used to save Merrick's life. Merrick fully realized the tremendous loss that he had unintentionally caused. He tried to fight down his remorse by arguing that it was not his idea. Why hadn't they just let him drown? Then no one would have been inconvenienced. But argue as he would, he could not escape the disturbing thought that at least unintentionally he had been responsible for the loss of one of the world's greatest men.

For weeks he brooded over the tragedy, but that did not bring Dr. Hudson back to life. Even Merrick's wealth could not replace Dr. Hudson's skill. Finally in desperation he hit upon the idea that he would personally replace the lost ability by making himself equally capable as a brain surgeon. His resolution grew rapidly and finally obtained the proportions of an obsession. The idea possessed him; it drove him day and night.

In studying Dr. Hudson's life, Merrick found that replacing

this great man was a more difficult job than he had originally anticipated. Dr. Hudson had been far more than a brain surgeon. He had made an even greater contribution in the fields of philanthrophy and human uplift. He had helped hundreds of people. Educations had been financed. His personal inspiration had banished many discouragements. He had saved the lives of many people who could not afford medical treatment.

Dr. Hudson had also had an interesting philosophy that did not allow his beneficiaries to tell of his good deeds. He believed that only when his gifts were unknown to others was his own personality properly enlarged and enriched. He reasoned that if a farmer's farm was too small to support him, he should get enough more land to fill his need. But what should one do if he had a personality insufficiently effective to make his life outstanding? His personality should also be enlarged, and this could only be done by giving. Dr. Hudson decided that he could make his greatest contribution to the world only through his own noble deeds.

Everyone knows that personality traits are modified by the influence of others, and there are two ways of expanding one's personality. The first is to copy the good qualities of others. That is, he may practice the abilities, imitate the graces, and develop the virtues of those around him. But Dr. Hudson believed with the scripture that "it is more blessed to give than to receive." He believed that an enlargement of his own personality could best be brought about by projecting it into the lives of others. To him it seemed similar to a blood transfusion where one man puts his life into other men. One man can also vitalize others by an effective projection of his personality. His ambition, love, and material means can be transfused to vitalize the success of those around him.

Dr. Hudson knew that if coagulation were to be avoided during the transfusion process, the blood being transferred must be kept free from any direct outside contact with the air. For a similar reason he believed that good deeds must be kept secret and the outside contact of publicity should be thoughtfully avoided. Jesus said, "Let not the left hand know what the right hand doeth." On several occasions Jesus had said to his own beneficiaries, "See that thou tell no man." People were advised by him to pray secretly in their closets so that too much outside contact would not make their prayers ineffective before God.

This may be a spiritual application of the insulation need that a wire has in carrying an electric current. Neither Volta's battery nor Faraday's dynamo amounted to very much until Du Fay discovered how to insulate the wire and prevent the current from being dissipated before reaching the object to be energized.

The greatest of all investments are the investments of the personality, and good works must not be grounded because of lack of insulation. The investment of one's self represents a far more important kind of altruism than mere financial generosity. However, the projection of good into the life of someone else is like any other kind of prime investment. It goes on earning compound interest forever. And if you are the one who gets it going, the credit belongs to you.

In his early life Robert Merrick had always paid for his recklessness with his money. And because his money was now useless, he was taking the only other alternative available, but he had determined that he would not allow the life's account of Dr. Wayne Hudson to show a loss. He would not only replace the ability of this eminent man, but he would replace all of his other benefactions as well.

With great zeal he undertook his well-planned course. His obsession rode him like the Old Man of the Sea. It hounded him by day and it haunted him by night. It worked him like a slave but it provided him with more than ample motive power. It was as though he had taken hold of high tension which when once touched he could not let go. But Robert Merrick received a peculiar delight from following the scent of his projected accomplishment. His previous temperament had demanded only self-indulgence to keep him satisfied with life. Now he was subject to a stronger kind of demand. Under the compulsion of this obsession, he rose quickly to the head of his medical school class. He could no more avoid leadership than he could avoid breathing or being young, for his obsession had plastered a mortage on his brain, his heart, his personality, and his hands. It had commandeered the time and attention he had formerly lavished upon himself. He was left no alternatives except to be the best doctor in the land.

At first he had merely had the idea, but now the idea had him, and it had become inescapable. It had reached out its curious tentacles and wrapped them about him. At the same time it had released within him an undreamed-of ability that propelled him irresistibly toward the goal.

In the years that followed, Dr. Robert Merrick became all that his obsession had hoped for and then some. But while this interesting case of Robert Merrick was intense, it is by no means unique. Other lives may have similar forces aroused within them. It would be very unfortunate indeed if great human service and magnificent personal behavior could only be brought about by the suffering of some great tragedy.

The Apostle Paul had his life's forces redirected to more worthwhile things by a heavenly vision. And thousands of others are touched by ambition, desire, conviction, faith, love, and worship, which are the attributes of God himself. These forces may react upon our lives like some God-given catalyst. Victor Hugo once said that the most powerful thing in the world is an idea whose time had come. It is also the most valuable. But more than almost any other thing we need something to get things going and release that miraculous God-given power within us. Every man owes it to himself to do something great and fine with his life, and our biggest problem is not a shortage of money or machinery or abilities or opportunities. Our biggest problem is to get a holy purpose supported by an overpowering ambition working in our hearts.

God has given us an upward reach, a divine desire for greatness, and he has also given us the ability to bring about whatever accomplishment we set our hearts on. Human beings have the exclusive right to ambition, but we ourselves must be the directing engineer.

During a debate on evolution, a biologist who was pointing out some of the physical likenesses existing between animals and men was asked to explain personality in the light of evolution. That is, how could he account for aspiration, ambition, and repentance by the theory written in his biology book? He replied, "I am a biologist, not a theologian." The solution of many of our problems demands that we also become theologians, because for many problems there are also answers. How else can we account for the wonders around us? How can we explain what happens to wild ducks in the fall to start them on their unerring flight across the continent to the Gulf Coast and beyond? And what is it that takes place in the spring of the year to reverse their compasses and send them flying back again to the northland? If this inner urge whispers timidly at first, it soon grows into something resembling an overwhelming obsession that governs the action of every individual bird and sends it on its long northbound migratory journey.

This overpowering urge does not exist only in the restless breast of the leader. It is a power that takes possession of all of the inhabitants of duckland and furnishes them with a drive so urgent and irresistible that not a single duck can disregard it; old ducks, young ducks, weak ducks, strong ducks, and sick ducks are all affected at the same time, in the same way, and to the same end. Under this spell they will fly as far toward their destination as their strength will permit. At all costs they must be true to their instinct and bring about a fulfillment of the divine urge so deeply planted within them.

But a far greater urge has been placed in the human heart, directing us to worship God and serve our fellowmen in such a way as to bring us all back safely into God's presence after we have finished our long migration across the world. Jesus pointed the way when he said that we should live by every word that proceedeth forth from the mouth of God. Just suppose that we should give ourselves over fully to this idea and be ruled by that power which governed the actions of the Master. He lived a sinless life and found it unnecessary to make a single exception to righteousness. Then he said to all of us, "Come, follow me." And the success of every human being must finally be judged by how well he carries out that single direction. Here is our opportunity for a most magnificent obsession, one that will wake us up in the morning and send us on our way with a desire for human uplift that cannot be put aside. This obsession says, "What can I give?" rather than "What can I get?"

A man was once preparing to retire and turn his professional practice over to his son. When, in the prime of life, his son died, the father went back to his task with an increased fervor—not for his own need, but to fulfill the compulsion he felt to reap a second professional glory for his son whose life had been cut short.

We have all profited much personally from the suffering, devotion, and even the deaths of others, including the pilgrims, the pioneers, and the prophets. And if you would like a magnificent challenge that dares you to complete the unfinished service of someone else, remember the life of the Great Physician. His years of mortality were terminated because of the swinging yardarm of our own personal sins, all of which he took upon himself.

A magnificent obsession to carry on the work he started will lift our own lives to greatness and eternal glory. Jesus gave us the cue when he said, "See that ye serve him with all your heart, might, mind and strength, that ye may stand blameless before God at the last day." This requires more than an ordinary amount of spiritual intensity working in our lives, and we ourselves must take the initiative in getting it going.

38

The Discipline of Language

THROUGH ITS monthly letter, the Royal Bank of Canada sent out an article entitled "The Discipline of Language." It pointed out the power that can be generated when words are properly used and understood. The function of some words is to inform, some provide entertainment, and some give encouragement. Some words persuade, some give cheer, and some may be used to defend a way of life. When we fail to use our language effectively, communication breaks down and our lives themselves tend to become inferior. Confucius once said, "If our language is not correct, then what is said will not be what is meant; if what is said is not what is meant, then what ought to be done will remain undone." Whether one is speaking, writing, or learning, the ability to pass ideas effectively from one to another is almost all important, as this is the process by which we teach, sell, inspire, and motivate.

The foundations of civilization itself are laid with words, and they underlie every activity in life. They are the indicators of our humanity, the measurement of our ability, and the tools of our success. Words convey affections, give expression to prayers, vitalize our ambitions, and record our progress. Our standards of living, our mastery of science, the quality of our faith, and the effectiveness of our know-how all come about because of our ability to get our ideas over. It is also true that the faulty use of words or the failure to communicate between family members, business associates, or the representatives of nations is a most serious menace to our every success and happiness.

After a prominent and very capable candidate for a high political office had been defeated in an election, he said, "I did not communicate." If the voters had been able to crawl inside his mind and discover what he thought and how he felt and what he was, he might have been able to get more votes. Unfortunately, most people are not mind readers, and when we lack the ability for effective communication, the darkness continues, so far as we are concerned.

The tremendous divorce carnage that desolates our society is largely a result of breakdown in communication. It is pathetic how little some husbands, wives, and children know about the hopes, ambitions, needs, and desires of each other. In the usual marriage relationship some giant Berlin walls are built between husband and wife, as well as between parents and children, with the result that the understandng that is able to get across is below the required minimums. One of our most common complaints is that someone doesn't understand us. Most hates, fears, disagreements, frigidity, mental and physical cruelties are the results of misunderstanding.

Because every human being needs love, acceptance, instruction, and encouragment, we should be able to cast ourselves into words. And just as we need food, rest, air, and drink every day, so we need words of inspiration, love, enlightenment, discipline, and correction every day. Some words of restraint and caution also serve a most important need. We can keep disorder and confusion out of our affairs by making sure that we are not misinterpreting the word signals or misusing the blueprint of those ideas by which we live.

In business or in life, few inefficiencies are so serious as poverty in our language. Every time a businessman does not express himself clearly and meaningfully, he loses business for his firm and wastes his own time. Husbands and wives fail each other for this same reason. The key to almost every success is the word *communication.*Even the greatest thoughts for which one has no words are often valueless. And those ideas and ambitions that are kept locked in the mind have no way of producing a pleasure or making a profit. When traveling in a foreign land, one must learn to use the currency of that country if he hopes to enjoy its benefits. The currency of life is language; and whether we are traveling or staying at home, we must have a good supply of negotiable words and know how to use them if we would receive the maximum value from life, for words are the basic currency in all of our exchanges.

It is through words that we gain knowledge, stir up ambition, arouse spirituality, and instill faith. Words are the tools of thought that we employ even with ourselves. They represent things, feelings, and activities. Words come in different colors, sizes, intensity, and shades of meaning. And we need to be as artistic and as scientific as possible, not only in their employment but also in their interpretation. Of course, to be completely exact is impossible, inasmuch as no idea or thing can ever be precisely or adequately represented by mere verbal symbols. A friend and and enemy would probably use different words to describe our conduct. It is frequently difficult to translate ideas from one language to another. We also have problems in translating our perception into language or our ambitions into words.

Suppose that you were to try to find words to explain what salt tastes like to one who has never tasted salt. Or how would you describe terror or anger to one who does not already know these emotions? Or how could you explain the difference in the pain of a toothache from that of a finger smashed in the door of your automobile, to one who is ignorant of both these experiences?

In the holy scriptures God has tried to make clear to us the difference between eternal happiness and eternal misery. But even the significance of his words may go over our heads with very little understanding coming from the most descriptive words that God knows how to use. We have a tremendous price exacted when we have to get the lesson from a personal experience rather than from the less expensive way of understanding that we get from words. Sometimes it is pretty difficult to enlighten our children in the most simple differences between wrong or right, without their having to fall back on the wastefulness of a personal experience. How unfortunate are those young people who have to learn the consequences of dishonesty or sloth or immorality from personal experiences. How effectively can we shape an idea for a business associate or develop an ideal for a student, or how can we understand in advance the blessings and emotions connected with celestial glory? In spite of the best intentions, we have some of our most serious problems with our communication. And because words are the best tools that we have, we should learn to make the best possible use of them by keeping our language of thinking and communicating under the most careful discipline.

The workmen engaged in building the Tower of Babel were craftsmen, skilled in their trades. If God had taken away their tools, they would have made some more; if he had deprived them of their skills, they would have learned them over again. But when he took away their means of communication with each other, then the building of the great tower was immediately abandoned. And so it is with the building of a successful business or a loving family or a happy life. When communication breaks down, progress comes to a standstill in many departments of our lives.

Of course, our words must be genuine and sincere and should always be supported by an adequate performance. Because our actions always speak louder than our words, we can develop our greatest ability for expression by translating every word into its highest form of activity.

Many people fall down because of the discord that is sometimes permitted between deed and creed. And because no one really lives as well as he knows how to live, our most serious shortcoming is our failure to translate our ideas and ambitions into their higher denomination of works. The central fact of life is that everyone, including God, will judge us primarily by what we do. No one is much of an expert in guessing at the meaning of words that haven't been spoken, or of deeds that remain unperformed. Even if we are equipped with the most adequate vocabulary to express every shade of thought and meaning in exactly the right word combinations, yet these words would have little value unless they are also accompanied by an intensity of feelings that can be translated into its most appropriate activity.

Often we let a wealth of words lie inert and unemployed; or sometimes, because of our own voluntary weakness in translation and communication, we allow coarseness or poverty to characterize that which might have been expertly and powerful done. Because every word has its own particular shade of meaning, there are actually no synonyms. Words may have a great deal in common, but there is something about each one that makes it unique. Words sometimes change in meaning to us as our own attitudes and behavior change. The word *love* may describe many things, from one's appetite for liquor to his adoration of God.

One of our greatest tragedies is that we are not on an intimate basis with great literature, which can be a very profitable kind of visual communication. We can choose from among the authors those who have a comparable spirit to that which we would like to develop. As we devour the words of William Shakespeare, John Milton, Winston Churchill, and Ralph Waldo Emerson, we may acquire some of their superior skills as architects of language. They not only organized great thoughts, but they were effective as translators and were masters of expression.

During the critical days of World War II, Winston Churchill made a number of great speeches. And probably more than anything else these speeches were responsible for saving the world from the mechanized might of the Nazis. In a communication to the British people, Churchill said, "We shall not flag or fail. We shall fight in France, we shall fight on the seas and oceans, we shall fight with growing confidence and power in the air, we shall defend our island, whatever the cost may be, we shall fight on the beaches, we shall fight on the landing grounds, we shall fight in the fields and in the streets, we shall fight in the hills; we shall never surrender." The great qualities of courage and determination that existed in Churchill's life were translated into words and broadcast to the people of the British Empire. Then in the hearts of loyal Englishmen they were changed back into the original virtues exhibited by Churchill.

Suppose we were to translate the Apostle Paul's famous sermon on love into our own lives, or suppose we were to appropriate for our own use the great ideas from the Sermon on the Mount or the Ten Commandments or the Lord's Prayer. Or suppose we were to communicate the expression "Father, thy will be done" into the working machinery of our lives. Those who can effectively read, memorize, and love the great scriptures can use them to lift themselves up to God.

The right words with appropriate feelings can discipline our lives to achieve the destiny that God has marked out for us.

Disciplined language demands more than merely adding words to our vocabulary. It is also a matter of forming attitudes and breaking slovenly habits of thought. It inspires us to avoid using second-rate words and ineffective idea combinations merely because they are handy. Our individual words and meanings should always fit the occasion. The electronics engineer does not use his trade language in explaining to his wife how to change a fuse. Sometimes we use a particular jargon that makes understanding difficult and communication ineffective. Our words often transform us into their own image. There are several willful language offenses that we are guilty of. One is obscurity and confusion. Sometimes we use negative words which represent negative thoughts. There is a great inventory of profane and ugly words that lead us away from our goals. This misuse of words and the abuse of ideas can cause a quick deterioration to take place in our own language, and then a serious negation takes place in our communication. When we fail to say our prayers or when we use speech to pervert our commitments to God, our language is misused, our abilities are weakened, and our ideas themselves may go down in value.

Without proper discipline and adequate exercise, our language takes on a kind of flabbiness or formlessness or mindlessness. When we are not living at our best, our expression may deteriorate into what the late James Thurber called "our oral culture of pure babble." Our expression and our performance depend to some extent upon each other. Some of our expression is best when we are living at our best. Expressions of patriotism increase our love of country. Even thinking is handicapped without expression. Someone was once asked what he thought about a certain thing, and he said, "I don't know; I haven't spoken on it yet."

We need to do more speaking about God and success and faith as we clarify our thoughts and give them power in speech. We need selected exercises in reading, and we need disciplined practice in thinking and speaking. Language itself may be enriched by the insight, imagination, and experience of those generations that have gone before us. We need to see how acknowledged masters use words, ideas, and emotions. The more we immerse ourselves in the work of the great writers of good language, the broader and more accurate our vocabularies will become and the more vigorous our activities. As the lives of great people have passed by, some of their ideas have been put down on paper, and we can help to build our own lives by using the tools that they have developed. Our constant prayer should be that God will help us to be able to effectively communicate with him both in our expression and in understanding his reply.

Section

V

Books of Inspiration

39

Books of Inspiration

L IFE IS made up of a great many
things. It includes a high sense of
appreciation of beauty, a sincere love of righteousness, and an
ability for exercising good judgment. It includes an awareness
of the importance of industry and an enthusiasm for following
those important laws of labor on which all success ultimately
depends. One of the most important elements in a good, happy,
and successful life is an ability to receive and give an adequate amount of that great quality known as inspiration.

Our earth itself is a giant magnet with a north pole and
a south pole. A great radio station receives and sends out various
kinds of messages. Every great human being also has this ability to receive and to read out uplifting satisfaction and ambitions. Not very much is actually understood about some of the
great sciences or philosophies having to do with mental telep-
athy, revelation, inspiration, and those various other means of
uplifting communication between individuals and individuals,
or individuals and higher powers.

Flowers have a kind of ability to inspire as they send out
their various messages of beauty. Their fragrance strikes our nostrils; their color contacts our vision and makes our hearts glad.
The fragrance, color, and beauty that have been given to flowers
were intended to be used to inspire and uplift others. No flower
was born to live unto itself alone, to bloom unseen, and to waste
its fragrance in an unappreciating environment. Birds were given
the ability to inspire us with their color, their form, their flight,
and their song. God gave a certain uplifting, creative power to the
foods of the earth that may build us up by giving us strength, vision, and the power to move and think and become. But our
spirits also need nourishment and strength.

The dictionary says that to inspire is "to infuse into." It is
a helpful input and means to enliven. It is to communicate uplifting messages to the mind and the spirit. Edward Everett Hale
once said that the best education is to be perpetually thrilled by

life. We need to be able to get a little more excited about things. We frequently associate inspiration with an intake or a breathing-into process that comes from God. And that is one of this word's very important meanings. God has given men many inspired dreams and visions. Sometimes complete ideas have been infused into the mind of some person with very little effort on his part. The scripture says that Jesus breathed on his apostles and said unto them, "Receive ye the Holy Ghost." (John 20:22.) Someone else has extended an invitation to the spirit by saying: "Come Holy Ghost, our souls inspire." But God has done a lot better for us than merely to provide us with a receiving instrument should he decide to give us some special prophetic message. He has also arranged for us to be broadcasting stations for his wisdom, righteousness, and inspiration.

The dictonary lists some of the synonyms for inspiration as animation, the ability to enliven, to exalt, to move, to motivate. And when God created us in his own image, he provided us with a great ability that we may develop by which we can inspire our own lives as well as the lives of others. We are aware that all good things come from God. God can put ideas bodily into our minds. We can also develop greatness in our minds on our own account. Paul referred to this situation when he said, ". . . be ye transformed by the renewing of your mind." (Romans 12:2.)

Everything, including man, was born small to begin with. The first automobiles all had to be cranked to get them started, but now most automobiles are equipped with self-starters, and certainly God would not put autombiles above his own children. Every day God is sending us food and vitamins and strength from his great central storehouse of the sun. And without God's support for our stomachs and our minds, we could not even live, let alone think or act. But with the right kind of diet, exercise, and thought, we may think some inspiring thoughts of our own. We have even learned how to preserve food so that its beneficial effects can be carried over from the growing season to last us during the long winter when nothing could live. And in about the same way, God has made it possible for us to carry inspiration over from one season to another and from one age to another so that our lives may be inspired from the past to meet their present needs. That is, we may open the great spiritual storehouse of the scriptures and draw therefrom the necessary inspiration to make our lives more productive in any desired field.

Through the scriptures we may in imagination go and stand at the foot of Mount Sinai and hear the words of God speaking to us in great power and authority. Or we may sit at the feet of Jesus and listen to the greatest human discourse ever given, in his Sermon on the Mount. We may use for our personal needs every inspiring thought and every great instruction that has ever been given in the world. We may use the physical energy deposited thousands of years ago in the coal beds of our earth to cook our dinner next Sunday. The yule log grows in the forest absorbing the sunshine of a hundred summers, and then by means of our Christmas fire we may release its stored-up energy in our living room to give warmth, good cheer, and happiness in the very dead of winter.

In a similar way, God has provided us with the ability to breathe into our own souls all of the inspiration that has been stored up in the great literature of our world. Ralph Waldo Emerson once said, "We live in the lap of an immense intelligence, and we may draw limitlessly from its strength for our own abundance."

When we hear great music we are lifted above ourselves, and the more familiarity and love we develop toward the thing that inspires us, the greater the uplifting force will be. The other day over television someone sang an old song that was popular fifty years ago, which I became very attached to in that early day but had allowed to pass out of my mind in later years. And as I heard it sung over television, all of these memories and pleasant feelings that I used to feel were reawakened and made me a different man than I was before. We can be inspired by great poetry and great literature and great examples.

Some time ago I watched a football game on television. The commentator who knew the players well explained that the quarterback was the emotional center of the team. He was their leader; he was their captain; he called the signals; he managed the team, infused their spirits, and was the team's personal leading performer. Then he was in a head-on crash that affected his eyes so that he had double vision and had to be taken out of the game. And while his team had run up a great score, the score was practically evened up in the third quarter when he was not there. The team's heart was gone. Their spirits lacked their former vitality. They were as though the dynamo connecting them with the source of their power had been shut down. By the beginning of the fourth quarter he felt well enough to go back into the game, and immediately his team again began to move and the game was won. The determination of his spirit was again transferred into them. The inspiration of one person can, under the right circumstances, be made negotiable in the spirit of someone else.

It was said by the Duke of Wellington that in his opinion Napoleon's presence on the field of battle was the equivalent of one hundred thousand additional troops. His very name acquired a mythical power, and his supreme confidence in himself was transferred as if by magic to those serving under his command. In trying to describe the striking power of the lion-hearted King Richard of England, Sir Walter Scott said, "He fights as if there were twenty men's strength in his single arm. It is fearful, yet magnificent, to behold how the arm and heart of one man can triumph over hundreds." I suppose that Richard's arm wasn't any stronger than any other warrior's arm, but that is not where strength comes from. Mr. Scott had said the arm and heart of one man, and Richard was fighting with his heart. He was fighting for England, and when one gets his heart into what he is doing, then things usually begin to happen.

We sometimes say of a team or an army or a nation that it is inspired. When it is inspired, a team plays over its head; an inspired nation is stronger than itself; an inspired individual has extraordinary strength. Winston Churchill during his old age would not have been a very good foot soldier, but the greatest strength usually comes from the mind and the spirit, and Winston Churchill inspired the soldiers of all the allied nations to do greater work and was a key factor in winning the war.

The Bible tells that God sometimes gives inspired dreams. He gave one to King Nebuchadnezzar and another to the prophet Daniel. God gave an inspired dream to Pharaoh that was interpreted by Joseph who was sold into Egypt.

In the latter days, the Lord has directed that a collection of sacred hymns should be compiled, that by being sung they might inspire the hearts and uplift the ambitions of those who sang them. The great musical masterpieces and the great paintings inspire the same feelings of exaltation today as they did when they were created. In fact, they might be much more inspiring to us because we have had time to learn to love them by living with them. The first time we meet a great person, we may not be unduly impressed; but as we get better acquainted and learn to love him and know of his good qualities more intimately, he greatly grows in our opinion, and so it is with great inspiration. The holy scripture is a great collection of inspiring ideas that may grow on us and become even more inspiring to us than they were in the days when they were new. The hymn "Come, Come, Ye Saints" can help us in our present-day problems just as it did in early pioneer days.

There is something inspiring about every life, and there are probably some things that are depressing. We can take those things to ourselves that lift us up and refuse those that tear us down. That is, we are not obligated to become friendly with gangsters unless we ourselves desire to. We can greatly inspire ourselves by selecting those books, those scriptures, great songs, great prayers, and the great companions that will lift us up. And our own ambition and determination to please God may be the greatest inspirers of ourselves.

Consciousness of a high skill in one's self gives him the greatest possible motivation for future accomplishment. I know a man who will not invest any money in anything that he does not have control over, as he feels that he has greater confidence in his judgment than he does in the judgment of other people. He knows that he himself is honest and that he is not lazy and will not make any serious mistakes or lose the company's money. He has an inspiring confidence in his own ability. And he thinks that if he has personal control of his possessions, he is safe.

The way to build up one's self-confidence is to build up a past performance that will entitle him to perfect trust in himself, where he knows by actual demonstration that he is stronger than anything that can happen to him. It is probable that all things and all people have inspiration in them. The flowers inspire by their beauty; the birds by their music; the books by their lofty ideals. The Lord has promised us that he would permit us to have his Spirit to be with us, but even his inspiration is not available to us unless we do our share in preparing the seedbed to receive the inspiration and give it strength.

The Bible is not an inspired book to many people because they are not inspired readers. There would be little inspiration in the solar system for an angleworm that lives ten inches below the surface of the earth, because it would know nothing about the solar system. A poem would mean nothing to someone who didn't understand it, and the greatest scriptures would be meaningless to those who did not believe them.

And so as a part of our collection of books to read from, we need some great books of inspiration to store up our enthusiasm and make us better than we are. We should never get in the habit of living in the dark, dingy basements of life; we should live on the upper floors where the sunlight of inspiration can get through to warm our hearts.

So we turn to the great masters who have conveyed their most elevated ideas to us, and as we run their thoughts through our own minds, we are inspired with a permanent enthusiasm so that we tend to think permanently inspiring thoughts.

40

Babylon

ONE OF the most significant and memorable cities in the history of the world was the ancient city of Babylon. It was founded about 2200 B.C. on the plains of Shinar by Nimrod, the powerful, defiant, rebellious grandson of Ham, who was the son of Noah. This great world capital from its very beginning was famous for sin, confusion, and disobedience to God. Its very name has become a synonym of wickedness, and it will probably remain the symbol of unrighteousness as long as time lasts.

Jesus used the name Babylon to denote corrupt Rome, apostate Jerusalem, and the entire empire of Satan, both in ancient and modern times. Any place that reaches a high state of corruption, where the powers of men are wholeheartedly antagonistic to the kingdom of God, there is Babylon.

This city built on the lower Euphrates in southwestern Asia was first called Babel. It was located only a few hundred miles south of Mount Ararat, where Noah's ark had landed. And it was not very long after the flood before a group of ungodly men started to build the tower that they expected would reach to heaven. It was here that God confounded the languages and scattered the people over the face of the earth.

Nimrod, the founder of Babel, was not entitled to the priesthood because of his lineage from Ham, but he laid the foundations of a heathen culture that has cursed civilization for four thousand years.

For the present we will skip over many centuries of Babylonian history and look in upon it at the height of its glory in the days of King Nebuchadnezzar. Nebuchadnezzar had spent the forty-four years of his reign fortifying and beautifying the city and making it the greatest capital on the earth. It was the world's center of commerce and industry. It was famous for wealth, luxury, and evil. Even by the standards of our day it was a city of enormous size. It was square in shape, each side measuring 15 miles in length. It was a city made impregnable to any war machine of that day. It was protected by massive walls 335 feet high and 85 feet thick. Even on their top the walls were wide enough that four chariots abreast could drive around them. Its streets were 120 feet wide, running at right angles to each other. Inside the city walls were farmlands sufficient to support the inhabitants indefinitely in case of a siege.

The city also included many beautiful parks and a great variety of flowers. The proverbial hanging gardens of Babylon were man-made imitations of mountains, provided at great expense to cure the Empress Amytis of her homesickness for her native land of Elam. Babylon was built across the great Euphrates River some distance above where it emptied into the Persian Gulf. This river, one-half mile in width, ran under the walls of Babylon and passed through the city, providing the water to maintain the city's beauty and the agricultural and culinary needs of the people. The river was spanned by ferries and drawbridges. The city itself included many beautiful buildings, palaces, and temples made of colored brick and costly tiles, which were decorated with precious metals and valuable jewels.

In the very center of all this splendor and power stood the great temple of Bel, which was one of the ancient wonders of the world. And enthroned therein, in all of his glory, sat Nebuchadnezzar, the king. As part of his program for enriching and beautifying Babylon, Nebuchadnezzar had captured Jerusalem, pulled down the luxurious temple of Solomon, and brought its rich treasures and ornaments back to Babylon. He had also taken captive over a hundred and fifty thousand of the leading Israelites and compelled them to serve in his own country.

Nebuchadnezzar is probably remembered most because of his relationship with the prophet Daniel, who has among the captive Hebrews brought from Jerusalem. The book of Daniel was written primarily about this relationship. It was in the days of Daniel that Nebuchadnezzar had had his famous dream. When the king awoke the next morning, he knew that he had received an important message, but it had gone from him, and he had no way of knowing what it meant. After the greatest magicians and astrologers of Babylon had failed, the Lord made known to Daniel the king's dream and its interpretation. Then Daniel said to the king, ". . . there is a God in heaven that revealeth secrets, and maketh known to the king Nebuchadnezzar what shall be in the latter days."

Then Daniel told the king of his dream wherein he had seen a great image set up before him "whose brightness was excellent . . . and the form thereof was terrible." The head of the image was of fine gold. His breast and arms were of silver. His belly and his thighs were of brass. His legs were of iron. His feet were part iron and part clay.

Then Daniel said to the king, "Thou sawest till that a stone was cut out without hands, which smote the image upon his feet that were of iron and clay, and brake them to pieces." Then by way of interpretation Daniel said to Nebuchadnezzar, "Thou, O king, art a king of kings: for the God of heaven hath given thee a kingdom, power, and strength, and glory. And wheresoever the children of men dwell, the beasts of the field and the fowls of the heaven hath he given into thine hand, and hath made thee ruler over them all. Thou art this head of gold."

Then he told of the succeeding kingdoms that would arise later and replace Babylon and its successor nations, until in the last days when the God of heaven should set up a kingdom which shall never be destroyed, and the kingdom shall not be left to another people, but it shall break in pieces and consume all these kingdoms, and it shall stand forever. (See Daniel 2.)

The king bestowed great honor upon Daniel, but he himself had not sufficiently learned his lesson, and so the Lord gave another dream to Nebuchadnezzar about himself. In interpreting this dream, Daniel said, "O king, and this is the decree of the most High, . . . they shall drive thee from men, and thy dwelling shall be with the beasts of the field, and they shall make thee to eat grass as oxen, and they shall wet thee with the dew of heaven, and seven times shall pass over thee, till thou know that the most High ruleth in the kingdom of men, and he giveth it to whomsoever he will."

Then Daniel said, "O king, let my counsel be acceptable unto thee, and break off thy sins by righteousness, and thine iniquities by shewing mercy to the poor. . . ." But the king decided against Daniel's counsel, and later as he walked in his palace he said, "Is not this great Babylon, that I have built . . . by the might of my power, and for the honour of my majesty?" Who could possibly drive him from among men? He was the greatest king of the mightiest kingdom ever known. But even while the words were in the king's mouth, there fell a voice from heaven, saying, "O king Nebuchadnezzar, to thee it is spoken; The kingdom is departed from thee." The same hour was the thing fulfilled upon Nebuchadnezzar. Nebuchadnezzar was stricken with madness, and then his son Belshazzar ruled in the place of his father.

Finally when Daniel's prophecy had been fulfilled and the Lord's purposes were satisfied, Nebuchadnezzar said, "And at the end of the days I Nebuchadnezzar lifted mine eyes unto heaven, and mine understanding returned unto me, and I blessed the most High, and I praised and honoured him that liveth for ever, whose dominion is an everlasting dominion, and his kingdom is from generation to generation: . . . and none can stay his hand." (See Daniel 4.) What a pity that Nebuchadnezzar could not have learned this great lesson a little earlier in his life!

But it appears that like some of us, each generation of Babylonians tended to repeat the sins and make the errors of the previous generations. And so Belshazzar followed in the unrighteous footsteps of his great father, and like his father, Belshazzar was also required to pay the penalties of his sins. And on what was probably the most important day in the history of this great city, Belshazzar made a feast to a thousand of the lords and nobles of his kingdom. To make the occasion complete, Belshazzar commanded that the vessels of gold and silver that Nebuchadnezzar had taken from the temple in Jerusalem should be brought, that the king, with his princes and their wives might drink therefrom. And as they drank and were merry, they praised the idol gods of Babylon.

Then the record says, "In the same hour came forth fingers of a man's hand, and wrote over against the candlestick upon the plaister of the wall of the king's palace: . . . Then the king's countenance was changed . . . and his knees smote one against another."

The news of this mystery was communicated to the king's mother. She came to the banquet hall where the drunken lord of Babylon sat trembling among his frightened guests. The queen mother reminded the king of the wisdom found in Daniel by his father Nebuchadnezzar; accordingly, Daniel was sent for and was offered gifts to read the handwriting on the wall.

Daniel said, "Let thy gifts be to thyself, and give thy rewards to another; yet I will read the writing unto the king, and make known to him the interpretation." He said, "O thou king, the most high God gave Nebuchadnezzar thy father a kingdom, and majesty, and glory, and honour. . . . But when his heart was lifted up, and his mind hardened in pride, he was deposed from his kingly throne, and they took his glory from him: And he was driven from the sons of men . . . till he knew that the most high God ruled in the kingdom of men, and that he appointeth over it whomsoever he will. And thou his son, O Belshazzar, hast not humbled thine heart, though thou knewest all this."

Then from the writing on the wall Daniel read to the king these fateful words: "God hath numbered thy kingdom, and finished it. Thou art weighed in the balances, and art found wanting. Thy kingdom is divided, and given to the Medes and Persians." (See Daniel 5.)

To the great Belshazzar this must have seemed unbelieveable. What could be more natural than for him to rethink the thoughts of his father, "Is not this great Babylon, that I have built . . . by the might of my power, and for the honour of my majesty?" Great Babylon had been built to last forever. It was protected by the greatest army and the strongest fortifications. Who could ever hope to batter down these walls, or break through the massive gates of brass, or cut off the inexhaustible food supply?

But at that very instant Cyrus, the Persian, was eight miles north of the city, turning the river Euphrates from its course to permit his army to march under the city walls on the riverbed. This accomplished, the great gates of brass were opened from the inside with little or no resistance. And while the nobles and princes of Babylon were drunken with wine, the Persians marched through the open gates, and the magnificent, luxurious, beautiful capital of the world with all of its wealth and immorality fell into the hands of the enemy.

Then the scripture records the end of the king of Babylon as well as his kingdom by saying, "In that night was Belshazzar the king of the Babylonians slain." (Daniel 5:30.) Belshazzar, like his father, had built his house upon the sands. Both had failed to learn this lesson: that unless the Lord shall build the house, they labor in vain who build it.

The ruins of ancient Babylon still remain. In fulfillment of the ancient curse and prophecy, the city has never been rebuilt. But spiritual Babylon is yet to be destroyed, and time is running out. In our own day the Lord has said, "Go ye out from Babylon. Be ye clean that bear the vessels of the Lord." (D&C 133:5.) "Go ye out from . . . the midst of wickedness, which is spiritual Babylon." (D&C 133:14.)

Daniel advised Nebuchadnezzar to turn to righteousness. For similar reasons we should eliminate sin and confusion from our individual lives. It seemed necessary for each generation of Babylonians to commit all of the sins and make all of the mistakes personally. But their history is a type of what sometimes happens in individual lives. We also seem to learn little from the past.

Nimrod was the great-grandson of Noah and knew the lessons of the flood, yet he used his great strength to reestablish the evil which the Lord had tried to destroy. We have another common problem in that so frequently we glory too much in our own strength and, Nebuchadnezzar-like, we say, "Is not this great Babylon, that I have built . . . by the might of my power, and for the honour of my majesty?"

Following such a course we may also someday see the handwriting upon the wall, saying, "God hath numbered thy kingdom, and finished it. Thou art weighed in the balances, and art found wanting. Thy kingdom is divided, and given to the Medes and Persians."

May God help us to learn the lessons taught by evil and disobedience, that in consequence we may build our own houses upon the rock of righteousness.

41

Joan of Arc

IN THE early 1940s President Franklin D. Roosevelt wrote to Winston Churchill and said, "It is fun to live in the same decade with you." When we love a great or noble quality, we usually personify or embody it in some fitting person. Embodiment enables us to see the great trait with our eyes and hear it with our ears and more effectively love it with our hearts. Because Winston Churchill has dominated our century and is the embodiment of certain great virtues, it is also fun to be a part of his world.

I recently felt some similarly pleasing emotions as I read an account of the life of Joan of Arc. It was written by Sieur Louis de Conte, who was born in the same village and was constantly with her in the war as her page and secretary. The account was published in two volumes by Mark Twain under the title of *Personal Recollections of Joan of Arc*. In all the annals of our time her life stands out as one of the most striking embodiments of goodness, nobility, and greatness, and it is fun to be a part of the human family with her.

Her biography itself is unique. It was written in court and comes to us under oath from the witness stand. It was taken from the records of the great trial held in the year 1431 at which she was condemned to be burned alive. Every intimate detail of her short and eventful life is still preserved in the National Archives of France.

Joan of Arc was born in the little village of Demremy, France, in 1412. Throughout her childhood she was extraordinarily healthy and happy. She was wholehearted in her play. Her merry disposition was supplemented by a warm, sympathetic nature. She had frank winning ways, was genuinely religious, and was greatly admired and loved.

At this period France was suffering the cruel pains of its Hundred Years War with England. France had lost almost every battle. Eight thousand Englishmen had wiped out sixty thousand Frenchmen at Agincourt. French courage had been paralyzed, and France had been reduced to little more than a British province. For Joan, who carried France upon her heart, the continual atrocities of war greatly sobered her spirit and frequently reduced her to tears. Then in her thirteenth year Joan began to hear voices, telling her that she would be God's instrument in setting France free. Among her instructors were Saint Margaret and Saint Catherine. Three years were required to prepare her for her mission. At first she offered objections. She said to her instructors, "But I am so young to leave my home and mother. How can I talk with men and be comrades with soldiers? I am only a girl and know nothing of war or even how to ride a horse. How can I lead armies?" Her voice was often broken with sobs, but finally she accepted her call and said, "If it is commanded, I will go. I know that France will rise again, for God has ordained her to be free."

The voices told her to go to the governor of Vaucouleurs, who would provide her with an escort of men-at-arms and send her to the Dauphin, who was the uncrowned heir to the throne. In leaving her village home, Joan said, "I am enlisted. God helping me, I will not turn back until the British grip is loosened from the throat of France." When the governor heard her message he said, "What nonsense is this? You are but a child." But Joan said, "Nevertheless, I am appointed by the king of heaven to lead the armies of France to raise the British siege of Orleans and crown the Dauphin at Rheims."

When the news reached the Dauphin that an unlearned seventeen-year-old peasant maid was coming to see him with a divine commission to free France, he appointed a committee of court advisers to hear her message. Confronting the committee, she said, "Forgive me, reverend sirs, but I have no message save for the ears of his Grace, the Dauphin." Their arguments and threats were useless.

After they had left in great anger, she said to her friends, "My mission is to move the Dauphin by argument and reasoning to give me men-at-arms and send me to the siege. Even if the committee carried the message in the exact words with no word missing, and yet left out the persuasions of gesture, the supplicating tone and beseeching looks that inform the words and make them live, then where were the value of that argument and whom could it convince?"

This untaught child had just discarded her shepherd's crook, and yet she was able to penetrate the cunning devices of trained men and defeat them at their own game. She would soon stand unafraid before nobles and other mighty men; she was fully prepared to clothe herself in steel and become the deliverer of France. The Dauphin said to her, "Tell me who you are." Joan said, "I am called Joan the Maid. I am sent to say to you that the king of heaven wills that you should give me men-at-arms and set me at my appointed work. For I will raise the siege of Orleans and break the British power." But how could she win victories for France where the nation's best-trained generals had had nothing but defeats for over fifty years? But Joan had said that "when God fights, it is a small matter whether the hand that holds the sword is big or little." This unlearned girl said to the Dauphin, "Be not afraid, God has sent me to save you."

Everyone knew that in her heart there was something that raised her above the greatest men of her day. Whether she came of God or not, they could feel that mysterious something that was later to put heart into her soldiers and turn mobs of cowards into armies of fighters. Her men forgot what fear was when they were in her presence. Her soldiers went into battle with joy in their eyes and a song on their lips. They would sweep over the battlefield like an irresistible storm. The Dauphin knew that that was the only spirit that could save France, come from wherever it may.

Joan won the confidence of the Dauphin and the court with her sweetness, simplicity, sincerity, and unconscious eloquence. The best and the most capable among them recognized that she was formed on a grander plan and moved on a loftier plane than the ordinary mass of mankind. And whence could come such sublime courage and conviction but from God himself?

Finally Joan was given her command. In a public proclamation the Dauphin said, "Know all men, that the most illustrious Charles, by the grace of God, King of France, is pleased to confer upon his well-beloved servant Joan of Arc, called the Maid, the title, emoluments, and authorities of General-in-Chief of the armies of France."

A suit of armor was made for her at Tours. It was of the finest steel, heavily plated with silver, richly ornamented with engraved designs, and polished like a mirror. She was miraculously provided with a sacred sword long hidden behind the altar of St. Catherine's at Fierbois. She herself designed and consecrated a sacred banner, which she always carried with her into battle.

As the war march of Joan of Arc began, the curtain went up on one of the most unusual of all military careers. Louis Kossuth said that "since the writing of human history began, Joan of Arc is the only person of either sex who has ever held supreme command of the military forces of a great nation at age 17." She rode a white horse and carried in her hand the sacred sword of Fierbois. It was also the symbol of the authority and righteousness that she always maintained. She once said to her generals that even the "rude business of war could be better conducted without profanity or any of the other brutalities of speech." Some could not understand why Joan continued to be alert, vigorous, and confident while her strongest men were exhausted by heavy marches and exposure. They might have reflected that a great soul with a great purpose can make a weak body strong and able to bear the most exhausting fatigues.

Once with an almost impossible objective ahead, Joan said to one of her generals, "I will lead the men over the wall." The general replied, "Not a man will follow you." Joan said, "I will not look back to see whether anyone is following or not." But the soldiers of France did follow Joan of Arc. With her sacred sword, her consecrated banner, and her belief in her mission, she swept all before her. She sent a thrill of courage and enthusiasm through the French army such as neither king nor general could produce. On May 8, 1430, by sheer strategy and force, she broke the siege at Orleans. This anniversary is still celebrated as Joan of Arc Day. It is the day that she drove out the British and saved France. Then, at the head of her troops, she marched to Rheims and crowned the Dauphin King.

With her mission accomplished, Joan planned to return to her family in Domremy, but she was treacherously betrayed and sold to the British. Her long trial of over a year began. For many weary months she was kept in chains. She was threatened and abused. The judges and jurors were carefully selected enemies. Trumped-up charges of witchcraft and sorcery were brought against her. No one doubted that she had seen and conversed with supernatural beings. She had made many prophecies and had done many things that could not be explained otherwise. But her enemies argued that her success came from Satan, and therefore she must be destroyed. Church influence and civil power were used to discredit her. She was promised her freedom if she would deny her voices and her mission. But Joan was immovable. She said, "If I were under sentence and saw the fire before me or even if I were in the flames themselves I would not say other than what I have said at these trials, and I will abide by my testimony until I die."

A full year had now passed since she had gone speeding across the plain at the head of her troops, her silver helmet shining, her silvery cape flutting in the wind, her white plumes flowing, and her sword held aloft. But Joan of Arc would ride no more, and as the fires were being lighted around the stake at which this nineteen-year-old French peasant maid would be burned alive, she was again given a chance to regain her liberty by denying what she believed. In choosing the fire rather than her freedom she said, "The world can use these words. I know this now—every man gives his life for what he believes; every woman gives her life for what she believes. Sometime people believe in little or nothing, and yet they give their lives to that little or nothing. One life is all we have, and we live it as we believe in living it, and then it's gone. But to surrender what you are and live without belief is more terrible than dying, even more terrible than dying young."

Twenty-four years after her death, the Pope appointed a commission to examine the facts of Joan's life and award a judgment. The commission sat at Paris, at Domremy, at Rouen, and at Orleans. It worked for several months and reinvestigated every detail of her life. It examined the trial records and hundreds of personal witnesses, and through all of this exhaustive examination Joan's character remained as spotless as it had always been. Someone said that for "all of the qualities that men call great, look for them in Joan of Arc and there you will find them." Joan was canonized a saint. The greatest praise was placed upon the official record of her life, there to remain forever.

It has been said that she lived in the most brutal, wicked, and rotten age since the Dark Ages. She was truthful when lying was the common speech of man. She was honest when honesty was a lost virtue. She maintained her personal dignity unimpaired in an age of fawnings and servilities. She had dauntless courage when hope had perished in the hearts of her countrymen. She was spotlessly pure in mind and body when most of society was foul in both. In nineteen short years this untaught girl had become the

deliverer of France, the savior of her country, the genius of patriotism, and the embodiment of sainthood, with a martyr's
crown upon her head—all of this when crime was the common
business of mankind.

She was perhaps the only entirely unselfish person whose
name has held a high place in profane history. No vestige or suggestion of self-seeking can be found in any word or deed of hers.
When she rescued her king and set the crown upon his head, she
was offered many rewards and honors, but she refused them all.
Although she was the companion of princes, the general of victorious armies, and the idol of an applauding and grateful nation,
yet all she desired was to go back to her village and tend her sheep
and to feel her mother's arms about her.

The work of Joan of Arc may fairly be regarded as ranking
among the greatest in history. She found a great nation lying in
chains, helpless and hopeless under an alien conqueror, its treasury bankrupt, its soldiers disheartened, its king cowed and prepared to flee the country. But when she laid her hand upon this
withered nation, its people arose and followed her. Her soul was
the embodiment of nobility and righteousness. And it was said
that she was the most lovely and the most adorable embodiment
of good that any age has produced.

42

The Lost Bible

O NE OF the principles of effective teaching is by comparison. Jesus used this powerful aid in his parables. We see light things best on a dark background, and it is one of our human principles that we usually appreciate things more after they have been lost. For example, no one ever really appreciates his freedom or his health or his opportunities until they are threatened or until they are no longer available. And in about the same way, we appreciate great books when they are not available. We have heard many stories of people who have had a great hunger for the Holy Scriptures intensified in their hearts when they have been prisoners of godless dictators and have been forbidden access to the Holy Scriptures. And we might do ourselves great good where in a process of imagination we deprive ourselves of the great scriptures.

For example, there is an ancient legend that tells of a time when the world lost the Bible. Not only did the book itself disappear, but all traces of its influence were taken completely from the earth. Its doctrines had vanished, its philosophy, its commandments, its history, and its religion were all as completely erased from the records of the world as though they had never existed. The priceless archives appeared as though vandals had pillaged them, slashing and despoiling the classical works of the world. The art galleries now displayed mostly a lot of empty frames. The valuable religious canvases had been taken away, leaving no trace of the thrilling artistry that had been inspired by the Bible.

Much of the finest music in the world was silence; it had evaporated as though it had never existed. The mighty oratorios such as *Messiah, The Creation,* and *Elijah* were out of circulation forever. They had not only been removed from the libraries and galleries, but they had also been completely expunged from the minds and hearts of men. Beautiful hymns that for ages had expressed the hopes, the fears, and the devotions of millions were now silent. The beautiful Christmas carols, Easter anthems, and songs of Thanksgiving were now no more.

Libraries had been gutted and the writings of Shakespeare, Milton, Tennyson, Carlyle, Longfellow, and countless others were dull and drab as they now lacked their former inspiration and beauty. The masterpieces of oratory were minus their most potent passages. Law books made little sense, for the fundamental principles of right and justice had been eliminated. The great documents of human rights such as the Magna Charta of Great Britain, the Constitution of the United States, and the Declaration of Independence were now as sounding brass. Great values had become jumbled and confused. The precious gifts of the spirit were blurred and cancelled out, and in their places there was nothing but blankness.

When the Bible was lost, according to the legend, the Holy Spirit was also snuffed out, and in its absence, man no longer grew tall of soul, gentle of spirit, courageous of heart, just and honest toward his fellowmen, faithful in life, and fearless in death. Life itself had become flat, empty, and purposeless, for God, the author of the Bible, had also vanished, and man had no one left to worship but himself. The natural laws by which the universe had been governed now had no author and no master, but everything was left to chance, and confusion reigned.

Fortunately this is only a legend. Actually we still have the Bible. The book of books is still on the shelf where it has always been. The word of God is still available where we can turn to its greatest passages with a moment's notice. How fortunate we are to have this holy book in our immediate possession. It has given more inspiration to more people than any other book that was ever printed.

The fate of the nations themselves hangs on the holy scriptures. Napoleon on St. Helena said, "The Bible is not merely a book—it is a living power. . . . Nowhere as in the Bible can be found such a series of beautiful ideas and admirable maxims which pass before us like the battalions of a celestial army. . . . The soul can never go astray while it has this book for its guide." The influence of this volume reaches into every corner of our lives. The writings of Shakespeare alone contain 550 Bible quotations and allusions. The poetry of Tennyson contains 330 Bible references. The works of Emerson are filled with Bible passages and philosophy. Jesus himself quoted eighty-nine times from the Old Testament scriptures.

But although the Bible itself is safe and sound, yet there are many individuals to whom the Bible is still lost. What good does it do for one to have physical possession if he does not have mental and spiritual familiarity? A recent survey revealed that ninety-two percent of all American homes contain a Bible, but 72.5 percent of the people living in those homes said that they seldom, if ever, read it. Thirty-four percent of those questioned could not name a single book in the Bible. One man who could quote the batting averages of every important major league baseball player in the United States confessed that he could not quote one single verse from the word of the Lord. He had a Bible but he knew nothing of its message.

This situation reminds us of the Forty-Niners who over a century ago started out for California, seeking gold. Many of them died of thirst while crossing the great American desert. Frequently their bodies were found near waterholes. They could have saved their lives if they had only known that there was water within their easy reach.

Our spiritual situation is very similar. Jesus talked a great deal about the living waters that would save us from spiritual death. But many are dying of spiritual thirst with the waterholes right under our noses. Many eternal deaths occur because those concerned have lost the Bible.

Some time ago the late Dr. Adam S. Bennion gave a series of Bible lectures. The first assignment made to the class members was for them to *find* their Bibles. They were not required to open them, or dust them off, or read anything out of them—just get them located. I suppose that in a little different sense, that is about the number one need of our day—for every person in the world to find the Bible; not just to locate the book itself, but to discover its doctrine and love its inspiration. Suppose that we could just make the proper use of the Sermon on the Mount and the Ten Commandments. Suppose that we could really discover the message of the Golden Rule or find the lessons hidden in the Parables and the Beatitudes, and then put every instruction in force in our daily program.

Most of the sin, degradation, and suffering in this world and in the world to come are and will be because of our misfortune in losing the Bible. We have lost its repentance, its righteousness, and its wisdom. Sometimes we lose the Bible a little bit at a time by deliberately discarding those parts that don't suit our fancy.

This is one of the places where without question the communist leaders of Russia excel us as they have thrown away the Bible all at once. Even though the book itself may still be available, in Russia its great doctrines have been repudiated and its Christian ordinances have been maliciously discarded. Not only has the Bible been officially lost in Russia, but in harmony with the legend, the author himself has been banished from every part of his own earth presently occupied by the Russians.

One of their astronauts went out into space and when he returned he assured his fellow disbelievers that there was no God because he had looked around out in space and could not find him. The fact that the Russian leaders now have no higher authority to go by than themselves certainly has much to do with the fact that they seem to have lost much of their sense of right and wrong. To bring about human slavery is one of their most cherished goals; they would deprive every human being of his God-given free agency without a moment's hesitation if they thought they could. In fact, they threaten that they are now posed and ready to destroy the world if their ultimatums are not followed. The problem that threatens Russia, like that which destroyed Nazi Germany, is that their leaders have lost the Bible. This has been the problem of the nations of the past; it is the most threatening problem of the nations in the present.

On February 22, 1852, before the New York Historical Society, Daniel Webster said, "If we and our posterity shall be true to the Christian religion, if we and they shall live always in the fear of God and shall respect his commandments, we may have the highest hopes for the future fortunes of our country. It will have no decline and fall, but it will go on prospering and to prosper. But if we or our posterity reject religious instruction and authority, violate the rules of eternal justice, trifle with the injunctions of morality and recklessly destroy the political constitution which holds us together, no man can tell how sudden a catastrophe may overwhelm us that shall bury all of our glory in profound obscurity. Should that disaster happen, let it have no history. Let the horrible narrative never be written. Let its fate be that of the lost books of Livy which no human eye shall ever read. Or the missing Pleiad of which no man can ever know more than that it is lost and lost forever."

If we are to succeed as individuals or as a nation, we must find the Bible and we must find the Bible's author.

God promised to spare Sodom and Gomorrah if ten righteous men could be found therein. Maybe he would also spare us the devastation that has been foretold if we would turn our lives to him. One of our most important needs is for the great Christian churches to find the Bible. There are presently some 250 Christian denominations claiming to base their entire religion upon the great book. They say they accept the Bible as the inspired word of God and the only authoritative rule of faith and practice. But many of the greatest doctrines taught by Christ and mentioned in the Bible are missing from their creeds. It is a very simple matter to accept the Bible when it is closed, but to reject the fundamental Christian doctrines that are exposed to view when the Bible is open.

Ninety-five percent of all the people in America claim to believe in God. Yet many have no clear conception of the kind of God they believe in. Almost everyone believes the Bible when it is closed. But when the Bible is opened, how much do we believe of the divinity of Christ, the atonement, the personality of God, the antemortal existence of spirits, the literal bodily resurrection, the degrees of glory, the eternity of the family unit, the authority of the priesthood, and the thrilling doctrine of eternal progression? It has been said that if Christ should come back to earth today he would certainly not be able to recognize in the contending sects led by unauthorized men the one Lord, one faith, and one baptism concept that he established. He promised severe punishment to anyone who added to or subtracted from his doctrine. (Revelation 22:18-19.)

A few years ago one of the greatest sectarian religious leaders of our day wrote a book in which he compared the doctrines taught in the Bible with what is presently being taught by popular religious leaders. This man pointed out from the scriptures that the God of the Bible was a personal God. There could be no question about that. Jesus taught that God was his Father (John 1:14), that Jesus was the first begotten Son of God in the spirit (Hebrews 1:6, Romans 8:29), and the Only Begotten in the flesh (John 3:6). But this minister making the survey said, "We don't believe that any more." Then he explained what the survey indicated was presently believed about God by the ministers of popular Christianity. One of them said, "No one can possibly know about God. He is absolutely unknowable, indiscernible, and undiscoverable. He is not limited to boundaries, and we can be sure that he has no body or shape." Another minister said that God was like a giant electronic brain. Many believed him to be some incomprehensible, mysterious essence that filled the universe that no one could understand. Another referred to him as a mobile, cosmic ether. Jesus prayed, "Our father which art in heaven." (Matthew 6:9.) Jesus said to Mary, ". . . go to my brethren, and say unto them, that I ascend unto my Father, and to your Father; and to my God, and your God." (John 20:17.)

Jesus was literally begotten by his Father (Luke 1:35); he had a body like his Father (D&C 130:22); he resembled his Father (John 6:46, 14:9); he prayed to his Father (John 17:5). He did the will of his Father. He taught the doctrine of his Father (John 7:16), and his Father's voice spoke approval of his work (Matthew 3:17, 17:5).

The minister handling the survey said that those who wrote the Bible believed in a literal, bodily resurrection. There could be no question about that. The body of Jesus came out of the tomb and was seen by many during the forty days between his resurrection and ascension. He said to Thomas, "Reach hither thy finger, and behold my hands; and reach hither thy hand, and thrust it into my side: and be not faithless, but believing." (John 20:27.)

Summing up some of the other great doctrines of Christ, this minister said, "The virgin birth is no longer an accepted historic fact. The second coming of Christ is an outmoded phrasing of hope. The inerrancy of the scriptures is incredible." Then this minister commented that "almost nothing is left of this great volume of scripture that if accepted could save the world." But through disbelief, disobedience, and false teaching, many churches and many individuals have in very large part lost the Holy Bible, and consequently they have lost themselves and their blessings.

The Church of Jesus Christ of Latter-day Saints declares that God the Father and his Son, Jesus Christ, have again visited the earth and declared again that the Holy Bible is the word of God and that every single doctrine is important. May God help us in our individual investigation to find the Bible and every one of its life-giving truths.

43

A Book of Songs

AS EACH of us attempts to make his way toward his own projected success, happiness, and accomplishment, he ought to be inspired and motivated by having the assistance of some books filled with especially selected songs. We ought to have personal access to a good book of hymns. We ought to regularly sing some good patriotic songs. We ought to know some love songs, and we ought to have some great philosophies that we love that have been set to music. There is a very important passage of scripture in which the Lord himself has said, "For my soul delighteth in the song of the heart; yea, the song of the righteous is a prayer unto me, and it shall be answered with a blessing upon their heads." (D&C 25: 12.)

Singing is also an excellent way to build up our own spirit and enthusiasm. It is a way to make ourselves happy. The wise man Solomon said, "A merry heart doeth good like a medicine. . . ." (Proverbs 17:22.)

Singing also acts as a great motivational power. It strengthens our faith and helps us to keep our objectives firmly in mind. It strengthens our faith and helps us to keep our objectives firmly in mind. Great ideas that have been cast into effective language and whose words have been rhymed and set to music can help to increase every accomplishment and give us greater power in our souls.

In his first inaugural address, President Dwight D. Eisenhower said that the great driving forces of the world are not intellectual but emotional. And singing patriotic songs is one of the best ways of building up that driving force of loyalty into our hearts. By singing the great religious songs, we may develop and expand our faith.

Great men and women are the most wonderful creation that God himself is capable of producing. And as God fashioned us in his image, he so constituted our natures that we may grow best by our own expression. Our bodies, our minds, our spirits, our voices, and our many other faculties are all strengthened as they are exercised.

Addison said that "good music is the only sensual gratification in which mankind many indulge to excess without injury to their moral or religious feelings." The great literature of the world, including the holy scriptures, constitutes a vast storehouse of those ideas and written emotions as to how we may make our lives more profitable, more useful, and more happy. And when the right number and quality of these thoughts have been measured, metered, weighed, harmonized, rhymed, and set to music so that we may effectively run them through our souls, then we may transform our lives to meet our own highest specifications.

Former British Prime Minister William E. Gladstone once said, "Music is one of the most forceful instruments ever discovered for governing the mind and the spirit of man." With the right kind of music we can control our moods, give our emotions greater power, and more accurately direct our own destiny. And those ideas that have the greatest influence for good with us are those that we know the best and love the most. In the early days of the Church, the Lord thought this idea important enough that he gave a great revelation suggesting that a careful selection of great hymns should be made and compiled into a book. These may be memorized and sung by us as a group or as individuals. This idea was built upon by Brigham Young who, while leading the early pioneers across the plains, appointed William Clayton to write "Come, Come, Ye Saints," to give extra enthusiasm and ability to members of the Church as they sought their new home in the unknown West.

The other day, I carefully read through a volume of these especially selected hymns and sang some of them to myself. At the top of each page directions had been given as to how these hymns should be sung. It said that some should be sung with enthusiasm, some should be sung with great feeling, some should be sung quietly and reverently, some should be sung majestically, some martially, and some solemnly and prayerfully. It indicated in the hymnbook that some of the hymns should be sung with feelings of gladness, some should be sung energetically, some boldly, and some thoughtfully and suppliantly. And as I tried to sing these words in the spirit suggested, I found the corresponding attitudes building up in my heart.

One of the important thrills that I get from attending church is to hear people sing the great songs of Zion, especially when they sing them with joy, thanksgiving, and jubilation as they are supposed to be sung. But this joy can be greatly increased in me when I myself know the words and music of the songs and can sing them with a great depth of feeling and enthusiasm. The singers should always get much more out of the songs than those who merely listen to them being sung by others. This is especially true when those who listen only partly understand or partly believe the great truths that are sung about. Sometimes I feel very badly as I watch some people sing in church, because you can tell they don't know the words or the music. They sometimes barely move their lips, or they mumble the words, or they don't feel the spirit and consequently they don't get out of it the intended benefit. So many people miss the great jubilation and fervor that is available to us in the great music. Some of our musical prayers are very weak and lack meaning. It naturally follows that very largely the blessings are lost that these songs are capable of calling down upon our heads.

It has always been interesting to me that the life of Jesus Christ was begun as a great concourse of heavenly beings assembled on the hills of Judea singing songs of praise and great joy. He was born to be the Savior of the world and the Redeemer of mankind, and this great multitude of heavenly hosts sang thrilling anthems and "Glory to God in the highest, and on earth peace, good will toward men." (Luke 2:14.) His life was also closed with a song. He gathered his disciples about him in the upper room for their last supper together. This was his last meal in mortality. The scripture tells us that he instituted the sacrament and gave important final directions to the members of the Twelve. Then the record says, "And then when they had sung an hymn, they went out into the mount of Olives." (Mark 14:26.)

It is one of the great commands of God that we should remember the Sabbath day and keep it holy, and a part of every worship service should be made up of beautiful, meaningful, inspiring music. The Lord wants us to go to church and he wants us to sing and pray and teach and worship effectively when we get there. He also wants us to understand and live the principles of the gospel, and it is in our interest to frequently and regularly run these doctrines of salvation through our souls to the accompaniment of that appropriate music that builds up our feelings.

And we can do ourselves great good by stabilizing the philosophies of faith, the words of encouragement and worship in our lives by running them through our minds and hearts again and again. One of the important laws of learning is repetition, and we gain the greatest amount of enjoyment from the hymns when we sing them frequently and expertly with great joy and faith. Inasmuch as we can't know all of the great songs, it is important that each one of us make his own selection, memorize the words, and learn to sing them effectively. We might include such masterpieces as "I Need Thee Every Hour," "We Thank Thee, O God, for a Prophet," "O My Father," and "God Be With You Till We Meet Again." By means of our great hymns we can increase the order, enthusiasm, righteousness, and spirit of our lives.

At Christmastime we get the spirit of the Master's life by singing such great Christmas carols as "Silent Night," "O Little Town of Bethlehem," "Oh Come, All Ye Faithful," and "Far, Far Away on Judea's Plains."

There is a great scripture which says that governments were instituted of God for the benefit of man, and we can increase the quality of our citizenship by singing those songs characterized by great loyalty and patriotism to our government. We ought to sing our inspiring national anthem and "God Bless America," "My Country 'Tis of Thee," and "America the Beautiful."

Everyone should also have in his heart some songs of love, some songs of courage, some songs of accomplishment. These should be thoroughly memorized in the appropriate spirit. Every time great ideas go through our minds and hearts, they purify us and exhilarate our accomplishment. They produce great ambitions in our hearts and give us health in our bodies.

Great songs increase our health, our success, and our happiness, and frequently we ought to hear our own voices singing these great ideas in a pleasant, beautiful, motivating way. The thoughts themselves don't need to be our own in order to uplift us. However, we can make the greatest songs our personal possession by loving them and knowing how to make them a more important part of us. We can get an intimate possession of the greatest ideas that have been composed and set to music by the greatest men.

The finest masterpiece of creation came into being on the sixth day when God formed man in his own image, but God also endowed us with a set of his attributes and potentialities. He gave us these potentially magnificent brains, these miraculous personalities, this great ability for growth, and a natural potential for power. He gave us a language as the finest means of communication with our own spirits and emotions.

Music is one of the most useful of all of these great inventions of God, and he has especially prepared his children to take advantage of it by giving them a voice box, a feeling of harmony, and many great potential musical possibilities. We have such mechanical instruments for making music as the piano, the violin, the harp, the trumpet, and the drums. But none of these equal the musical device that God himself has built into the hearts, throats, and voices of human beings. A piano or a drum can make musical sounds, but God made man a musical being. He fully equipped him with a heart and a voice and a mind all prepared for the most harmonious music. And this includes not only musical notes but also words, meanings, feelings, and expressions. Canaries, the winds, and the rain can make musical sounds; but the greatest music comes from God and his children. The Lord himself loves music and has great delight when we sing, and he wants us to have those important blessings that music can bring upon us. He has given us the ability to develop every other facet of our lives through the harmony, the rhythm, the inspiration, and the beauty of music.

It is thought that everyone desiring to be a successful businessman or an inspiring teacher or a good parent or a devoted Christian or any other variety of a great human being should have in his immediate possession some good books to sing from and to delight in.

44

The Man Without a Country

O N AUGUST 13, 1863, a reader of the *New York Herald* might have observed in an obscure corner among the obituaries the following notice: "Philip Nolan died on board the U.S. Corvette Levant on the 11th of May, 1863, buried at sea, latitude 2 degrees, 11 minutes South, longitude 131 degrees West." But the casual reader would have had no way of knowing the tragic life that was concluded by this solitary notice. Edward Everett Hale has thrilled us with his story of this life under the title of "The Man Without a Country." Certainly it contains an appropriate philosophy for our times.

Unfortunately for Philip Nolan, he had allowed his life to become entangled with that of Aaron Burr, who was a gifted and remarkable man. During the Revolutionary War Aaron Burr had served his country with loyalty and distinction. His pleasing manner and unusual ability gained friends for him wherever he went. But Aaron Burr also had an ambitious, jealous nature, which led him to challenge Alexander Hamilton to a duel in which Hamilton was killed. Hamilton disapproved of duels and is said to have fired his shot into the air. Everyone condemned Burr for his act, and he lost the popular favor in which he had previously been held.

In his bitterness, Aaron Burr had drawn away and conceived a plan to establish a new nation west of Mississippi River, with himself as emperor. He secretly went among some of the officers of the army to enlist their aid, leading them to believe that he had an army behind him and an empire ahead of him. In 1805 he met Philip Nolan, a fine young officer in the American army. Burr's talk fascinated young Nolan, and Burr enlisted him body and soul in his cause.

The conspiracy was put down by the government, but not before enough damage had been done to make necessary an important treason trial, which was held at Richmond. Philip Nolan was one of those involved with Burr in the court-martial. Nolan was guilty enough, but he was also confused, disillusioned, and sick at heart. He was acquitted and spent the rest of his life abroad. Nolan was caught in the trap of his own rashness, for when the president of the court asked Nolan if he had anything to say for himself that would indicate that he had been faithful to the United States, he was seized by a fit of frenzy and cried out, "Damn the United States! I wish I may never hear the name of the United States again."

The court was shocked. Colonel Morgan, who was presiding, called a council in his private chambers. In fifteen minutes he returned to the room, his face white as a sheet. He said, "Prisoner, hear the sentence of the court. Subject to the approval of the President it is the decision of the court that you shall never hear the name of the United States again."

Nolan laughed, but he was the only one who did. The whole room was hushed in a silence dead as night. Then Colonel Morgan said, "Marshall, you are instructed to take the prisoner to Orleans in an armed boat, and deliver him to the naval commander there. You are to see to it that no one ever again mentions the United States to the prisoner. You will receive written orders this evening. The court is adjourned."

From that moment until the day that Philip Nolan died on May 11, 1863, he never heard the name of his country spoken again. For fifty-five long and lonely years, he lived as "the man without a country."

He was put aboard an outgoing government vessel and was never permitted to come within a hundred miles of American territory. He was transferred over twenty times from one vessel to another. With each transfer, the official orders to the captain of the outgoing ship read as follows:

"You will receive into your custody the person of Philip Nolan, late lieutenant in the army of the United States. On trial by court-martial, he expressed with an oath, the wish that he might never hear of the United States again. He was sentenced to have his request fulfilled. The execution of this sentence is now entrusted to you. You will take the prisoner on board your ship and keep him there with such precautions as shall prevent his escape. You will provide him with such quarters, rations and clothing as would be proper for an officer of his late rank were he a passenger engaged in government business. You will make any arrangements agreeable to yourself regarding his society. He is to be exposed to no indignity of any kind nor is he ever to be unnecessarily reminded that he is a prisoner. He is to be confined only so far as to make certain that under no circumstances shall he ever again hear of his country or see any information regarding it. You are to specifically caution all officers under your command to take care that in the various indulgences which may be granted, this rule shall never be broken. It is the intention of the government that he shall never again see or hear of the country which he has betrayed and disowned. Signed Respectively yours, W. Southward, for the Secretary of the Navy."

Nolan was never permitted to talk with anyone unless an officer was present. All reading material was carefully censored. He chose to wear a regular army uniform but he was not permitted to wear the army button which bore the initials of the country that he had scorned. He had unrestrained association with the officers aboard as he and they might choose, providing only that all kept strictly within the limits of the sentence. Mostly he ate and drank in his cabin by himself. Including Nolan, all cooperated as best they could in this unusual situation.

Nolan was permitted to read foreign newspapers, but someone must go over them first and cut out any advertisements or stray paragraphs that alluded to America.

On one occasion the ship that carried "Plain Buttons," as he was often called, ran down a little schooner carrying a load of contraband slaves. Officer Vaughan was sent to take charge of the captured schooner and set the slaves free at some convenient location. The officer sent back to the ship for someone who could speak Portuguese. When no one else responded, Nolan said that he understood the language and he would be glad to interpret for the officer if the captain wished.

The conditions aboard the slave boat were horrible beyond imagination. Officer Vaughan had their handcuffs and anklecuffs taken off. He told Nolan to try to make the slaves understand that they were to be set free. When this information was made clear to them, the slaves began yelling with delight, leaping, dancing, and kissing Nolan's feet.

Officer Vaughan said, "Tell them that I will take them to Cape Palmas." With this news the slaves became dejected. Officer Vaughan inquired what the trouble was. Drops of sweat stood out on poor Nolan's white forehead, as he relayed their message. With trembling voice Nolan said, "They don't want to go to Cape Palmas, they say, 'Take us home; take us to our own country; take us to our own houses, and our own pickaninnies and our own women.' "

Then with an agony almost equal to that of Nolan's, Vaughan said, "Tell them yes, tell them that I shall take them to the Mountains of the Moon, if they wish. Tell them that even if I have to sail the schooner through the desert, they shall go home."

And after some fashion Nolan told them so. And again they fell to kissing his feet. However, Nolan could stand the strain no longer, and he asked Vaughan if he might be excused to go back to the ship. On the way Nolan said to the officer accompanying him, "Young man, let that show you what it means to be without a family, without a home, and without a country. If you are ever tempted to say a word or do a thing that shall put a bar between you and your family, your home, or your country, pray that God in his mercy will take you home to his own heaven that very instant. Stick by your family, boy. Forget you have a self, while you do everything for them. Think of your home, boy; write and send, and talk about it. Let it be nearer and nearer to your thought, the farther you have to travel from it. And when you are free, rush back to it as those poor black slaves are doing now. And fight for your country, boy"—and the words rattled in his throat—"and for that flag."

Then he pointed to the ship. "Never dream a dream but of serving her as she bids you, though the service carry you through a thousand hells. No matter what happens to you, no matter who flatters you or who abuses you, never look at another flag, never let a night pass but that you pray to God to bless that flag. Remember boy, that behind the men, behind the officers, the government, and even the people, there is the country itself, your country, and that you belong to her as you belong to your own mother. Stand by her, boy, as you would stand by your mother."

Then in a whisper, as if he were speaking only to himself, Nolan said, "Oh, if someone had said that to me when I was at your age."

Long ago Nolan had repented of his folly and had accepted the fate for which he himself had asked. He was nearly eighty

years of age when he died at sea. The first time the doctor entered
his stateroom, Nolan was lying in his berth, looking very frail.
He smiled pleasantly as he gave the doctor his hand. As the doctor
glanced around, he saw the shrine that Nolan had made of his
quarters. The stars and stripes were triced up above and around
a picture of George Washington, and Nolan had painted a majestic eagle with its wings overshadowing the entire globe. As the
doctor was taking in the scene before him, Nolan said, "Here, you
see I have a country after all." Then he pointed to a great map of
the United States that he had drawn from memory. He said,
"Doctor, I know that I am dying. I have no home to go to. Surely
you will tell me something about my country before I die." Seeing that the doctor was remembering the sentence, Nolan raised
his hand and said, "Stop! Don't speak till I have said what I am
sure you know, that there is not in this ship, that there is not in
America—God bless her!—a more loyal man than I. There cannot
be a man who loves the old flag as I do, or prays for it as I do, or
hopes for it as I do. It has thirty-four stars in it now. I thank God
for each one of them, though I do not know their names. I thank
God that there has never been one star taken away. I thank God
that there has never been a successful Aaron Burr. What a
wretched dream to look back upon after such a life as mine.

"But," said he, "tell me, tell me something, tell me everything before I die." Then his guest said, "I will tell you everything
you ask." Then a happy smile crept over Nolan's white face, and
he pressed the doctor's hand and said, "Tell me their names," and
he pointed to the stars in the flag. Then the doctor told him the
story of immigration and steamboats and railroads and telegraphs
and inventions and books and literature, of colleges and West
Point and the naval academy.

Philip Nolan was a Robinson Crusoe, hearing for the first
time the answers to his accumulated questions of over half a
century. He was told the story of Abe Lincoln and how he had
worked up through the ranks from a backwoods cabin. The tired
old man drank in every word with unbelievable enjoyment. He
said, "God bless Abraham Lincoln." Gradually Nolan grew more
and more tired and more silent. He was handed a glass of water,
but he merely wet his lips. Then he asked for the *Book of Public
Prayer,* which lay close by, and with a smile he instructed his
guest that it would open at the right place—and so it did, showing a double red mark running down the page; and the doctor

knelt down and read as they repeated together, "For ourselves and our country, oh gracious God we thank Thee, that notwithstanding our manifold transgressions of Thy Holy laws, thou has continued to us Thy marvelous kindness," and so on to the end of this psalm of thanksgiving.

Then together they repeated the more familiar words at the end of the book, saying, "Most heartily we beseech Thee with Thy favor to behold and bless Thy servant, the President of the United States, and all others in authority." Nolan said, "I have repeated those prayers night and morning, it is now fifty-five years." Then Nolan said he would like to go to sleep. He was happy now and wanted to spend his last moments as he had spent most of his life, alone. He drew the doctor down and kissed him and said, "Look in my Bible when I am gone."

An hour later when the doctor quietly stepped back into his room, he found that Nolan had breathed his life away with a smile. There was a slip of paper in the Bible on which Nolan had written his last request. It said:

"Bury me in the sea; it has been my home, and I love it. But won't someone set up a stone in my memory at Fort Adams or at Orleans, that my disgrace may not be more than I ought to bear? Say on it,

In Memory of
Philip Nolan
Lieutenant in the Army of the United States.
He loved his country as no other man ever loved her;
but no one deserved less at her hands.

May God bless us, that we may forever be loyal to that country to which we also owe our allegiance and our gratitude.

45

Little Journeys

THE ANCIENT Chinese had many very interesting customs. For example, if you had visited in one of their homes, and if you had let it be known that you greatly admired some particular article, you may have found that the Chinese would wrap that article up and send it to you as a present. You admired it, and in their eyes that made it yours.

We may think of this custom as being a little strange or unusual, and yet life has a custom that is almost identical to it. There is a fundamental law of attraction that says, whatever you truly love and desire, you get. That is, if you love honesty, you get honesty. If you love faith, you get faith. If you have a deep and abiding admiration for greater character qualities, life wraps them up and sends them to you free of charge. This is also the procedure by which we get our friends, our abilities, and our material possessions.

This means of acquiring valuable property reminds us of the Federal Homestead Act of 1862. The government wanted to get some of its public lands into the hands of the people. But before the homesteader could get title, he had to live on the land, and not until he had made certain improvements would the government put the land in his name.

We remember another application of this law used by King Midas, of the ancient Greek state of Phyrsia. Midas had an overwhelming love of gold, and the Grecian deity Dionysus believed with the ancient Chinese that that should give him title. He therefore granted the wish of Midas that everything he touched would turn into beautiful, sparkling, valuable yellow gold.

But anyone can have this gift, so that everything that he touches with his love and industry will turn into gold.

Elbert Hubbard made an interesting use of this important success principle. Following the Chinese custom, he visited the homes of many great men, not to admire their material possessions, but to admire the character traits that made them what they were. Important qualities of personality have much more value than mere material wealth. Personality can create wealth, but wealth cannot create personality; therefore, personality is greater than wealth. Midas got gold because he loved gold. That is the law. It is not only what you possess, but what you love, that makes you wealthy, just as it is what you love that makes you great. In fact, this old Chinese law works best in the field of personal greatness.

Mr. Hubbard picked out what he considered to be the ten best people in each of seventeen fields of activity. When he had assembled this company of 170 of the wisest and most successful people who had ever lived, then in the spirit of this Chinese custom he visited them one at a time. Some had been dead for many centuries. Some lived in foreign lands. But the effectiveness of this law is not limited to any nationality, religion, or time. In fact, the law works best at a little greater distance. That is, you may live on the same street or even in the same house with great men or women without ever really getting acquainted with them or profiting very much either by what they think or by what they are.

Jesus said, "A man is not without honor save in his own country."

The benefit received from the operation of this law does not even require one to make a personal visit to his prospective benefactor. That marvelous invention called the printing press makes the greatest men and women fully available to everyone in every part of the world. A book may contain in life-size proportions a man's innermost thoughts and feelings. In the great biographies every virtue may be found fully developed, and we may delve into this primal element of human personality to our heart's content. We may inspect the life of a particular man in his youth and then turn the calendar of his years ahead to his old age so as to understand the consequences as well as the deeds.

Through the lives of others we may experience poverty, sin, helplessness, despair, and even death under every imaginable circumstance. Or, we may turn events back to their beginnings and examine the antecedents that brought these particular conditions into being. By this process we may learn how to reset the state of our own lives so as to avoid the pitfalls in which others have been ensnared. From this interesting research in human lives we may identify and isolate those factors that bring about "the happy endings," where peace, prosperity, and joy predominate. We may research or presearch every department of human success and failure until we thoroughly understand the relationships of causes and effects.

We may lift up our eyes to the peaks of the most magnificent accomplishment. We may be thrilled by the greatest success. The love thus generated will serve as the roadway on which our own success may travel. Great literature gives us the ability to go backward or forward, across time or space, so that we can see at one glance the seed and the fruit, the motive and the result, all in their proper relationships to each other. We can learn to fashion our own lives in the light of the mistakes and successes of others.

Mr. Hubbard carried on this interesting study in human nature for fourteen years. During this period he lived 170 different lives. He put them under the microscope to discover what made them good or bad, successful or unsuccessful, loved or hated. He studied them from all angles; he weighed, sorted, and classified the facts. Best of all he made his research available to others in fourteen large volumes of miniature biographies called *Little Journeys into the Lives of Great Men.* As we study human life in all of its myriad forms, we will be attracted by certain qualities that we desire to have. If our admiration is real and our desire has great enough intensity, then life gives us a clear title to whatever our love touches.

The law never fails. All we need to do is to understand how to operate it effectively. For example, we do not fall in love with anyone or anything until we know something about them. If great lives are to be of value to us, we must put ourselves in harmony with them, so that love will have a chance. Great literature is our key to life's gold mine. But we must learn to command the shaft by which we draw out that gold.

Carlyle once said that the history of the world is written in the biographies of its great men. What has a greater value? What is it that makes the past important to us? Is it the land that people have occupied, is it their material goods, or is it the people themselves? Take away the people from any country and what would be left? Try to picture Egypt without Moses, or Babylon without Daniel. How would we measure the influence of

Greece without Demosthenes, Socrates, Plato, and other intellectual and moral giants of her golden age? What was Carthage without Hannibal, or Rome without Caesar? Think of France without Napoleon and Victor Hugo, or England without her great men. Try to imagine the United States without Washington, Lincoln, Edison, Henry Ford, and the Wright Brothers. What significance would ever attach to Nazareth without Jesus?

In this wonderful realm of thought and feeling, great men and women still hold an influence in the world that is more important than when they were actually living in it. This power also holds sway over our individual lives and makes the past the most dominant force in our future.

When Alexander the Great went to conquer the world, he left his living schoolmaster, Aristotle, behind him, but he took the works of dead Homer with him. It is said that Alexander developed more courage by reading Homer's account of the deeds of Achilles than by anything that Aristotle ever taught him about bravery or fortitude.

The study of biography is a sort of detective work by means of which we may shadow destiny itself. We may select from the most wonderful variety of virtues to suit our every need, but we may also have the association of the finest men and women who ever lived, and we may have them on our own terms without the necessity of waiting weary hours in outer offices for the mere chance of snatching one hasty, unsatisfactory interview. We may come to know the best men in any field better than their contemporaries knew them, better than we know our own intimates, and, unless we are masters of self-scrutiny, better even than we know ourselves.

The study of biography is also one of the most delightful forms of enjoyment. Real men and women are far more interesting than the greatest characters of fiction. Of all the myriad novelists writing for a thousand years, no one has ever created one character comparable to Abraham Lincoln or as fabulous as J. P. Morgan.

Through the use of biography we may have the facts, motives, ambitions, and accomplishments of men laid out in endless exhibit before us. We may know things about them that even their closest friends did not suspect. We also have the judgment of time shining upon their acts so that we can value their deeds in

the light of the consequences. We know the end from the beginning and the beginning from the end. We study with the advantages of foresight and hindsight. We have the evidence and the
proof, the act and the consequences, the motives and the deeds
placed side by side. At one glance we can see the acorn and the
oak, the seed and the fruit. A great man from the past can frequently do more to stimulate our thoughts and arouse our ambitions than he could have done in person. From his biography
we can get the spirit of his success plus the principles and
methods by which it was brought about.

Ideas and personality traits are born of parents, just as is
anything else. And when we get on the right basis with the right
kind of great men, we soon feel a new life stirring within us. New
ambitions are born, new aspirations are aroused, and new personality qualities are developed. Life will give us title to any quality
that we can identify, providing only that we love it sufficiently.

Who can estimate the tremendous human uplift that has
come to people from reading the lives of the great prophets? The
scriptures have been called "God's Who's Who." They describe
the thoughts and the deeds, as well as picture the personality
traits of those who are important to God. What a thrilling possibility is contained in the biographies of the holy scriptures, the
constructive use of which reaches its highest pinnacle in the life
of Christ. Millions of lives have been completely changed by living with his example, absorbing his faith, and loving his righteousness. In the conquest that we are all conducting for our own
personal success and happiness, we can count a tremendous ally
in the habit of making some little journeys of our own into the
homes of the great men who live in the pages of the holy scripture.

Isn't it interesting that even the great Simon Peter didn't
find the Master on his own power? Andrew, the brother of Peter,
and one of his friends first heard the testimony of John the Baptist regarding Jesus. Then they saw Jesus going down the path
and ran after him. When they had overtaken him they said,
"Where dwellest thou?" Jesus said, "Come and see." The scripture
says, "They came and saw where he dwelt, and abode with him
that day. . . ." That is, Andrew and his companion made a journey
to the abode of Jesus. Then after they were satisfied that Jesus
was divine, the record makes this significant statement: "[An-
drew] findeth his own brother Simon, and saith unto him, We

have found the Messias . . . and he [Andrew] brought him to Jesus." (See John 1:38-42.) These humble men became apostles of the Lord because of one "little journey" into the presence of a great man. Jesus has never withdrawn his invitation. He is still saying, "Come and see." And in accepting the invitation we may avail ourselves of the greatest blessings in the world.

Suppose, therefore, that we organize ourselves for our own little journeys into the lives of the great; and in the process we should remember that whatsoever we really love and admire, life wraps it up and sends it to us free of charge.

46

The Greatest Use of Life

S OME TIME ago I heard a prominent real estate man talking about his business. He has listings on many pieces of real estate, and he analyzes the situations surrounding each one and tries to determine what its most profitable and productive use may be.

It is interesting that various tracts of land are not all equally suited for the same use. One area may be particularly adapted as a residential area. Because of its location and other conditions, another place could be best used as a shopping center. Another can be best used as a site for a skyscraper or a manufacturing plant. This may not be the same kind of land that could be best used for the runway of an airport. Some pieces of land may find their highest utility as an agricultural area, or they may best serve as a cattle ranch. There are two or three sections in the United States that have become famous for growing potatoes. It takes a particular kind of land area to serve as an irrigation reservoir. Some intensive commercial possibilities may make the land sell for a higher price than if the land were used to produce the beauty of some flower gardens. And so this great real estate man does a lot of thinking and dreaming and planning as to how he can get the most valuable utilization of all of this land by using every inch of it so as to bring about its maximum potentiality. A mountain side that would not be very practical for the center of a great city may serve admirably as a ski slope.

In doing some of his own land planning, God has separated some of his important land areas by great oceans. He put the Rocky Mountains in one place and the Mississippi River valley in another. Some people travel long distances in the winter to slide down mountain slopes on skis, and many mountain climbers will go a long way to scale the Tetons or the Matterhorn.

Mountains have also been used to inspire people by their majesty and beauty. God came down to the top of Mount Sinai in a cloud of fire to give the people the important substance contained in the Ten Commandments. Jesus often went to the mountains. The greatest discourse that has ever been given was the Sermon on the Mount. Jesus was trransfigured with Moses and Elias on a high mountain and appeared in shining garments before Peter, James, and John. And the resurrected Jesus ascended unto his Father in heaven from the top of the Mount of Olives.

God did some very important land planning as he covered our earth with this miraculous layer of top soil—looking forward to our great agricultural, horticultural, and livestock industries. Then he laid out the terrain to provide areas for great irrigation reservoirs. He laid out the oceans in such a way that they could accommodate a vast aquatic life. He gave wings to a large segment of his creation so that they might utilize the air, the atmosphere, and the treetops to their best advantage.

Then God formed man himself out of the dust of the ground and breathed into his nostrils the breath of life, and man became a living soul. By this process of human creation he brought about an even more important problem by making it necessary for us to do some planning of our lives. The most valuable thing there is in the world is human life, and Jesus indicated that the worth of one human soul may be greater than the wealth of all of the earth. With all of life's possibilities before us, God said, "Thou mayest choose for thyself." This makes our primary life occupation far more important than that of the land planner, as we must lay out the detail providing for the greatest possibility of ourselves.

Someone has said that planning is the place where man shows himself most like God. It might be pretty difficult to think of something more God-like than the planner. He is the thinker, the organizer, the dreamer. He is the one who draws the blueprint for life and builds the roadway on which every success will travel. And how we plan our lives determines almost every other worthwhile thing in the world. Sam Walter Foss said,

> Bring me men to match my mountains,
> Bring me men to match my plains,
> Men with empires in their purpose,
> And new eras in their brains."
> —"The Coming American

Some well-planned and well-directed lives may be like the giant Tetons, while other lives following the path of least resistance may end up as swampland, as a breeding place for yellow fever and malaria. Some have been called mountaintop men. They live at their best. Their lives reach the highest use of which they are capable. It may be that of a Moses to give the Ten Commandments, or a Thomas A. Edison to light our world, or a great poet to inspire our minds with music, or a Henry Ford to give us transportation.

William James, the great Harvard psychologist, once said that the greatest use of life is to spend it for something that outlasts it. Temporary benefits are sometimes not very important. The author of *The Rosary* referred to "an intense love that was not maintained as a barren gain and a bitter loss." And sometimes instead of engaging in those mountaintop employments of great value, we spend our time in digging a pit and then falling therein, so that our temporary joy may become a permanent and bitter loss. And we would need to qualify Mr. James a little bit because of the many things that outlast life. Some of them are evil. The scripture speaks of eternal damnation and eternal misery and everlasting suffering and outer darkness with weeping, wailing, and gnashing of teeth.

Many years ago, I had the privilege of helping to build a church to be the center of spiritual learning, where people came to uplift and inspire each other. This is a place where ideals could be formed and where lives could be changed in righteousness. Many of those who helped to build this church have already passed away, but their work continues. Somebody has put this idea into verse. He said:

> The work that you have builded oft with
>   bleeding hands and tears
> And in error and in anguish will not perish
>   with your years.
> It will last and stand transfigured 'till the
>   final reign of right
> And will merge into the splendors of the city
>   of the light.

That is, this church house may actually continue until the millennium. And in the process, it will uplift the lives of countless people, many of whom will be the posterity of the original builders.

We sing a song in which we say:

This house we dedicate to thee,
Our God, our father's God.
Wilt thou accept and deign to bless
The path our feet have trod?

Wilt thou thy servants here inspire
When in thy name they speak?
And wilt thou bless each contrite soul,
Who here thy face doth seek?

Here may our sons and daughters come
And find that peace which swells
From grateful hearts, when touched by thee
Wherein thy Spirit dwells!

And may pollution ne'er have place
Within this shrine we give;
And in it through the years to come,
Awake the dead to live;

Live to thy kingdom; live to thee
While time shall pass away;
Then greet again with praise and song,
In heaven's eternal day.

It is another of the great uses of life to organize a family and exercise this great power of procreation where it is possible for us to beget children in God's own image, and through this miraculous power help to endow them with God's attributes and potentialities. Then we can help them to develop characters sufficiently strong to withstand the pressures of life. Then we can share with them the great treasures of the gospel and build integrity and righteousness and eternal life into them which will extend far beyond the boundaries of mortality.

Those conditions of life which have attached an "until death do you part" clause may not have equal value with those that reach beyond the boundaries of life. Harry Emerson Fosdick has said that if the death of the body forever ends all there is of human life and personality, then the universe would be throwing away with utter heedlessness its most precious possession. A reasonable person does not build a violin with infinite care, gathering the materials and shaping the body of it so that it can play the composition of the masters, and then by some whim of chance caprice smash it to bits. Neither does God, the great architect of life, create this wonderful masterpiece of flesh and bones, brain and spirit, personality and vision, which we call a human being, and then when it has just begun to live, throw it utterly away. Human life was built for eternity, and it was intended that the volume of our lives should increase as we go along.

We might think of the progress a man makes within the narrow limits of this life. We regard him as he lies in the lap of his mother, a newborn babe. He has eyes to see but cannot discern objects. He has ears to hear but cannot distinguish sound. He has legs that are unable to bear the weight of his body, much less walk, and yet within the span of one short life, what a change may be wrought! From such a one may come one likened to Demosthenes or Cicero or Pitt or Burke or Fox or Webster, who shall compel listening senates to hear him and by his master mind dominate their intelligence and their will and force them to walk in channels that he shall mark out for them. Remove from his path the incident of death, or better yet, contemplate him as raised from the dead and give to him in the full splendor of manhood's estate immortality and eternal existence. What may we not hope that he may accomplish?

Grant immortality to man and God for his guide—what is there in the way of moral, spiritual, or intellectual accomplishment that he may not aspire to? If in the span of one short life men may rise up out of infancy to become the masters of the elements of fire and water and earth and air so that they well nigh rule them as gods, what may they not expect to accomplish in a few hundreds, or thousands, or millions of years? To what heights of power and glory may they not ascend? Jesus tried to project the possible future of some of the Pharisees living in his day by saying to them, "Ye are gods, and all of you are children of the most High," and they accused him of blasphemy.

Alexander Pope said, "Seeing we are here but for a day's abode, we must look elsewhere for an eternal resting place where eternity is a measure, felicity the state, angels are the company, the land is the light, and God is a portion and inheritance."

The greatest use of life is not to become drug addicts or failures or ne'er-do-wells. God did not create this great earth with all of its laws and opportunities without having some important destiny in mind for those who would be permitted to live here upon it, and he did not endow us with these magnificent brains and give us these miraculous personalities and then expect us to waste our lives in failure. The greatest use of life is not to corrupt the morals of other people or to lead ourselves along that broad way that leads to eternal death. It is not to give our wives nervous breakdowns or seduce our friends or lead our children astray.

The greatest use of life is for us to fill the measure of our creation, that the offspring of God may sometime hope to become like their eternal heavenly parents. And so we spend our lives as we look forward to those great experiences that will outlast it. The poet said,

> Beyond the sunset, O blissful morning,
> When with our Savior heaven has begun.
> Earth's toiling ended, O glorious dawning,
> Beyond the sunset when day is done.
>
> Beyond the sunset no clouds will gather,
> No storms will threaten, no fears annoy.
> O day of gladness, O day unending,
> Beyond the sunset, eternal joy.
>
> Beyond the sunset, O glad reunion
> With our dear loved ones who've gone before,
> In that bright homeland we'll know no parting
> Beyond the sunset forevermore.

And so we come back again to that important idea that the greatest use of life is to spend it for something that outlasts it, to build up our families, make our wives happy, inspire our friends, and help us all to become even as God is.

47

Poetry

SOME OF life's greatest pleasures and many of its most important meanings come from language. It would be difficult to visualize our lives or imagine our satisfactions without the ability to express ourselves. Language takes several forms, and it may be written, spoken, heard, or thought. Included in our language we have all kinds of persuasion, conversation, debate, religious discussion, and political declarations. Then there is an extra-special kind of language that we call "poetry." Poetry has a little more elegance and a little greater punch than ordinary language.

Someone has said that "poetry is language dressed up in its best clothes." It is one form of speech that is a little more refined. It has a little more spirit, a little more music, and a little more beauty than regular forms of literature. Poetry can sometimes say more and say it with greater effectiveness. It adds perception to life, widens our horizons, sharpens our spiritual contacts, elevates our spirits, raises the temperature of our enthusiasms, and increases the joy content of our experiences.

Poetry fills some important inspirational and emotional needs and helps us to live more fully with a greater awareness of life's values. It provides a motivation that enables us to get greater performance from ourselves. The poet assembles from many sources what has been felt, observed, learned, or imagined. Then he selects, combines, reorganizes, and refines them in such a way that he may create some brand new experiences that appropriately stimulate and satisfy us. A poet may develop a greater insight so that he can pass on to us a better understanding of our world and a finer appreciation of its people. Charles Elliott Norton has recommended that whatever our occupation may be and however crowded with affairs our hours are, we should not fail to spend a few minutes each day in refreshing our inner lives with a bit of poetry.

Ezra Pound defined great literature as that language which has been charged with meaning to the utmost possible degree.

This definition might also serve as a good description of our poetry. We may enjoy the refined thoughts of others without investing the time or becoming involved in the expense or risk that we would need to put into our actual experience.

Someone has said that every day we ought to think a good thought, read a great poem, listen to some inspiring music, absorb a great scripture, and do a noble act. We have a daily need for something to encourage us, raise our sights, wind up our faith, and fill our ambitions with power. And it has been pointed out that in their ability to upgrade our lives, the poets stand next to the prophets.

Walt Whitman points out that "to have great poets, we must also have great audiences." He says that the Greeks were great during their golden age because their audiences yearned for poetry. Certainly every inspired book needs an inspired reader. In our day we have such a great collection of fine poetry, and from these poems we may select the inspiration and imagination about our most exalted human concepts and the high ideals of life as they are presented in their most beautiful forms.

Anciently one who was thought to be worthy of bearing the laurel or wearing the crown of the muse of poetry was given the title of poet laureate. Later this title was used to honor other eminent poets. It has also been conferred by some universities on poets of noted ability. In England, an outstanding poet was appointed by the sovereign to be a member of the royal household, and his duty as poet laureate of England was to compose odes and poems for national occasions and for the inspiration of members of the court.

A poet is not bound to write poems only about those things that have actually happened. He is free to exercise his imagination over the entire range of his emotional powers so as to touch all of the fundamental principles of truth. This may include all of the useful truth that has been expressed in fables, parables, history, or fantasy. And by the integrity of his treatment, the details of all of these fundamental avenues of truth are made available to us in dynamic form to uplift us by their strength and beauty. Someone once said that the poetry of Coleridge is the blossom and fragrance of the greatest human thoughts and passions translated into the language of the emotions.

The values in great ideas may be more easily incorporated in our ambitions when they are dressed in beautiful, rhythmical, poetical language. Great poetry is characterized by harmony and by those emotional qualities that appeal to the feelings and stimulate the imagination. Wordsworth spoke of the vocal raptures of poetry. Keats said, "I will fly to thee on the wings of poetry." John Milton said, "He who would do laudable things ought to be a true poem in himself." Every life is supplied with a poetic vein, but we must learn to command the shaft by which the gold is withdrawn. Of course, many of the most excellent poets have never versified. But everyone should develop those qualities of harmony, expressiveness, artistry, and an ability to elevate the spirit that is said to belong to poetry. Even by reading and memorizing poetry we may train ourselves to feel extra beauty, develop more music in our hearts, and acquire the spirit of a more effective expression. When we feel the harmony and music of poetry, we can improve our lives and make these extra virtues a permanent part of us.

Of course, great prose too can step up the intensity of our reactions and increase the range of our vicarious experiences. In its various forms, our language is almost all-important to our success. It can help in clarifying life's meanings and give our emotions greater power.

Language is the instrument of persuasion; it is the chief ingredient in all kinds of advertisements, propaganda, bulletins, sermons, and political declarations. But that special language called "poetry" can also be used as a kind of sugar-coated, nice-tasting pill by which some wholesome truths can often be made more palatable. Language, like people, affects us more powerfully when dressed up in a significant attire that is pretty and colorful. Like other forms of literature, poetry has an interest in every kind of human experience, whether it is beautiful or ugly, strange or common, noble or ignoble, actual or imaginary. And when such ideas are artfully transmitted, the various uplifting ideas can be made to serve our best interests more effectively.

Even such experiences as sickness, death, pain, and suffering, which in real life may be unpleasant, can be made to seem both pleasurable and profitable through fine poetic thoughts. In real life, getting soaked in a rainstorm may not be very pleasant, but in poetry it can become a happy occasion. Sometimes when we cry in actual life, it means that we are unhappy, but many people cry while reading a great poem as a manifestation of their joy. Ordinarily, we don't like to be frightened in real life, whereas sometimes we go to the movies or read a book with that very purpose in mind. Even righteous wars can give us joy when we read about them in elevated language afterward. We sometimes go to a great lecture to receive a challenge that we are unable to give ourselves.

Sometimes when we are dull, bored, unperceptive, and lifeless, we can be made responsive and brought back to life by the music and driving power of a great poem. Poetry may help us to focus our attention and organize our experience in such a way as to get greater understanding and produce more satisfactions.

To understand success is one of the first steps toward attaining it. Here again, poetry can be helpful as the most condensed and concentrated form of literature. Poetry can usually say the most in the fewest number of words. Elevated thoughts cannot be adequately expressed in degraded language. One may read poetry while lying in a hammock sipping a cool drink, while low music is playing in the background. But while engaged with great ideas, his mind should never assume that attitude. Poetry may soothe and relax, but its primary function is to arouse and awaken.

Sometimes an idea can be used to shock us into activity. Poetry might serve as a substitute for a sedative, but it fills a greater need while maintaining us in a state of animation. Poetry is the language of love. And to get the greatest amount of good out of poetry, one should fall in love with love's spirit and language. Then everything around him seems more beautiful and worthwhile. Then even the most trivial things can seem of great consequence.

When one person loves another person, the importance of the beloved is greatly increased in the mind of the lover. Great truths and great ideals also are magnified by feelings of love. Poetry has a greater power to move us because it is able to make the maximum use of the music and emotion of language. A good poet chooses his words for their sound, their meter, their cadence, and their music to reinforce their meaning.

Edgar Allan Poe describes poetry as music combined with a pleasurable idea. Some people may disagree on the amount of attention poetry deserves, but certainly our success can be helped by getting a love of rhythm and the beauty of meter more deeply rooted in us. Rhythm is related to the beat of our hearts, the pulsations of our blood, the intake and outgo of air in our lungs. Everything that we do naturally and gracefully, we do rhythmically. There is a rhythm in the way we swim, the way we ride a horse, the way we swing a golf club or use a baseball bat. The term rhythm refers to any wave-like recurrence of motion or sound. In speech it is the natural rise and fall of language. All language is to some degree rhythmical, for all language involves some kind of alternation between accented and unaccented syllables. We need some kind of rhythm in our lives that we can tap our foot to, so to speak.

In every word or more than one syllable, one syllable is accented or stressed by giving it more prominence in pronunciation than the others. The word *meter* means measure. The rhythm and the sound of language can be harmonized to produce the music of poetry. Not only is this music enjoyable in itself, but it also reinforces meaning and intensifies our finest communications.

Poetry engages the responses of the whole man in his senses, his imaginations, his intellectual powers. It does not merely touch him on the side of his nature. The mission of great poetry is not merely to entertain its devotees, but to inspire more measure and help them reach greater accomplishments. With great poetry, we can get some fresh insights and a renewal of life itself into our human experience, and a person can develop a broader and a deeper understanding of his fellowmen as well as of himself by the music that good poetry can put into his soul. A study of poetry delights our hearts, ornaments our lives, supplies us with information, and increases our success ability.

48

Lives

Oof the world goes under the title
NE OF the most influential books
of *Plutarch's Lives.* Plutarch was a great Greek moralist and biographer who lived for seventy-five years beginning in A.D. 45. He studied in Athens, visited Egypt, and spent some time in ancient Rome. He made his greatest contribution to the world by writing the biographies of famous Greeks and Romans. He said, "My method is to study their history, and by the familiarity thus acquired, to habituate my memory to receive and retain images of all that is best and worthiest in their characters." He said, "To write their lives is like actually living and associating with them." We also may receive them into our minds as our guests. We may entertain and be entertained by each in turn. And as we view their statures and judge their good qualities, we may select that which is most noble from each.

Plutarch said that he first commenced writing biographies for the good of others, but he continued to write them for his own sake. He said, "The virtues of a great man serve as a sort of looking glass in which I may see how to adjust and adorn my own life. I am thus able to free myself from any ignoble, base, or vicious traits. And what greater pleasure can one have?" And we might echo his exclamation and ask, what indeed? There is nothing so important as life, and Plutarch devoted himself to the study of that mysterious human element out of which all of our lives are fashioned.

Of course, the very heart of success centers in the individual himself, and it is of primary importance to us that we know as much as possible about the basic elements from which our lives are made up. Plutarch had some ideas and procedures to which we might very profitably give the most serious consideration.

There is in modern medicine a very interesting practice known as vivisection. This is the act of cutting into the tissues of a living animal in order to study the workings of its vital organs. Vivisection is not for the purpose of killing the animal; it merely provides the education by which the doctor hopes to keep others alive. From the practice of vivisection the investigator is able to learn how life works, and where it may go wrong, or how it may be improved.

Plutarch was a kind of vivisectionist. He cut into the experiences, attitudes, and personality traits of men to find out what makes them great and good, wise and successful. And as a good doctor can learn medicine by comparing diseased and healthy bodies, so we can promote our success in life by a kind of laboratory comparison of the similarities and differences in human lives.

In a long series of studies Plutarch compared the lives of noble Greeks and Romans. He wrote up his findings in some interesting biographies that he called *Parallel Lives*. For example, he wrote up the life of Theseus, who settled Athens, and then set him side by side with Romulus, the founder of Rome. He studied Lycurgus, Solon, Pericles, Cato, Pompey, Tiberius, Demosthenes, Cicero, Demetrius, Antony, and dozens of other great Greeks and Romans. Then he compared them with each other. He appraised their virtues, weighed their faults, and, fully labeled, he placed them all on public display. He did some interesting personality vivisections that others might also learn "how to adjust and adorn their own lives." Sometimes seeing a wrong in the life of someone else teaches us how to prevent it from occurring in us.

On the other hand, the greatest influence in the world is the power of a good example. We need better working models for our lives to go by. Byron hurried across Europe searching for an ideal to adore. When we see man at his noblest, we are able to appropriate the very essence of his courage and faith to produce a sublime effect in our lives. As a usual thing, those who enshrine no ideals experience no growth.

What a glorious gallery of stimulating pictures we have in the biographies of great human beings! Your library can be a wonderful storehouse where hundreds of the great of all time are looking down upon you, awaiting your command. We may lift up our eyes to the peaks of their accomplishment and get from them the ability to draw ourselves upward. These great men have all undergone the test of time. We do not have to accept their acts without knowing the consequences in advance. It also helps us to understand our own lives better when we see our human characteristics in operation in others. The fine distinctions in values that are so difficult to make in ourselves are easily recognized when we study them in other people. Once the solution has been worked out, we can more easily apply the principle to ourselves.

Biographies are the histories of individual lives, considered as a branch of literature, the delights of which are among the most pleasant and profitable of all human intercourse. No entertainment is as cheap as reading, nor is there any pleasure as lasting. Have you ever had the experience of lingering in front of a house at night where the lights are lit and the blinds undrawn? Each floor of the house shows us a different section of human life and being, and we wonder who and what they are. What are their names? their occupations? their thoughts and abilities? And then some enterprising biographer searches out the answers to every question and every ambition. He lights up their lives as the electricity lights up the houses in which they live. Then we see them going about their daily affairs, toiling, failing, succeeding, hating, and loving until they die.

Our own futures can be greatly enriched by the poetry, music, art, and history that show themselves in other lives. Through the stimulation that can come by the study of biography, we can learn not only about the surface of life, but we can also study it in depth and breadth as well. We may get valuable knowledge and vicarious experiences from those who have soared the highest as well as from those who have dived furthest into life's depths. At the closest range we are able to scrutinize both failures and successes, both good and bad. We can learn as much from the villain as from the hero. One teaches us the quicksands to be shunned; the other holds up the goals to be attained.

Sometimes we can learn faster from the experiences of others than from our own. Because of troublesome blind spots where we ourselves are concerned, our progress may be extremely limited when we have no other model to go by but ourselves. Isn't it interesting that the thing that we know less about than anything else in the world is our own individual selves. We don't know very much about where we came from or what the purpose of our life is. We do not know very much about our eternal destiny. We did not even discover the circulation of our own blood until about 300 years ago. We are familiar with the prevailing winds and the currents of the ocean. We are not so familiar with those powerful influences moving in our own lives. Twenty-five hundred years ago Socrates said, "Know thyself." Confucius said, "To understand yourself is the key of wisdom." And we can usually understand ourselves best when we see ourselves reflected in others without the hindrance of our personal prejudice or the distorted vision of self-interest.

What wonders are available to us in books where the wisest men from every land look down from library shelves waiting patiently to answer our questions and enrich us with their wisdom. During their lifetimes these men were inaccessible and impatient of interrogation. But the thoughts that they did not uncover to their bosom friends are here fully written out for us, the strangers of another age.

It has been said that "books are embalmed minds." In a good book we may have the very essence of a good man, where his virtues are spotlighted and his faults are forgotten. "Through the great literature we can feel the fascination of moving to and fro over the vast reaches of time, as imperially as the astronomer moves through space. Such flights are exhilarating. They involve us in no peril, they attach to us no responsibility. They begin and end by our own fireside at our own convenience."

These hours should be greatly expanded in most of our lives. As we do this important research, we become experts in the responses of the human heart, whether they are Greek or Hebrew, Babylonian or English. "Biography abounds in religion, pathos, sympathy, and loving kindness. It contains a portrait of man's innermost feelings. It shows the beauty and wisdom of God attempting to reappear in the lives of men." Here we have a gallery of spiritual ideas in which we may meet Socrates, Moses, Shakespeare, and Mahatma Gandhi. We may even meet Christ himself. We may go with them as on some sacred mountaintop of life to be transfigured, as it were, and spend some wonderful hours dressed in the shining garments of the mind.

Because of the unique terms that exist between author and reader, we are able to associate with sinners no less than with saints, and to receive a helpful contribution from each. We are all curious to learn how men subject to our passions, contradictions, and disabilities have succeeded or failed in this great experience called life. Having entered the realm inhabited by those who live to us through the magic of biography, we soon meet friends for whom we have sought in vain among our actual living associates.

Access to these great leaders in the flesh would have been impossible, but through their biographies the most humble among us may have an absolute freedom of selection from a limitless variety that no one could have enjoyed among the living.

We can research the life of Napoleon or Bismarck or Lincoln. We can relive the experience of Booker T. Washington in his biography entitled *Up from Slavery.* Then we may transfer our mental residence to the palace of Queen Victoria and live again in *Leaves from a Journal.* We can know the pathos and paradox of human passion involved in the fearful agony of Faust's final doom, and share his despair as he waits for the midnight bell which is to be the signal of his eternal destruction.

In his *Hearts of Men,* H. Fielding said, "I would have you go and kneel beside the Mohammedan as he prays at the sunset hour and put your heart in tune with his and wait for the echo that will surely come. Unenviable is he whose heart ne'er ran over with silent admiration for the great of old. Those dead but sceptered sovereigns who still rule our spirits from their urns. They pass to us across the sea of time, their most cherished ideals and ambitions, and no matter what the cares or torments of your day may have been, at evening you can enter this magic city, forget the present, and follow in imagination those careers that closed in time so long ago, yet still live on with undimmed lustre on the timeless domain of the imagination. And during all of this delightful exploration, you can be learning more and more about human nature, that mysterious, primal element in which you yourself have your being." We can learn what a precious privilege it is to live, to understand, to think, to feel, to be, to love, and to enjoy.

It has been amply demonstrated that everything we hear, everything we read, everything we feel, every sermon, and every ambition leaves an impression upon our lives so that we are never quite the same thereafter. In our own right, we can live only once, but through others we may live a thousand lives and become expert architects in building our own eternal existence. With Plutarch, we may borrow from others all that is noblest and most worthy. "He is a rich man who can avail himself of all men's faculties and draw benefits from the labors of men in distant countries and in times past." By this process we may become citizens of what has been called the "celestial city of fine souls."

Think of the unlimited treasures available to us in the holy scriptures. Here we can live with the great prophets, memorize their philosophy, and even absorb the spirit made available to us through the words of God himself. There is a sacred song that says, "I walked today where Jesus walked." And wouldn't it be a thrilling experience to go and stand on the very spot of ground where Jesus stood, while we undertook to capture the spirit of his life. And while it may not be practical to walk today where Jesus walked, there is something much more important that we can do, and that is, we can think today what Jesus thought. We can fill our minds and actuate our lives with the very attitudes that made him the Master of men. We are all aware of the fact that Jesus died for us. We are not so conscious that he lived for us also, that he is our example, that by reliving this life we can transfer his thought and motivations for our own success.

"He who merely knows right principles is not equal to him who loves them." May we love the good and be effectively moved by the great powers placed in our hands by the magic of biography.

So, thrice—fair lady, stand I, even so;
As doubtful whether what I see be true,
Until confirm'd, sign'd, ratified by you.

Then, in an inspiring reply, Portia said:

You see me, Lord Bassanio, where I stand,
Such as I am: though for myself alone
I would not be ambitious in my wish,
To wish myself much better; yet, for you
I would be trebled twenty times myself;
A thousand times more fair, ten thousand times
More rich;
That only to stand high in your account,
I might in virtues, beauties, livings, friends,
Exceed account. . . .

—Act III, scene 2

Portia was a beautiful, wealthy young woman of great character. And yet for Bassanio she wished herself to be a thousand times better even than she was. This would be a great philosophy for all married people to absorb and use. However, their joy did not last very long, for just as Bassanio and Portia were about to make the plans for their marriage, a letter came from Antonio telling Bassanio that by some mysterious tragedy, all of his ships had been lost at sea. The great Merchant of Venice was now a ruined man. And he wrote to tell Bassanio that he would count it a great favor if Bassanio would come to see him before he died.

Shylock had made it clear to everyone that he intended to go the limit in collecting the forfeit. Many futile efforts to intercede had already been made by Antonio's friends and fellow merchants. The Duke himself had tried to dissuade Shylock from his purpose by paying many times the amount of the loan, but all settlements had been refused by Shylock.

Then Portia said to her betrothed Bassanio, "First go with me to church and call me wife,/ And then away to Venice to your friend." When Portia was told that the amount of the loan was only three thousand ducats, she said, "What, no more? Pay him six thousand, and deface the bond;/ Double six thousand, and then treble that,/ Before a friend of this description/ Shall lose a hair through Bassanio's fault." She said, "For never shall you lie by Portia's side/ With an unquiet soul." She then put all of her resources at Bessanio's command and said, "When [the debt] is paid, bring your true friend with you along."

After their hurried marriage, Bassanio set out immediately to do what he could for his friend. But Portia also wanted to help. She was not only very beautiful and very wealthy, but she was also very resourceful. She had a relative by the name of Bellario, who was a famous lawyer to whom the Duke had appealed for help in settling this difficult contest between Shylock and Antonio. Everyone wanted Antonio released, but Shylock insisted on the bond, which gave him the right to put Antonio to death. This was a difficult case for the court, for if it disregarded the law and set aside any legal agreement, then the great merchants who traded in Venice would scorn Venetian laws and laugh at Venetian courts.

As the time came for the trial, the Duke convened the court, and they were waiting for Judge Bellario to arrive. But instead, Portia and her companion Nerissa came in his place. These young women were both disguised as men, and Portia brought a letter from Bellario introducing her as a learned young doctor from Rome by the name of Balthasar, and Nerissa was his clerk. In his letter, Bellario regretted the fact that he was ill and unable to come, but he highly recommended young Balthasar, whom he had appointed to come in his place.

The disguised Portia was enthusiastically accepted as the judge. The court was called to order, and Portia made it clear that she was thoroughly informed on the issues. Then Portia said to Shylock, "Of a strange nature is the suit you follow;/ Yet in such rule that the Venetian law/Cannot impugn you as you do proceed." She said to Antonio, "Do you confess the bond?" He said, "I do." Portia said, "Then must the Jew be merciful." Shylock replied, "On what compulsion must I? tell me that." Then Portia gave an inspiring speech on the importance of mercy, and Shakespeare always puts enough music, logic, and poetry in his thoughts to give them greater meaning. Portia said:

> The quality of mercy is not strain'd,
> It droppeth as the gentle rain from heaven
> Upon the place beneath: it is twice blest;
> It blesseth him that gives, and him that takes:
> 'Tis mightiest in the mightiest: it becomes
> The throned monarch better than his crown;
> His sceptre shows the force of temporal power,
> The attribute to awe and majesty,
> Wherein doth sit the dread and fear of kings;

> But mercy is above this sceptred sway;
> It is enthroned in the hearts of kings,
> It is an attribute to God himself;
> And earthly power doth then show likest God's
> When mercy seasons justice. Therefore, Jew,
> Though justice be thy plea, consider this,
> That, in the course of justice, none of us
> Should see salvation: we do pray for mercy;
> And that same prayer doth teach us all to render
> The deeds of mercy. I have spoke thus much
> To mitigate the justice of thy plea;
> Which if thou follow, this strict court of Venice
> Must needs give sentence 'gainst the merchant there.

Shylock said: "My deeds upon my head! I crave the law,/ The penalty and forfeit of my bond." He was reminded that the money was available in amount many times that of the debt. But he insisted on his bond, and Portia insisted that the law of Venice must not fail. She said:

> It must not be; there is no power in Venice
> Can alter a decree established:
> 'Twill be recorded for a precedent,
> And many an error, by that same example,
> Will rush into the state: it cannot be.

Shylock was so pleased with the wisdom of this young lawyer that he said, "A Daniel come to judgment! . . ./ O wise young judge, how I do honour thee!"

Portia said, "I pray you, let me look upon the bond."

Shylock replied, "Here 'tis, most reverend doctor, here it is."

After examining it, Portia announced that the bond must be paid, and she bid Antonio to bare his breast so that the forfeit could be collected. Portia then said to Shylock: "A pound of that same merchant's flesh is thine:/ The court awards it, and the law doth give it."

Shylock was very eager to begin the operation. He had his scales and equipment ready. But Portia said,

> Tarry a little; there is something else.
> This bond doth give thee here no jot of blood;
> The words expressly say 'a pound of flesh:'
> Take then thy bond, . . .
> But, in the cutting it, if thou dost shed

> One drop of Christian blood, thy lands and goods
> Are, by the laws of Venice, confiscate
> Unto the state of Venice.
> . . . nor cut thou less nor more
> But just a pound of flesh: if thou cut'st more
> Or less . . . of the twentieth part . . .
> Thou diest and all thy goods are confiscate.

This put a little different light on the subject for Shylock, and he then decided that he would take the offer of three times the amount of his bond and let the matter drop. But Portia said:

> Tarry, Jew:
> The law hath yet another hold on you.
> It is enacted in the laws of Venice,
> If it be proved against an alien
> That by direct or indirect attempts
> He seeks the life of any citizen,
> The party 'gainst the which he doth contrive
> Shall seize one half his goods; the other half
> Comes to the privy coffer of the state;
> And the offender's life lies in the mercy
> Of the Duke only.
>
> —Act IV, scene 1

This was a happy ending for Antonio and his friends, though a very unhappy one for Shylock. The Duke pardoned the old man before he could ask, and Antonio refused his share of the money-lender's wealth, but he stipulated that Skylock make a will giving it to Shylock's daughter, Jessica, upon his death.

Like Portia's great plea for mercy, Shakespeare created many important speeches and uplifting philosophies that may become an important part of us. In great literature we can see both the good and the bad of life. And the villain may serve our interests quite as well as the hero. The villain shows us the quicksands to be avoided, whereas the hero points out the pathway to be followed. Through the holy scriptures, the greatest literature, we may go and live in a great new world with the most interesting people. The scriptures also supply us with the greatest moral principles, the most inspiring philosophies, and the finest life-saving religious doctrines. Through them we may instruct our minds, fill our hearts with a love of right, charge our spirits with power, and be motivated to save our souls.

50

The Albatross

I N 1798 Samuel Taylor Coleridge wrote his great epic poem entitled "The Rime of the Ancient Mariner," which one prominent critic has said is in all points one of the greatest creations in all of literature. James Russell Lowell has said: "In the 'Rime of the Anient Mariner' Coleridge has written one of the most poetical poems in the language which is not only unparalleled but unapproached in its kind."

This great literary work tells some of the experiences of this ancient mariner and his crew as they sailed their ship through distant southern seas. One day as they journeyed pleasantly upon their way, a great albatross appeared out of the ocean mists and, with an attitude of the greatest friendliness, hovered about their ship and accompanied them on their way.

The albatross is the largest of the sea birds. It lives in southern zones and is capable of long continued flights so that it is often sighted great distances from land. To these sailors far from home this great bird was a very pleasant sight, and they considered it as one of the best of good omens.

In that day it was supposed by some that an albatross brought good fortune to the mariners and success to their causes. Among other things it made the breezes blow, and it assured the sailors of good rains to provide fresh water to drink. It also favored the attainment of their other needs. Therefore, when the albatross appeared the sailors greeted it as if it had been a "Christian soul," and they "hailed it in God's name." For days it followed their ship and hovered around it. Occasionally it came aboard for food and to engage in a kind of fraternal association and play with the sailors. It frequently perched on the mast and shroud for evening vespers, and it was generally good company.

Following an evil impulse, the ancient mariner drew his great crossbow, shot the harmless, friendly albatross, and thereby destroyed their omen of good fortune. With no friendly bird to follow their ship, their favorable fortunes began a sharp decline.

Because the friendly bond of fellowship that had existed between man and beast had been broken, the breezes stopped blowing, the heavens dried up so that no rain fell, and soon the ship and all aboard were marooned on a hot, dead ocean. The ancient mariner had violated that reverence for life that should exist for man and beast and bird, and because a law had been broken and a crime had been committed, a natural vengeance must surely follow. Mr. Coleridge said:

> Down dropt the breeze, the sails dropt down,
> 'Twas sad as sad could be;
> And we did speak only to break
> The silence of the sea!
>
> All in a hot and copper sky,
> The bloody Sun, at noon,
> Right up above the mast did stand,
> No bigger than the Moon.
>
> Day after day, day after day,
> We stuck, nor breath nor motion;
> As idle as a painted ship
> Upon a painted ocean.
>
> Water, water, everywhere,
> And all the boards did shrink;
> Water, water, everywhere,
> Nor any drop to drink.
>
> The very deep did rot: O Christ!
> That ever this should be!
> Yea, slimy thing did crawl with legs
> Upon the slimy sea. . . .
>
> And every tongue, through utter drought,
> Was wither'd at the root;
> We could not speak, no more than if
> We had been choked with soot.

Because the ancient mariner had caused the sorry plight of of his sailors by killing the albatross, they naturally felt very unkindly toward him. Therefore, he said of their attitude:

> And I had done an hellish thing,
> And it would work 'em woe:
> For all averr'd I had kill'd the bird
> That made the breeze to blow.
> Ah wretch! said they, the bird to slay,
> That made the breeze to blow!

Then in punishment for his crime the dead albatross was
hung about the neck of the guilty ancient mariner. He said:

> Ah! well a-day! what evil looks
> Had I from old and young!
> Instead of the cross, the Albatross
> About my neck was hung.

But all on board the stranded ship continued to suffer many
disagreeable things that his sin brought upon them, and even
death itself visited the ship. Again the ancient mariner said:

> There pass'd a weary time. Each throat
> Was parch'd, and glazed each eye. . . .
>
> One after one, by the star-dogg'd Moon,
> Too quick for groan or sigh,
> Each turn'd his face with a ghastly pang,
> And cursed me with his eye.
>
> Four times fifty living men
> (And I heard nor sigh nor groan),
> With heavy thump, a lifeless lump,
> They dropp'd down one by one.
>
> The souls did from their bodies fly,—
> They fled to bliss or woe!
> And every soul, it pass'd me by
> Like a whizz of my cross-bow! . . .
>
> Alone, alone, all, all alone,
> Alone on a wide, wide sea!
> And never a saint took pity on
> My soul in agony.
>
> The many men, so beautiful!
> And they all dead did lie:
> And a thousand thousand slimy things
> Lived on; and so did I.
>
> I look'd upon the rotting sea,
> And drew my eyes away;
> I look'd upon the rotting deck,
> And there the dead men lay.
>
> I look'd to heaven, and tried to pray;
> But, or ever a prayer had gusht,
> A wicked whisper came, and made
> My heart as dry as dust.

> I closed my lids, and kept them close,
> And the balls like pulses beat;
> But the sky and the sea, and the sea and the sky,
> Lay like a load on my weary eye,
> And the dead were at my feet.
>
> The cold sweat melted from their limbs,
> Nor rot nor reek did they;
> The look with which they look'd on me
> Had never pass'd away.
>
> An orphan's curse would drag to hell
> A spirit from on high;
> But oh! more horrible than that
> Is the curse in a dead man's eye!
> Seven days, seven nights, I saw that curse,
> And yet I could not die.

After days of enduring this awful living death in company with the slimy things that were crawling over the rotting decks marooned on this rotting sea, the ancient mariner got into his heart a new feeling of sympathy for God's other creatures so that he loved even the lowliest among them. His own suffering and this new feeling of godliness purged out his sins and restored that sympathetic relationship which should always exist between God's creations of man and man, and man and beast. The ancient mariner said:

> O happy living things! no tongue
> Their beauty might declare:
> A spring of love gush'd from my heart,
> And I bless'd them unaware:
> Sure my kind saint took pity on me,
> And I bless'd them unaware.
>
> That selfsame moment I could pray;
> And from my neck so free
> The Albatross fell off, and sank
> Like lead into the sea.

Now that the curse had been removed, the rain fell in abundance into their buckets. The dead men came back to life. Their throats were slaked, their brows were cooled, and a gentle, peaceful sleep was again made possible after the tiresome weariness of this awful suffering. A friendly wind now arose that would carry the ship and its crew back again to their own country.

A reminder of this awful experience always remained with the ancient mariner, and at intervals it would again return to burn in his memory. His only relief was to get someone to listen as he rehearsed his awful tale. He never knew in advance at what hour his suffering might again come upon him, but he must always be ready to tell again the story of his sin. He said:

> Since then, at an uncertain hour,
> That agony returns:
> And till my ghastly tale is told,
> This heart within me burns.

After giving the account to his most recent listener, he said:

> Farewell, farewell! but this I tell
> To thee, thou wedding-guest!
> He prayeth well, who loveth well
> Both man, and bird, and beast.
>
> He prayeth best, who loveth best
> All things both great and small;
> For the dear God who loveth us,
> He made and loveth all.
>
> The Mariner, whose eye is bright,
> Whose beard with age is hoar,
> Is gone; and now the wedding-guest
> Turn'd from the bridegroom's door.
>
> He went like one that hath been stunn'd,
> And is of sense forlorn:
> A sadder and a wiser man
> He rose the morrow morn.

The stimulating ideas that we get from great literature serve an important place in all our lives.

Good poetry is often very effective in producing a sublime feeling in us in the place of the images given us by the poet. The thoughts from our great literature frequently help us to feel the elemental truths of life as they strike some responsive chords in us. Some of these thoughts should also become embedded in us.

This idea that a part of the punishment of the ancient mariner was for the dead albatross to be hung about his neck to represent his sin reminds us of Nemesis, the Greek goddess of divine retribution. It is one of the universal laws of life that an unseen avenger is constantly standing guard in the world to make sure that no sin ever goes unpunished. This idea of burdening the sinner with his own sin also accords with that graphic way which some of the ancients had for punishing wrong. When any crime was committed, the criminal was tied to his crime. If one should kill, he had to pay for his evil by being chained to the corpse of his victim. Then wherever he went, forevermore he must drag with him the putrefying remains of his sin. There was no possible way that he could disentangle himself from the results of his evil act. If at a later date he should decide to kill again, another dead body would be added to his awful burden.

This punishment is terribly severe, and yet life has a plan of retribution that is exactly like that. The facts are that we must always be chained to our sins with no possible escapes permitted. If a person becomes an alcoholic, his punishment is that a ruinous, driving thirst attaches itself to push him farther and farther down the road to despair. If one fails to study, his sentence is to be chained to his ignorance. He cannot lay it off for even an hour. His own albatross is hung about his neck. If one tells lies, his judgment is that be becomes a liar. And so it is with every other sin. The Apostle Paul may have had this awful custom in mind when he said: "O wretched man that I am! who shall deliver me from the body of this death?" (Romans 7:24.) And with some of our albatrosses about our necks we might say, "Who, indeed?"

One of the important characteristics of the people of our day is that we are leading ourselves down with the dead bodies of so many serious sins. It would be a great source of embarrassment if each of us had to go about his daily affairs with this appropriate albatross hanging about his neck. And yet that is exactly our present situation. Disloyalty is an albatross that is presently dragging our great nation down toward its doom. Atheism is an albatross that is destroying our chances for eternal life. Immorality is an albatross which is placing an awful encumbrance upon millions of human beings.

Recently a broken-hearted mother reported that her fifteen-year-old daughter had taken up the life of a hippie. She had previously been very active in her church class. She had been a scholastic and social leader in her school. Then with some peculiarly dressed, uncombed, evil-smelling companions she had become addicted to dope, lust, and irresponsibility. She now is a mental case in the hospital psychiatric ward, suffering from a venereal disease and from several equally serious venereal attitudes.

Some doctors and social workers are trying to get her well enough to send her to the reform school. It is easy to understand that wherever she goes forevermore, both she and her mother must drag with them this girl's dead and decaying albatrosses.

Nicotine is an albatross. It not only hangs itself around our necks, but it discolors our fingers, gives us a foul breath, puts cancer in our lungs, and contaminates the very atmosphere that others around us breathe.

Rebellion is an albatross. How pathetic when people hang a load of irresponsibility around their own necks and insist on the immoral pleasures of idleness and sin! They want a prestige and recognition that they have not earned, and if someone objects to their evil ways, they think they are being persecuted. An individual can live without integrity, industry, or faith in God, but not very well. How terrible is the mistake that some make of thinking that happiness can be found in idleness, begging, immorality, irresponsibility, and sin! The betrayal of Judas Iscariot not only hung an albatross around his neck, but it also caused him to put a rope around his neck and hang himself.

Atheism is an albatross. What a heavy, dead weight we have to carry when we load ourselves with disbelief and disobedience! And what a tremendous advantage is the privilege we have of relieving ourselves through repentance! Like the ancient mariner, the albatross of all our sins may, like lead, drop off into the sea and we can again pray and worship God and love all of his creatures. But if we make the chains of our evil too strong, then even hell itself may not be able to burn out our sins or free us from those monstrous things that we sometimes permit to fasten themselves upon us.

51

Acres of Diamonds

D R. RUSSELL H. Conwell was a Union officer in the Civil War. Later he became the founder and president of Temple University in Philadelphia. In the eighty-three years of his life, which closed in 1925, he did many praiseworthy and constructive things. But it has been said that everything considered, the most remarkable thing in his life was his famous lecture entitled "Acres of Diamonds." So far as is known, "Acres of Diamonds" has been the most popular single lecture ever given in the world. The same lecture was presented to American audiences by Dr. Conwell on an average of 200 times each year for over twenty-five years. The total income from admissions was in excess of four million dollars. The money was largely used by Dr. Conwell to help deserving young people acquire an education.

The five thousandth lecture was delivered in Philadelphia, where it had been given many times before, yet the proceeds from this single lecture was over nine thousand dollars, and many people had to be turned away.

A substantial amount of the interest in this lecture came from Dr. Conwell himself, who was a man of great personal inspiration and accomplishment. But the lecture contains a great idea that is just as important now as it was in Dr. Conwell's day.

The theme of this four-million-dollar message centers around an ancient Persian farmer by the name of Ali Hafid. Ali Hafid owned a large farm made up of orchards, grain fields, and gardens. He had money out at interest and he was a wealthy and contented man. He was contented because he was wealthy, and he was wealthy because he was contented.

But one day Ali Hafid had a visit from a Buddhist priest who was one of the best-informed men of his time. That evening the priest sat before the fire with Ali Hafid and told him about the world and how it was made. He explained that the most valuable thing in the world was a diamond. The priest explained that a diamond was a drop of congealed sunlight. It was a deposit of carbon from the sun. The old priest told Ali Hafid that if he had one diamond the size of his thumb, he could purchase the entire community in which he lived. And if he could find a diamond mine, he could place his children upon thrones.

After Ali Hafid had learned about diamonds, he thought of nothing else, and that night he went to bed a poor man. He had lost nothing, but he was poor because he was discontented, and he was discontented because he now thought of himself as being poor. He now wanted diamonds more than anything else in the world. He lay awake all night thinking about these precious gems and how he could get them.

He inquired where diamonds might be found. The old priest did not know, but he told Ali Hafid that some place in the world there were plenty of diamonds, and all that anyone had to do was to find them. Ali Hafid made up his mind. He sold his farm, left his family in charge of a neighbor, took his money, and started out to search the world for diamonds.

He began his explorations at the mountains of the moon. Afterward he traveled throughout Asia. He searched in Palestine. He went on into Europe. After years of searching, his money had all been spent and he found himself in rags, wretchedness, and poverty. Then one day he stood on the shores of the bay of Barcelona in Spain as a great tidal wave came rolling in between the pillars of Hercules. The poor, afflicted, suffering Ali Hafid fell a victim to the awful temptation to cast himself into the incoming tide. He sank beneath its foaming crest, never to rise again.

Back home the man who had purchased Ali Hafid's farm was one day letting his camel drink from the garden brook. As the camel splashed its nose into the shallow water of the clear stream, Ali Hafid's successor noted a curious flash of light coming from the white sands of the stream. He pulled out a stone that had an eye of light reflecting all the hues of the rainbow. He took the stone into his house and laid it on the mantel. Some time later when the same old priest came to visit Ali Hafid's successor, he saw the light flashing from the mantel and told the owner that this stone was a diamond. Then together they rushed out into the garden and stirred up the white sands with their fingers, and lo, there came up other beautiful gems even more valuable than the first.

This is said to be a historically true account of the discovery of the great Golconda diamond mine, the most magnificent diamond mine in history, even excelling the famous Kimberley mine itself. The Kohinoor and the Orloff diamonds of the crown jewels of England and Russia came from this mine. At the very time that Ali Hafid was longing for diamonds, he was living on top of the greatest diamond mine in the world. If he had just dug in his own garden, instead of wretchedness, starvation, and a suicidal death in a strange land, he would have literally had acres of diamonds. For every part of that old farm produced valuable gems which have since decorated the crowns of the greatest monarchs of the world.

We feel very sorry for Ali Hafid; in our minds we can see him wandering homeless and friendless further and further away from the very thing that he sought. He wanted diamonds more than anything else in the world, and yet he left the very thing that he wanted most in exchange for lonesomeness, starvation, and death in a far-away land.

Dr. Conwell stirs up our interest and imagination with many other examples of this same principle in operation. It is probable that the main interest in Dr. Conwell's lecture was not the pathetic sight of Ali Hafid taking his leave of the very things that he wanted most. The greatest interest probably arose from the fact that the actions of Ali Hafid so much resemble the course that we ourselves so frequently take. A large percentage of our own population is continually rushing from one place to another seeking for things that we never find. We stop for only a brief period and then we are on the move again. This constant unrest is caused by a strange inclination among us to think of success and happiness as lying in some distant country, to be found only under unusual circumstances. The grass usually looks so much greener on the other side of the fence that it draws our attention and our interest away from those more important things that lie right under our noses. We look for some great deeds to do in some far-away foreign land and we neglect our own acre of diamonds with all the possibilities that are just begging to be uncovered in our own backyard.

This four-million-dollar lecture suggests that most of our opportunities are not found in the distance, but usually in the vicinity of our birth. In fact, opportunity may be found wherever one really digs for it and usually in no other place. Henry Ford found acres of diamonds by digging in his own tool shed. Thomas A. Edison found his acre of diamonds in the experiments of his own laboratory. The people of two thousand years ago believed that no good could come out of Nazareth, and yet Jesus went from the carpenter shop to become the Savior of the world. So far as is known, Jesus never traveled more than 200 miles from the place where he was born. And so it is with us. It has been said that "no one is ever born whose work is not born with him." Yet how futile it sometimes is to urge one to start digging in his own home town and make good right where he is. The chances always seem so much better if we could cultivate the distant acres that lie beyond our reach.

We sometimes feel that we would be great if only we could be elected to some important political office or by some other means have the power of exceptional accomplishment placed in our hands by someone else, whereas if we would dig a little deeper in our own backyard, we would find some important inspiring purpose for our own lives. It is a serious mistake to wait for some great deeds to do in the future when there are so many little deeds that need to be done in the present.

In ancient Athens one of the requirements for appointment to a great position was to have first filled some lesser positions well. We need to learn to dig a little deeper into our own acre right where we are. In the early days of this country many people lost their lives in the gold rush across the great American desert on their way to California. The same thing happened in the Arctic wastes of the Yukon, while those who died frequently left great undeveloped treasures in their own home towns.

Some of us never become aware of our greatest treasures. The most likely places to look for diamonds is under our own feet and within ourselves. In fact, God has implanted in every man the very things that he seeks. If you seek the kind of faith that moves mountains, look within yourself, for God has already implanted in your own heart the seeds of faith and power waiting only for you to make them grow. If you seek the courage that will make you one of the giants of your day, don't look in Barcelona or Paris, or London, for it is already within yourself awaiting only your command. Every man has within himself a vein of greatness; he has only to learn to command the shaft that draws out the gold.

One young man said he would like to be an orator, but no

one would elect him to an office great enough for his talents to be utilized. If you want to be an orator, start speaking your piece now. Oratory is not bestowed by political election or special appointment. Oratory as well as office depends on how well you have developed those particular acres inside yourself. Those who are not great before they get into office will not be great when they get in. Just begin digging where you are, and you will be surprised what will turn up. Demosthenes had a speech defect, but he started to dig and he finally became the greatest orator in the world, not in spite of his speech defect but because of it. His defect made him learn to dig.

Dr. Conwell tells of meeting Fred Douglass, the black orator and journalist of American slave days, who six months before his birth was pledged by his white master to a creditor in payment of a debt. And for the first part of his life Fred Douglass did not even own his own body. Then some friends of his took up a collection of $750 and purchased Fred Douglass and made him a present of himself. The father of Fred Douglass was a white man; his mother was a Negro slave. Mr. Douglass said, "I never saw my father and I remember very little of my mother except that once she tried to keep an overseer from whipping me, and the lash cut across her face and spilt her blood over me." The plot in life that Fred Douglass was asked to cultivate did not at first seem very promising, but he dug long and deep and uncovered his own acres of diamonds.

The story of Fred Douglass is in one way the story of every man. We first need to get possession of ourselves. In the beginning God gave man dominion over everything upon the earth, including himself, and when we really start taking possession things begin happening. There are very few poor people in the United States who do not keep themselves poor by their own shortcomings. Shakespeare said, "The fault, dear Brutus, is not in our stars, but in ourselves, that we are underlings." Life did not really intend that Demosthenes should be a poor speaker just because he had a speech impediment. The defect was just to stimulate him to dig. It is all wrong to allow a weakness to become permanent.

Dr. Conwell tells of a man who used to sit on his front porch and smoke away his wife's small income in idleness. Then this man would get up in prayer meeting and ask sympathy for what he called the Lord's poor. Dr. Conwell said that he thought the Lord was not very pleased with this kind of poor people. We must not mistake sloth, ignorance, and indifference for humility and piety. God wants all of us to be numbered among the Lord's rich; otherwise he would not have hidden so many wonderful gifts within us.

Dr. Conwell said that the very apex of his life's thought is that people should do their best right where they are with the wonderful gifts that God has already given them. He said, "Arise, ye millions of Americans. Trust in God and believe in your opportunities and in yourselves." Dr. Conwell's principle of greatness will work for everyone. Whatever you have to do, put your whole mind and soul into its doing. The greatest of all wealth is eternal life, and it also comes by this vigorous digging process. As Jesus said, ". . . see that ye serve him with all your heart, might, mind and strength, that ye may stand blameless before God at the last day." (D&C 4:2.)

Ali Hafid sought for diamonds because he believed them to be the most valuable things in the world, but Jesus said, ". . . seek ye first the kingdom of God, and his righteousness; and all these things shall be added unto you." (Matthew 6:33.) Jesus said the kingdom of God is within you, and that is where most of the digging needs to take place. A little of the light and glory of God in our lives dwarfs into insignificance all of the brilliance that came from Ali Hafid's brook. It is a great day in our lives when we determine to dig a little deeper into the acre that God has given into our personal care.

52

A Gift of Books

THE MOST important fact in the universe is God. The second greatest value is found in great human beings, and ranking in third place would undoubtedly come our treasury of great books. We think of God as many things. Isaiah looked forward to the coming of Christ, and said, ". . . and his name shall be called Wonderful, Counseller, The mighty God, The everlasting Father, The Prince of Peace." (Isaiah 9:6.) He is called the Redeemer, the Savior of the world, the Great Physician, the Great Teacher; but as one of his highest titles he is called the Giver of all good gifts.

The scriptures tell us about some of God's great gifts to us, such as the gift of life, the gift of tongues, the gift of prophecy, the gift of healing, the gift of faith, the gift of industry, the gift of salvation. It also speaks of God's greatest gift, which is the gift of eternal life in his presence. This idea of giving gifts is a very good one for us to follow also, as great human beings are also judged primarily by what they have given to the world and to their families, to their friends, and to society generally.

To commemorate the birth of Christ into the world, the wise men came out of the East bearing gifts of gold, frankincense, and myrrh, which they laid at his feet; and each year as we celebrate the anniversary of his birth we renew this ancient custom by giving gifts to each other. We give gifts of flowers, gifts of toys, gifts of food, gifts of clothing, and gifts of many other things. There are also several passages of scripture indicating that we should seek out the best gifts to present to ourselves.

This custom of giving gifts sometimes becomes very difficult, because some people already seem to have everything. Even with ourselves, there are frequently not many things that we really need or want. In our important role as givers, it is necessary to remember that some gifts are better than others. An unknown poet has said:

> I gave a beggar of my store of wealth, some gold.
> He spent the shining ore and came again and yet again,

Still cold and hungry as before.
I gave a thought and through that thought of mine he
    found himself,
The man supreme, divine, fed, clothed, and crowned with
    blessings manifold,
And now he begs no more.

Certainly great thoughts can be among our most valuable gifts.

Victor Hugo once said that there is nothing as powerful as an idea whose time has come. An idea's time always comes when we can get a harness on it and get it working for us, and one of the very best sources of great ideas is in books.

A book is probably the greatest invention of all time. Abraham Lincoln once said, "What I want to know is in books, and my best friend is the one who will get me a book I haven't read." What we want to be is also found in books, and we can become what we understand and love. Through books we can be born again many times, and each time we can be born better and more successful.

Someone once asked Phillips Brooks, "When were you born?" And he said, "I will tell you about it. It was one Sunday afternoon about 3:30 just after I had finished reading a great book."

A book is one of the greatest wonders of creation. The greatest human being may spend his entire lifetime learning the secrets of some outstanding success and then make it available in a book to all nations and all future generations of individuals.

The great God of creation has caused his prophets to write down the important laws of eternal life as they have been made known throughout the ages. We have books of scripture, books of poetry, books of music, books of science, and books of literature that are available for our own use or to give to our friends.

Someone has said that the only real gift is the gift of yourself, but try to imagine Albert Einstein or Ralph Waldo Emerson or the Apostle Paul trying to give their great success and personality secrets away except in books. It would take many years for even the least accomplished person to personally give himself completely away.

I have in my library the supreme essence of a hundred lives that I myself have written down from all that I have learned about them in all my reading of many books. Their great intellects inspire me as through the most friendly eyes they look down upon me from my bookshelf, awaiting my command to offer me friendship or assistance.

Carl Sandburg spent many years giving to me the essential parts of Abraham Lincoln in a set of books which can do wonderful things for me if I absorb them effectively. And I remember that Lincoln himself borrowed millions of dollars of greatness from the life of Washington through a book. There are parts of myself that I may give to my children or grandchildren or future generations of my posterity. But in a book I may write out for them those things that I would like to have them remember. And through a book, long after I am gone, I may counsel and try to inspire my posterity. Through books I may give them some gifts of the greatest ideas and the highest ideals. I may give them gifts of courage and gifts of faith and gifts of understanding. Jesus said, "It is more blessed to give than to receive." And I would like to give my posterity some gifts of books and a power that they might get out of the books all that there is in them. What an inspiring thing it is to me to know that I may present to any of my friends or loved ones *The Life of Christ* by Cannon Farrar, or those 804 pages written by the apostle James E. Talmage under the title *Jesus the Christ.* Or I may make someone a gift of a sacred volume of holy scriptures giving the words and conversations and revelations of God himself. What a thrill it would be if we could understand and fully utilize the benefits of such a gift.

On a lesser level the greatest man can give to everyone in the world simultaneously his most constructive secrets. But lacking those abilities ourselves, we may still make a gift to many persons all that is best and most profitable to know in the life of any other person who has ever lived.

Samuel Smith was the first missionary of the newly restored Church of Jesus Christ of Latter-day Saints. He tried to get the Reverend John P. Green to buy a Book of Mormon for sixty cents. John P. Green didn't buy the book, but he told Samuel that he would keep it and try and help him sell it if he could. However, the Reverend Green did not sell the book; he read it and then he loaned it to a friend of his whose name was Brigham Young, and he read it. And Brigham Young loaned it to a friend of his whose name was Heber C. Kimball, and he read it. And this one sixty-cent Book of Mormon brought these three great families, now numbering many thousands of people, into the Church and caused a spiritual renewal in the lives of many thousands of people.

It may have been a sixty-cent Bible that Abraham Lincoln used to read at night on the dirt floor of a backwoods cabin before the open fire. And think of the value that has come into the world as a consequence! Norman Vincent Peale wrote a great book, *The Power of Positive Thinking*. Of this book, five-million copies have been printed. Each one may have been read by several people, and if they have read it well, think what the eternal consequences will be.

Undoubtedly Moses was a very busy man, and had I lived in his day it might have been pretty difficult for me to have gotten a personal interview with him where he could spare me enough time to give me a substantial part of the information that I would like to have. And yet I have easily available twenty-four hours a day, all of his writings, and many other things that have been written about his life that will inspire and help me.

I was not present at Mount Sinai when God gave the Ten Commandments, and yet I can believe them as wholeheartedly as though I were present. In addition, I can give someone a Holy Bible, which not only has the lifework of Moses recorded, but also the lifework of the other great prophets since time began, including the greatest discourses by the Master of men himself. The ancient prophets have long since departed this life, and yet through the holy scriptures I can summon them at any hour to speak to me from the dead with all of the vigor, enthusiasm, and authority that they possessed at the peak of their careers.

Walter Dill Scott once said that mental attitude is more important than mental capacity. We hear a great many people complain about their lack of mental capacity, and yet through books I can make available to my friends the finest attitudes, the most expert instruction, the most beautiful poetry ever written by any of the greatest men and women who have ever lived in the world. I know of a man who has put 3,000 hours into writing a book for which he had spent a lifetime in study, experience, and research. In addition to the great number of people who have bought this book, he has personally given away 30,000 of these books, so that just their reading time in absorbing this information would total nine million hours of 4500 years, or a hundred working lifetimes. The possibilities of this idea boggles our minds when we think of what Abraham Lincoln and many other people have gotten out of one book.

As has been said, "The greatest gifts are of ourselves." In giving ourselves we may give our love, our interest, our attention, our praise, our help, and we can make all of our knowledge available to anyone receiving this gift. But if we do not have all of the great resources in ourselves that we would like to have, we may give away through their books the greatest wisdom of the greatest men who ever lived, including God himself.

And so we come back again to the wonderful story of Christmas as we try to absorb the spirit of the wise men who, at great expense, traveled across the desert to lay their gifts of gold and frankincense and myrrh at the feet of the newborn king. And following their example, we may present to our loved ones, our friends, and any other person, this great gift of books.

And if we are good readers, we can not only get out of the book all of the wonderful things that are written therein, but we can also get an additional benefit from those important things that the book inspires us to think about and do.

May God bless the great books and all of us who read from them and live by them. For this I humbly pray in the name of Jesus Christ.

INDEX